D1426436

I BELONG HERE

I BELONG HERE

A Journey Along the Backbone of Britain

Anita Sethi

BLOOMSBURY WILDLIFE
LONDON · OXFORD · NEW YORK · NEW DELHI · SYDNEY

BLOOMSBURY WILDLIFE
Bloomsbury Publishing Plc
50 Bedford Square, London, WC1B 3DP, UK
29 Earlsfort Terrace, Dublin 2, Ireland

BLOOMSBURY, BLOOMSBURY WILDLIFE and the Diana logo are
trademarks of Bloomsbury Publishing Plc

First published in Great Britain 2021

A catalogue record for this book is available from the British Library

ISBN: HB: 978-1-4729-8393-0; PB: 978-1-4729-8395-4;
eBook: 978-1-4729-8396-1

2 4 6 8 10 9 7 5 3 1

Map on page 6 by Julian Baker

Typeset in Bembo Std by Deanta Global Publishing Services, Chennai, India
Printed and bound in Great Britain by CPI Group (UK) Ltd, Croydon CR0 4YY

To find out more about our authors and books visit www.bloomsbury.com
and sign up for our newsletters

In memoriam Sophie Christopher
(1990–2019)

To everyone who has ever felt like
they don't belong

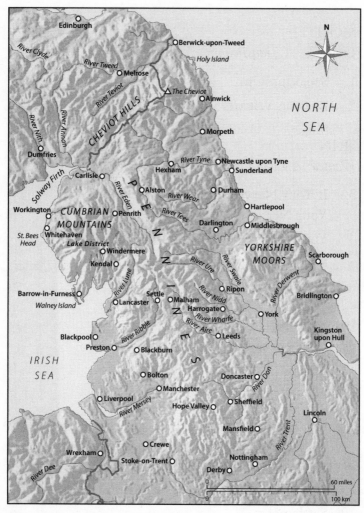

A map of the Pennines.

Contents

FEET
*The Way: North Pennines to Hadrian's Wall
  (via Manchester)*

A Place Called Hope

I watched the wings as they soared through the sky – so sure of itself, so confident was the curlew as it caressed the clouds, so in its element. Where do I belong? Such a perennial question of existence and I remember the flight of that curlew I saw in the Pennines when I consider the quest for a sense of belonging. The bird belongs in its fine feathers and in its nest and in the air, flying through the sky with such ease and grace. The fish belongs in its spectacular scales and in its watery habitat. The bulb belongs in soil, in its state of becoming, growing towards the light. How could I feel a sense of belonging in my own body, in my own self, in the world?

What does it mean to belong? What does it mean to feel like you don't belong? How can nature help us to find a greater sense of belonging, and how can we ensure people care enough to realise that nature and wildlife belong as much to the world as humans do?

A definition of 'to belong' is to be in the right place; we all belong here in the world, our shared home. If the conditions that make up our belonging on earth are removed completely, we will ultimately perish. Belonging is a need, like water and air and food – vital elements in the natural world that every living organism needs to survive, making us realise that we are not apart from but a part of nature; nature flows through our very veins, fills our lungs, and pulses in our hearts. As well as water, air, food and shelter, we have felt more than ever what else we need, what is essential and what is not. Is it possible to survive without friendship and community? Without love and language? Without basic care and respect for each other and for wildlife? Without civil rights? These elements also make up our belonging. This book was born during a time when our primal need to belong – and ways in which some of us are brutally denied the basic elements of belonging – has been evidenced in the extreme.

Everyone needs to feel a sense of belonging, and without it arises a deep loneliness and isolation that can affect the mental health – and such loneliness has seeped through my life since childhood.

All my life I felt like I didn't belong, and I grew used to that sense of unbelonging; being an outsider has shaped my life in many ways and made me become a writer. But there comes a time when it's necessary to say: I belong here. It might come when someone is trying to push you from a place, to eradicate you. It might come when your basic rights are being denied. It might come when you are struggling to breathe clean air, when you are struggling to breathe at all. It's exhausting having to prove and explain why we belong, yet so often have I had to do so on account of multiple macro and microaggressions. Ultimately, I hope for a world in which every creature great and small is accepted and I don't have to say it at all.

I was on a journey through northern England in early summer 2019 when I became the victim of a hate crime, when a man attacked my right to belong here, with words that hurt the very heart of me. The North is my home, having been born and bred in Manchester – the TransPennine Express train even passed through the city on its route from Liverpool to Newcastle. The hate crime was a vicious attack on my right to exist in a place on account of my race. I was called 'Paki cunt' and told to 'get back on the banana boat' and 'go back to where you're from' – and yet this country *is* where I belong.

Hate crime is on the rise in our hostile environment. After the attack some advised me to stop travelling alone due to the dangers, and I experienced panic attacks and anxiety at the thought of travelling by myself. But I was intent on not letting a hate crime stop me moving about freely and without fear in a country where I belong. I was eager to continue travelling alone as a woman, asserting my right to exist.

One day I was looking at a map of the North and there, along the route of my train journey, falls the Pennines, 'the backbone of England', with its nature reserves, national parks, and Areas of Outstanding Natural Beauty (an area of countryside designated for conservation due to its significant landscape value). My heart quickened as I looked at the miniature mappings of its mountains and rivers. The TransPennine Express journey had run a route tantalisingly close to such Pennine areas, but it would take walking and local railways to fully explore it. I longed to journey through the natural landscapes of the North, transforming what began as an ugly experience of hate and exclusion into one offering hope and finding beauty after brutality.

Go back to where you're from. This is where I'm from. I'm from the North. The glorious North. Our emotional connection with certain places runs deep and forceful as a river, and during and after the hate crime I felt how profound my connection was with the North. Although a racist had viciously told me to leave, I felt a magnetic pull drawing me back – not to get further from it but even deeper into it.

My journey is one of reclamation, a way of saying, to adapt the Woody Guthrie song title, 'this land is my land too' and I belong in the UK as a brown woman, just as much as a white man does. Journeying through the so-called backbone of England also feels symbolic, a way of showing backbone myself and that I will not let having been the victim of a race hate crime curtail my movements through the world, despite the trauma and panic attacks that followed.

The nature of trauma is that it lives on after the traumatic incident. The man who racially abused me was arrested, charged, pleaded guilty and was convicted of a racially aggravated public order offence, using threatening, abusive, insulting words and behaviour. After I heard my abuser had pleaded guilty, I felt the oxygen return to my lungs. But in the days and weeks that followed, I still experienced anxiety attacks, feeling the room closing in on me as my breathing became rapid and my heart pounded. I saw the man's face flash through my mind. I felt a crushing pain at the suggestion that I had no right to exist in a place that is my home. At my lowest ebbs I wanted to cease existing. When I walked up through the carriages, the man had threatened to set fire to me. I had nightmares about choking on smoke. Sleeplessness left me exhausted. Even walking the streets of the city, I felt a sense of claustrophobia. That year I'd been racially abused twice while walking the streets, in Nottingham and London.

As my claustrophobia grew, I began to long for wide open spaces, to breathe freely in the great outdoors. I hungered for greenness.

I began to devour more and more maps of the Pennines and plot out a route, reading up about the Pennine Way, Britain's oldest long-distance footpath, which runs for 431 kilometres through the backbone of Britain. This path was the idea of the rambler Tom Stephenson who, in 1935, wrote about how he yearned for 'a long green trail' like those of the John Muir Trail through the Sierra Nevada mountain range and the Appalachian Trail in the eastern mountains of the US. I also saw that the Pennine range is not confined to the Way but stretches from the Peak District, up through the Yorkshire Dales and into the North Pennines, fringed by the foothills of the Lake District, with a westerly outpost in the Forest of Bowland.

I zoomed in on a map of the Peak District, where the Pennine Way begins, and where the North begins; its border. How glorious to glimpse a place named Hope. It's there I wanted to start my journey, walking through Hope Valley. The night before the hate crime, I had happened to stay in a place called Hope Street Hotel on Hope Street in Liverpool – my actual experiences turned out to be profoundly allegorical. Since then I tried to channel hope throughout, drawing on it at my lowest ebb.

I felt strongly that journeying again through the North had something to offer me, and I wanted to follow that gut instinct. Places where traumatic events occur take on even greater significance; they become a part of us, a deep wound in us, often paradoxically drawing us back to the wounded place to understand something about it, to transform it into a place of empowerment – and that's

how I felt about that TransPennine Express journey and
my journey of reclamation through the Pennines.

One day in mid-summer, I finally make a move. I get the
Hope Valley line from Manchester, reopened after storm
closure. I see flashes of purple rosebay willowherb through
the window. I step off the train in Edale, the gateway to
the Pennines, and feel the noise of the city fall away. As the
train engines fade, silence envelops me, but for birdsong.
I had been living in a flat on a busy main road, and it is
particularly welcome to feel a deep quietening both in
the outer world and in my head. I breathe in fresh air.

In a cafe called Penny Pot I sip sweet tea while looking
at maps left on the table. A volunteer from the National
Trust sitting at the next table sees me marvelling at the
maps and tells me more about Kinder Scout moorland
plateau and nature reserve. This part of the countryside is
about access and the right to roam, as it is here that the
Kinder Scout Mass Trespass of 1932 happened, which
helped to open up access to the countryside. Hundreds of
walkers who were mainly from Manchester trespassed en
masse on what was then private land and walked from
Hayfield to Kinder Scout, asserting their right to exist in
places from which they were excluded. Kinder Scout was
at the time used to keep grouse for rich landowners. The
walk was celebrated in the folk song 'The Manchester
Rambler' by poet and folk singer Ewan MacColl, who
marched during the protest and knew that walking could
be a radical and political act and lead to change; that
walking could be a way of saying: I belong here.

The Kinder mass trespass sparked a wave of transformation: three weeks later, 10,000 ramblers held a protest for the right to roam at the nearby limestone gorge of Winnats Pass, launching a movement that ultimately led to the creation of the first national park in 1951, the Peak District, and to the establishment of the Pennine Way and other long-distance footpaths. But it was not until the year 2000 that freedom-to-roam legislation was passed, securing walkers' rights to travel through open country – just two decades ago. I feel how far there still is to go for all to feel safe and free and welcome while walking in the world.

A National Trust leaflet in the cafe explains about the Be Kinder walking trail, an initiative from Jarvis Cocker and Jeremy Deller, both whom I later run into at the cafe: 'The self-led walking trail encourages people to think about the importance of being kind to this incredible natural habitat, as well as honouring the individuals who fought for our rights of way; allowing future generations to enjoy and protect this spectacular landscape for years to come.'

I had known little about this history when I boarded that Hope Valley line train into Edale; what a symbolic place it is to walk through as I assert my right to roam through the world.

Learning more about the North, my sense of place and identity deepens. As I walk through the moorland I feel more than ever that pioneering spirit from Manchester, and how walking is still a radical and political act.

The Pennines are an important water catchment area with many reservoirs in the headstreams of river valleys. The peat moorlands – landscapes of dark, rich peat soil which provide much of our drinking water – died off

due to industrial pollution, poisonous gases destroying
vegetation and damaging the peat. Hundreds of hectares
are being brought back to life by conservation and
restoration initiatives such as dams on the Kinder plateau,
rewetting the moor and helping heather to flourish, and
thousands of trees and cotton grass plants have also been
planted, benefiting biodiversity. Another extraordinary
species helping to bring the moorland back to life are
sphagnum moss plants, and millions have been planted
by volunteers. In damp areas the vivid green plants grow,
taking in carbon dioxide, storing water and enabling
habitats for other wildlife such as bird populations to
flourish – so astonishing is sphagnum moss that it is able
to hold twenty times its weight in water. Sphagnum
moss was used in the First World War as a wound dressing
due to its antiseptic properties; it is now healing the deep
wounds in the landscape created by erosion and pollution
that left bare peat exposed. But these crucial upland
landscapes are threatened due to climate change, the
species and habitats that live here highly sensitive to
environmental changes. Should climate change continue
at its current rate, peat moorlands would be decimated,
woodlands suffer drought, rivers and streams dry up, and
creatures which make a home here such as curlew and
lapwing be at risk of extinction.[1]

I think about the deep wounds in places and in people,
and how they might be healed.

I think about how we care for each other and for the
land in which we live.

I think about being kind to each other, ourselves, and
to the earth through which we walk. I had experienced
kindness as well as cruelty on that train journey during

which I was racially abused and am keen for it to be kindness that ultimately triumphs.

I continue to walk through the Kinder Scout moorland plateau, following 'trig points' used to measure the heights of mountains. I see butterflies – a brown angus, common blue, marbled white, red admirals, bright orange-and-black painted ladies and small tortoiseshells. I see creatures of many colours flutter by, oblivious to me. I relish being in the non-judgemental world of nature. I relish learning the new names of places and creatures, letting the beauty of them take the sting out of the abusive words I was called. I look out for rare wildlife like bilberry bumblebees, which started to return when the moorland began to come back to life.

The world opens out and my sense of claustrophobia lifts, as I breathe deeply. My anxiety no longer contracts the world to the size of a train carriage. Through walking and engaging with the world around me, my thoughts are shifted from anxious ruminations. Soon I am entirely alone in fields of flowers. I lie down in the grass and begin to weep. I savour these moments being close to the earth, a part of it.

I continue on the train to a place I'll be staying that evening.

'We will shortly be arriving at Hope,' says the train conductor. Then, a little while later: 'This is Hope.'

This is hope. This is what hope feels like. This is what it's like to be in a place of hope, acknowledging the existence of pain and panic but pushing through it. Gazing out over the valley from on high, I look back over my life and at other times when I have experienced abuse and either did not speak out about it or did report it but was not taken seriously. I realise how much hatred can become internalised, become self-loathing.

Walking through the world, I feel those emotions shift and lift. Walking does wonders for my wellbeing, and I walk until I can feel my limbs, the bones in my body, my heart beating, telling me I'm alive, I exist, and I begin to relish existing.

I realise how much my anxiety has been about my sense of place in the world. I feel a defiance to those who would have me disappear, a desire to keep on forging a place for myself in the world.

I think back to the situation on the train and how it was standing up from my seat and walking through the carriages that had been defining, followed by talking with the train manager to report what happened – it had been standing up and speaking up. It had been walking and talking. I reported the hate crime as I wanted to do all I could to stop anyone else having to go through what I went through. In the days that followed, a desire grew in me to continue turning hope into action.

I'm hungry to continue my journey through the North. I feel my mind open out as I look forward to walking through the Forest of Bowland, rising up through the Yorkshire Dales, and the North Pennines. 'You may kill me with your hatefulness, but still, like air, I'll rise,' wrote Maya Angelou. I want to continue rising, both geographically and emotionally.

My journey is far from over. I will not be silent. I will not stop speaking out, and I will not stop walking through the world, my home.

MOUTH

Onwards: A TransPennine Express Journey

1

Speaking Up

It was broad daylight when I boarded the TransPennine Express train in Liverpool en route to Newcastle, a day filled with the kind of bright sunshine that makes you feel nothing bad could possibly happen. I had walked to the station from the place I had stayed in called Hope Street Hotel on Hope Street – given such auspicious names, it was hard not to be filled with hope.

The night before I had managed some snatches of sleep despite lingering jetlag, and in the morning I pulled on my jeans, red jumper, and trainers, and filled myself with a full English breakfast. I slung onto my shoulder a canvas bag patterned with a giant Union Jack and the words KEEP CALM AND CARRY ON, purchased from Gatwick airport following my recent trip to the former British colony of Guyana where my mother was born. I had been invited there to give a reading from my contribution to an anthology called *We Mark Your Memory*, which explores why stories of immigration urgently need to be told to help eradicate the ignorance that breeds racism. I stepped back into the UK from a British Airways flight on the Monday of that same week and it was now Friday.

I had been in Liverpool to speak at a festival on a panel entitled 'The B-Word: Where Are We Now?' during which I had discussed my experiences of racism and how they have increased since the EU Referendum, as I have walked through the streets as a woman of colour. Yet there have been some who have tried to gaslight me, to deny racism even exists, as had happened in conversations that evening.

Despite the tense night before, emerging into the light of a new day and walking down Hope Street, I felt in high spirits. Hope filled my heart as I thought of the evening ahead: I was travelling to Newcastle to read at the northern launch of a new anthology, *Common People*, from my piece 'On Class and the Countryside' exploring inequality in access to nature, and evoking a memory of my first childhood trip to the Lake District from my home in Manchester. Hope coursed through my limbs as I put one foot in front of the other, the sunshine casting deep pools of shadow.

As each footstep pressed upon the earth, I thought of the history of this place, once a major slaving port. Liverpool grew wealthy in the eighteenth century in part due to ships transporting millions of slaves across the Atlantic Ocean, and benefited from its location near a network of rivers and canals upon which goods were traded, including textiles from Lancashire and Yorkshire. The International Slavery Museum in Liverpool describes the slave trade as 'undoubtedly the backbone of the town's prosperity'.[2] The city's landscape still bears the markings of slavery, from slave ships and enslaved people engraved into buildings to street names named after slave traders. The world's waterbodies have long been used as ways by which to exploit humans. The Bristol Harbour, which is fed by the River Avon, bore witness to the historic moment in which the statue of slave trader Edward Colston was toppled and pushed into its waters on 7th June 2020 by anti-racism protestors, having stood for 125 years. Places influence our sense of belonging and unbelonging, and for far too long slave traders have been celebrated in stone. Let's instead salvage what has been airbrushed from history and commemorate that. Let's make the moment Colston's statue splashed into the harbour the beginning of a reconfiguration of landscapes so they are something in which we can all feel a sense of belonging.

My own ancestors were shipped across the world to British colonies under the brutal indentured labour system that followed slavery. As I walked through the city that day, I thought of all those who came before me whose movements through the world were cruelly controlled and curtailed, how far we have come since then, and how far there is still to go for true equality.

At the station I found my pre-booked seat on the 12.25 p.m. train, and as it pulled out of Liverpool I recalled a school trip to the city to stand on a huge map of the United Kingdom and Ireland that floated in the Albert Dock and from where weather reports were presented, and that exhilarating sense of having something of the world beneath my feet as I gazed out beyond the map and over the water. I've long loved maps and sensed that every journey makes within us its own mappings from memory and emotion.

Next, the train stopped in Newton-le-Willows, Merseyside and onwards it growled, pulling into Manchester Victoria station. I felt the familiar connection to be stopped here in my hometown and the inevitable flood of memories at this station, gateway to teenage trips skiving school and visiting the hills surrounding

the city. I would get a bus through Rusholme, and a train
from this station towards Littleborough and Todmorden,
and feel peace at being on the train and watching the
world shift from grey to green, then walking and walking
until my muscles were sore and I could see the moorland,
marvelling that I was only half an hour away by train from
my hometown. I would walk by the foothills of the South
Pennines where Littleborough is situated in the Upper
Roch Valley and through Todmorden, at a meeting point
of Pennine valleys on the Lancashire–Yorkshire border
and surrounded by sandblasted gritstone. A friend and
I had first been up into the Pennine hills together when
I was thirteen as it was rumoured a popstar with whom
we were besotted lived in the area, but soon it was the
place itself rather than the popstar that became the star
attraction. I would dream of one day walking further and
deeper into those hills and higher up those mountains.

When I was back in my home city and a sense of
claustrophobia gripped me, I would think of the great
Pennine range out there and how my stress drained away
as I walked through it, how I felt stronger after walking,
my head clearer after breathing in fresh air, calmer
surrounded by the silence, so different from the constant
noise of the busy crossroads where I lived, harsh engines
roaring all day and night. It brought some solace knowing
those hills and mountains were there. They became part
of my inner landscape. So much did I treasure those
journeys that I kept a stash of train tickets from them for
years so that when I was grounded and could go
nowhere, or could not afford a ticket, and felt that inner
landscape slipping away as if a distant dream, I could
hold on to the tickets like talismans with dates and times

of the journeys imprinted on them and remember that the trips I made had been real after all.

The train pulled away from my hometown and I watched the concrete and brick and metal and memories blur into the distance. I felt again a pang of deep connection with this part of England, with the North, my birthplace, my home. I thought of how my father worked for the railways his entire working life. Train tracks run deep throughout my history, and the history of colonialism, and with them the racist and brutal treatment of humans. My grandfather worked for East Africa Railways in Nairobi for many years and my father grew up in railway quarters, the children of the area known as the 'railway children'. Tracing the history of trains even deeper, between 1895 and 1903 under British colonial rule, thousands of Indian indentured labourers helped build the railway line from Kenya to Uganda dubbed the Lunatic Express,[3] and around 2,500 workers died during their contract from the brutal conditions; man-eating lions also attacked and killed some of the rail construction workers during the building of a bridge over the Tsavo River. The railways are often cited as one of the great things the British Empire supposedly did for the world, but let's remember the blood, sweat and tears that went into bringing them into being.

I browsed some photos taken the evening before including of the News From Nowhere bookshop which I had been happy to finally visit since I had featured it in an *Observer* newspaper article. During my conversation with a bookseller, she recalled how the radical, feminist, community bookshop had been firebombed by racist thugs in the 1970s and targeted by members of the

National Front, and spoke of how there has been a resurgence of hostility with rising fascism – the previous summer the radical bookshop Bookmarks was attacked by fascists.

I began to practise my reading in my head for the coming evening, reliving being a small child visiting the Lake District for the first time, the awe of seeing such magnificent mountains, such vast lakes and hungering for them forever after, the wonder of first walking through a wilderness.

The train hurtled on, hours passed, and a migraine began pulsing due to loud music blaring in the carriage. A train conductor walked by and told a man sitting a few seats ahead of me to turn his music off. The conductor walked on, after which the man turned the volume up. The dull thumping made the pain in my head swell. I was impelled to open my mouth and speak. I asked the man if he would turn the volume down as it was giving me a migraine. The man turned around and looked at me with surprise then hatred. He stood up and burst into a hostile, aggressive torrent of racist abuse:

'Do you have a British passport? Get back on the banana boat. Paki cunt! Fuck off!'

I reached for my phone, nestled in my handbag next to my burgundy coloured British passport (its cover adorned with the golden words: 'EUROPEAN UNION. UNITED KINGDOM OF GREAT BRITAIN AND NORTHERN IRELAND'). I felt an imperative to keep calm and communicate what was happening. I turned my iPhone video on and caught some of his abuse and posted a seven-second clip on Twitter including him sticking two fingers up at me, his face contorted into a sneer, then putting his hands on his trousers and motioning as if he was about to 'moon' me. The man lunged towards me and my heartbeat hammered as I ducked behind my seat's headrest. The oxygen felt sucked out of the train carriage. The racial slurs stung like wasps. I felt prickles of horror spread over my skin at having been called those slurs, and in front of a whole carriage of people.

The woman sitting next to him told him to shut up and stop it, but he did not stop. When I had opened the Twitter app, my phone's video camera had automatically switched off. I turned on the voice memos recording facility instead since it is possible to keep that on while using other phone functions.

2:51 p.m.
This man has continued to racially abuse me throughout the train journey: I now have a voice recording of him saying 'these paki people who come over here on banana boats, strange people' – recording too long to share right now. There's also a whole train carriage of witnesses.

For a few moments I felt frozen in shock and bewildered that more passengers were not challenging him, that they remained silent. Then I felt the hope from this morning surge through me as I stood up and walked through the carriage past the man, who shouted abuse after me and assumed I was getting off the train. I was not, however, getting off the train. I did not engage directly with him but instead continued putting one foot in front of the other, each step fuelled by a fury of determination.

I knew in every bone in my body, in every fibre of my being that I had to report what had happened, not only for myself but to stop anyone else going through what I did. I knew I could not remain silent or still, I could not stop walking through the world.

I kept walking until I reached the end of the carriages and a door marked 'Staff'. I knocked on the door, hand curled into a fist, feeling my knuckles resounding and the sense of indignation and urgency rise. I have knocked on doors seeking help from authority figures before, in childhood days of attempting to report bullying, but in those instances the door either remained closed or the person who opened it and heard me did not listen, did not take action to help, which had put me off reporting and standing up to any abuse I experienced subsequently. The words had stuck like lumps in my throat and I had instead carried incidents around in me, secrets burning at the back of my throat in silence.

Trauma can stun us into silence. Those who have been violated verbally, sexually or physically, victims of domestic violence, veterans of war, the beaten or bereaved, those who have experienced loss including the loss of a sense of safety and belonging can end up losing language too – we're 'lost for words' by 'unspeakable' happenings. When we try to speak out and are not listened to, or are punished for doing so, this can become even more acute. For those who have experienced this and have recoiled into silence: I hear you.

For years I felt my voice trapped within me like a caught bird beating its wings. My heart would flutter ferociously when I was called on to speak in class, the blood rushing to my head and draining from my fingertips. I would be on the verge of fainting and struggle to breathe as my voice caught in my throat. I lived encased by silence, mute in class to the concern and consternation of teachers. Yet there was so much to say. It is often when we need it most that language can desert us. What keeps us silent? Shame. Taboos. Stigma. Pain. Fear.

It wasn't that I did not know how to speak. I had learned language at an early age; I share the humblebrag that I appeared in the *Manchester Evening News* aged twenty months old on account of my prodigious love of learning language. Yet a few years later, trauma froze the words before they could leave my lips. *Speak!* I would sometimes will myself, but still the words would clot and curdle and crash against the lump in my throat.

A mouth: an opening, a hole, a cave, an orifice, a passageway. The body is full of paths and passageways, and the mouth makes us realise how deeply we are connected with the natural world; breathing and speaking at all are made possible by trees that turn the sunlight into oxygen. To produce speech sounds, air travels from the lungs over the vocal cords in the larynx, thanks to the muscles in the chest that we use for breathing.[4] The tongue, the teeth, the lips, the soft and hard palate, the pharynx, 'the articulators', all play their part in the production of speech and every movement of the upper jaw reverberates through the backbone that begins in the neck. Many creatures great and small have mouths of a kind, from snouts to the beaks of birds. Even a river has a mouth.

As a child my tongue would feel leaden with the weight of unspoken words. I'd chew my lips until they were sore (a classmate had taunted me that I had 'lips like a slug'), and they were sometimes otherwise sore from where I'd been hit. I often tried to hide my mouth behind my hand. I was a gap-toothed child who later had

a pair of train-track braces in my mouth. In my silence
I loved to learn about ways in which wildlife speaks up –
the rhythmic clicking of dolphins; the pattern of sounds
that make up the 'whale song' of humpback whales; the
unique accent of sperm whales;[5] and the language of
birds and their glorious singing made possible by the
flow of air over the syrinx, their vocal organ.

I can't quite pinpoint the moment in teenagehood
when I broke my silence, though it coincided with the
removal of the train-track braces. One day I felt my
voice rise within me like a trapped bird, soaring out.
I spoke. I am now a professional speaker as well as writer.
But sometimes I can still feel the silence threaten again
and I have to fight against it. I now feel that speaking out
is an act of survival, even if it kills me – it would be a
worse kind of death to remain silent.

I know there can be a price for speaking out, being
called 'outspoken', putting one's head above the parapet,
rocking the boat. Literature, folktale and mythology bear
witness to a long history of silenced women: in Greek
mythology, after Philomela was raped, she had her tongue
cut out so she could not speak of her traumatic
experience; she later turned into a nightingale. As women
we have historically been conditioned to please and
placate, to be meek and docile, not to speak out. In our
contemporary age, women commentators and public
figures are susceptible to being trolled, harassed, gaslit
and 'victim blamed'. Greta Thunberg is trolled for
speaking out about the climate crisis, with bullying
comments about her mental health and appearance, yet
this does not stop her speaking out. This happens not
only to public figures but to many women who speak

out in their everyday lives. The fear of speaking out is
understandable. Misogynistic stereotypes are often hurled
at women who speak out: 'difficult', 'demanding',
'unkind', 'mouthy', 'lippy'. More so to women of colour,
who face stereotypes of the 'angry brown woman' or
'angry black woman', ad hominem attacks and character
assassinations, and violence.

'White privilege' has historically prioritised the words,
voices and morality of white people over people of
colour; it deems what they are saying of greater worth,
validity and truth. Conversations around race show the
challenges of speaking out and paradoxically how much
we need to do so. The term 'white fragility' coined by
Robin DiAngelo describes the potentially 'dangerous
emotional reaction' of white people – including white
liberal people – when they are told they have done or
said something that has unintentionally caused racial
offence or hurt, and how such defensiveness upholds
systems of white supremacy. I have experienced such
alarming defensive reactions and how calling out racism
can be regarded as more offensive than actual racism.
The reaction can be 'How dare you speak to me like
this?!' but dare to speak out we must. Raising
conversations around white privilege does not constitute
abusiveness as I heard a white man deem it, and no
moral or ethical code should exclude such discussions.
Such silencing behaviours impede true conversations
about race from happening, and therefore society
progressing to one of real equality free from racial
injustice. The reason other passengers on the train
journey were not themselves racially abused is due to
white privilege (I was the only person in the carriage

who was not white). Every white person needs to acknowledge such privilege and how it affects how they move around in the world. Understanding needs to be so much deeper than it is across the political spectrum. I dream of a world in which I can speak out without having my very existence threatened by doing so. 'Silence is violence' read many banners at Black Lives Matter protests, along with words of Martin Luther King: 'Silence is betrayal' and 'Our lives begin to end the day we stay silent about things that matter.'

Speaking out is not easy; it is always an act of courage. But there comes a time when it's even harder, more painful, to stay silent. That day on the train, this time, fury surged past frozenness and any fear I felt. I knocked on the door and when it opened, I spoke.

The elderly, bespectacled man who opened the door listened attentively as I reported what had happened. The member of train staff, Stephen, said he would accompany me to the carriage and asked me to point out the abuser. We walked back down the carriages, my heartbeat racing as we got closer. I pointed out the abusive man, then Stephen sat beside me a few seats behind the man, discreetly tapped the passengers seated nearby on the shoulders and jotted down what they had seen and heard, before leaving the carriage and ensuring the police were called.

'Do you want to move down the rows to the back of the train?' asked Stephen, still sitting with me.

'I shouldn't have to move,' I said.

'I know you shouldn't but I'm thinking of your safety.'

There was a brief pause in conversation filled by the man's abusive mutterings.

'Are you all right to sit here?' he asked again.

'I shouldn't have to move,' I repeated. 'I have as much right to exist here. I appreciate your concern for my safety but out of principle I'd rather stay.'

I was glad of his support but was also indignant at the thought of having to move from a space when I had done nothing wrong. My safety aside, why should I have to move from a space I was rightfully occupying, rather than the abusive man moving? I was inspired by Rosa Parks in those moments, who had refused to give up her space to a white person on a bus in Montgomery, Alabama in 1955, her refusal helping to end racial segregation on buses. 'The only tired I was, was tired of giving in,' said Parks. I felt a deep exhaustion but also steadfast determination. I held my ground. I felt all the times I had been mistreated as a woman of colour, been made to move from or feel unwelcome in a place – whether an actual or metaphorical place – and I was sick of it. All the years when I had not fully taken up space where I rightfully belonged, when I had been terrified of losing my place – so contingent and insecure are minorities made to feel about our place in the world – all those years gathered into a few moments in which I decided enough is enough, I belong here. I stayed put.

The train stopped in Darlington and through the window I saw two policemen. At the platform I pointed out the abusive man. Meanwhile a policeman got in the carriage and recorded bodycam statements from the passengers.

'I feel violated and disgusted. This country is my home,' I said to one of the policemen, back on the platform.

'Everyone in the carriage has said it was awful,' he said. 'It's not acceptable and it will be dealt with.'

I looked across the platform and saw the man who abused me standing in handcuffs. He saw me and tried to point at me, with a look of hatred.

3:25 p.m.
This man who racially abused me has been met by police at Darlington & the police say they have enough evidence to arrest him. Thanks to all my fellow passengers who gave witness statements. I gave a statement to police at Darlington & will be giving another one in Newcastle.

'If people think they can get away with it, nothing's going to change,' I said to the train conductor as I stepped back on the train after giving a verbal statement.

'You did the right thing,' he said.

A member of staff, Lewis, helped me carry my bag back onto the train then we walked down to my new seat in First Class, and in each footstep I knew something had shifted: I had spoken up and spoken out. The simple acts of walking and talking had created change and a movement from passivity. *There are good people in the world too,* I thought as I walked.

I settled into my seat and looked down at my phone. My tweets chronicling what happened had gone viral, with streams of supportive comments including offers to call for help, an intense debate raging about racism and Brexit, and some racist trolls gaslighting my experience, though they were massively outnumbered. I learned how much a tweet can be a modern-day message in a bottle reaching its reader instantaneously. I had felt very much alone – though in a peopled carriage – when sending the messages. I had felt language being used as a weapon against me, words used to try and hurt and degrade me. I had for a split second felt that silence threaten again to keep my voice caught in my throat. But no more that silent girl. I wanted to use language as a force for good. I felt again how important a tool words are, and the primal nature of communication. I then typed the words I felt were urgent to convey:

3:29 p.m.
Reminder: it is illegal to racially abuse someone and anyone who experiences it or witnesses it should report it as soon as possible.

2

Bearing Witness

Eyes. Dragonflies' eyes are so big they cover most of their head, allowing for 360-degree vision. Birds are able to see the earth's magnetic fields. Starfish have five eyes. Humans' eyes are impressive too and we should use them to look out for others not only ourselves. Even from before we are born we begin to see, opening the eyes and witnessing from within the womb. The word 'eye', the same sound as the letter 'I', and what we see can influence who we become. Whenever we open the eyes, we are witnessing the world in all its light and shade reflected and refracted from us, absorbed into us. What enters the eye, shapes the 'I'.

Ears. The creature capable of hearing the highest sound frequency of any animal in the natural world is the honeycomb moth, also known as the greater wax moth.[6] Elephants are excellent hearers too. Dolphins can hear from miles away and, like many creatures, use their faculties to protect not only themselves but others. 'Alarm signals' are sounds emitted as warnings by wildlife about impending danger. We witness with our ears as well as our eyes. Listen out for others, lend an ear.

Mouth. Every word we utter makes a journey, passing through soundwaves before being detected by the listener's ear and transduced into nerve impulses sent to the brain. The mouth – the organ through which we intake food for nourishment, and from which we emit words that can also be nourishing. Use your words to speak up for others, not only yourself.

We witness with all our senses; smell and touch and taste also help us witness the world. Such faculties are navigational tools, they can help us to find our actual and ethical 'bearing' – and can help us help others, too, to find their bearings, navigating away from those who would hate us and hurt us. They become part of our literal and moral compass.

We are a communicative species. Every living organism communicates in some way, and in the natural world, creatures have found all manner of ways, from bee dancing to birdsong. Squid use colour, patterns and texture changes. Treehoppers use vibrations. The natural world shows astonishing examples of mutually supportive communities. Trees 'talk' to each other through a vital communication network beneath the soil, mycorrhizal networks dubbed 'the wood wide web', letting their own needs be known but also helping others by transferring nutrients and sending warning signals.

A meaning of 'to bear' is 'to carry or move something to a place' – words are borne by the air from the mouth to the ear. A meaning of 'to bear' – to be able to tolerate or endure something unpleasant. At what point does something become unbearable? There are times when we cannot bear what we witness, when bearing witness alone becomes challenging.

I can't remember what I saw and bore first. What of the world and its wildness first flooded into my eyes and entered my heart. I will have witnessed the dark amniotic fluid within my mother's body – due to complications in there, I almost never made it out at all. I will have witnessed

the world reflected in my mother's and others' eyes.
I witnessed tears, rain, clouds reflected in puddles, brick
homes, concrete pavements, grass growing. I first witnessed
the fierce power of the sea on a trip to Blackpool and
I see now that carrying a sense of the wild within helped
me persevere. I witnessed myself bruised and beaten by
bullies. I witnessed the staggering beauty of a sunset.
I witnessed words graffitied onto a building telling me
I did not belong. I witnessed a ladybird crawl over my
skin so tenderly it seemed to disprove this. I witnessed the
world and its wildlife being wounded. I witnessed littered
parks, dirty rivers, smoggy skies, the canal's grimy surface.
I witnessed swallows migrating. I witnessed ones I loved
lose their life. I witnessed the persistence of blossom in
spring. I witnessed my hometown blown up by a bomb.
I witnessed a bulb planted in soil. I witnessed hurt skin
healing. I witnessed a daffodil opening with the morning
light. That day in May, as I journeyed through northern
England, I witnessed a man trying to wound me.
I witnessed a glimpse of greenness from the train window
that kept me going. Close the eyes, now. What we have
seen is there, still, within us. Our ears are witnesses too –
hearing from within the womb and, on being born, our
own screaming, as if life is already too much to bear. That
day in May I heard bad words try to bruise me. Our
bodies bear witness, too, hurt leaves its presence even in
our posture, the way we carry ourself, our bearing. My
body bore witness that day as it slumped against my seat's
headrest, as it remained shaken and tense even as I stood
up and walked.

There have been times I could not bear what I had
witnessed. Putting into words what we have witnessed

makes it more bearable, what remains untold becoming toxic, unbearable – for language can bear more than us. To communicate what we have witnessed becomes a mutual bearing. A shared witnessing. I see you. I hear you. I bear you. To bear witness to another's suffering moves the victim from a state of isolation to one of belonging. What would you do if you saw a stranger in distress? Would you be a bystander and look the other way? Or would you be a citizen and help? Do not witness and walk away. The silence and inaction of bystanders can be as traumatising as the violation itself, condoning what happened – silence is indeed complicity. Good Samaritan laws and duty-to-rescue laws exist in many countries and you can be prosecuted for failure to provide assistance, but in the UK, legislation could better reflect such moral and ethical duties. It is more a civic and moral duty rather than an act of generosity to speak up on behalf of someone being racially abused, showing that you belong to a community of equals. A person cannot possibly be an anti-racist if they think they should be repaid or are owed anything by the victim – that notion in itself is racist. The person who has been racially abused is not indebted, nor have they been saved by people of superior morality. The toxic 'white saviour' narrative is still deeply embedded in culture and society. It posits morality and agency in the white person, diminishing both from the person of colour, and puts a burden of debt on people of colour for not being white.

The origin of the word 'kind' is from Old English *gecynd* (kind, nature, race) from Proto-Germanic *kundi* (natural, native). The word 'kind' is related to 'kin' and

both have belonging embedded in their meanings. True
kindness is so important, extending kinship to all,
showing that all of us belong here. True kindness I felt
that day, in the sweet tea that someone made for me on
seeing I was distressed; in the hurt in my shoulder
alleviated when a train staff member lifted my bag back
onto the train; in altruistic concern shown for my
wellbeing. As I looked at the gorgeous glimpse of green
outside the train window, it felt that nature too was in
kinship with me. What kind of a world are we? What
kind of a world do we want to become? I hope for a
world in which the 'kind' (i.e. class or racial group) of
the person does not affect how others show real kindness
to them, in which we are all kind to each other,
recognising true equality.

The lens of the camera like an eye witnessing, its
audio an ear listening, and recording and providing
evidence; phone cameras are in our contemporary world
bearing witness to many injustices. A brown woman
abused on a train. The barbaric murder of a black man in
broad daylight. There will be many incidents happening
that have not been recorded on camera, shared and gone
viral, that have not been borne witness to.

Discrimination is still ongoing and systemic; everyday
racism and sexism are rife. Prejudice of all kinds is
pervasive. You might witness it walking the streets, in
the great outdoors, on public transport, in workplaces,
as both macro and microaggressions. While a victim can
try and have the courage to speak out, those who
witness discrimination should also speak up for them,
and the systems enabling such injustice need radical
reform. We are all living history, and all our actions will

have a reaction and reverberation. All of us can, in whatever small way, help to move the world forward for the better.

I sat in a small, windowless Interview Room in the police station not far from Newcastle train station, the sunshine of earlier seeming a distant dream. Claustrophobia engulfed me, the walls closing in and the air leached from my lungs, but I had to keep my nerve.

PC: Have you given a police statement before?

Me: I gave a statement to your colleagues in Darlington, they have it.

PC: On statement paper?

Me: No not on statement paper, they recorded it…it was verbal not a written statement. What happened is that they stopped the train at Darlington, they took the man off and I gave a statement.

PC: That's essential, that's a first account. This is how we formalise the process, by giving a written statement. Have you ever given a written statement before?

Me: No.

PC: It's pretty much identical to what you've gone through. What's your full name please?

I spelled out my name phonetically, shaping 'A' for apple, 'n' for night, shaping vowel and consonant until I felt language leaving me. My voice broke at the third syllable of my name, 'i', as I felt a rush of tears begin to well, and the beginnings of a panic attack.

Me: Sorry do you have a glass of water? I'm so so thirsty. I'm still really shaken.

My mouth was parched, the migraine had gathered in full force and a sudden wave of exhaustion hit me. My mouth felt so dry it was as if I would never again be able to form another word. The policeman returned with a cup of water. I took a sip and the cold liquid awakened me. I marvelled for a moment at the sheer miracle of water and its capacity to revive. I felt the water on my lips, tongue, the roof of my mouth, slipping down the back of my throat and flowing within until it was fully a part of me. I felt the cold water in my empty stomach. I was so grateful for the water. Meanwhile, my eyes dried again, thankfully. The dull thumping in my head lifted a little. I inhaled until I felt my heart rise, then exhaled.

PC: What's your surname?

It is such a primal feeling – spelling out your identity, letter by letter, in a police station, after being the victim of a hate crime, after having the core of the identity attacked and in such brutal language. I began again shaping sound into sense, hearing my name resound. This is who I am.

PC: What's your current job occupation?

I explained more about my occupation, and that I was in Newcastle to speak at the launch of a new book I am in at Waterstones at 6.30 pm, and how heartbreaking it is that we can't move around the country freely without suffering from racial assaults.

PC: So what can you remember about what happened today?

This is my name, this is what I do for a living, this is where I live, this is what happened as I was travelling through the world. I felt language return to me, and each word I uttered felt palpable, each word felt powerful, each word was bearing what had happened. I felt words in my brain, then on my tongue, behind my teeth, then enter the room. The room was so small it was as if I could feel my voice vibrating in the air, shaping sound into sense. It seemed as if every cell and every muscle in the body was engaged in helping the words out into the world, as if all the oxygen flowing through my lungs was intent on getting into language. *I*...A letter so strong and sturdy, upright. Today someone tried to bruise that self, to dent it, and not for the first time. It was an attack not only on me but on everyone of my skin colour. I felt the vowel in my voice. And how for so much of my life it had been a struggle to fully say it, to be it, all the forces that had tried to flatten it, extinguish it. I. I exist. I have a heart that beats. I have a right to exist and move around in the world safely, to belong. I shaped each word with care, feeling how important it was to convey what happened, for the truth to be known, and justice to prevail – and that by giving this testimony I might stop someone else having to suffer what I did. For being able to fully say 'I' enables connection with 'you' and 'we' and 'us'. This is why we learn to talk at all.

I answered many questions. What time did you get on the train? What time did the abuse begin? The sense of time can become sharpened and intensified when an aberration ruptures normality. Some moments come to stand outside of time, replayed in the mind – and in actuality given the recordings I made, which I played for the policeman, a few seconds becoming vital, becoming evidence. At any time during the journey did you feel he was going to come at you? So what happened when the train conductor asked him to turn the volume down? So he didn't have any headphones so he wasn't going to turn it down? So he asked you if you came over on the banana boat? Did passengers challenge him on his behaviour? So you left your seat to go and speak to the train manager? So the guard contacted police? Once you reported it did you return back to your seat? When you gave your first account was that on the platform as well? Was it on one of these [holding up recording device]? How would you describe this man… Physical features, attributes…? What kind of build? Approximate age? How tall? What was the closest distance between you two?

PC: A few signatures needed…and that's everything.

Me: These incidents are distressing, they leave you shaken. Thank you very much for being so thorough in taking the statement. So what's the process now?

PC: So he's been arrested now and depending on what his previous offending history is like depends on what the outcome will be. Most likely he'll be charged and go to court and he'll be sentenced from there.

Me: Will I have to go to court?

PC: That will only be the case if he pleads not guilty. If he pleads not guilty then you may well be summoned to court, but I find that pretty unlikely…

Me: Because there's so much evidence…

PC: Yes.

I gathered my belongings before stepping back outside, taking a deep breath and blinking at the bright light of day. After so long in a windowless room, I was elated at the sight of the sky. As I walked on, I knew that a crucial step had been made but I knew too that this was not the end of the journey. As I walked, I recalled the last time

I had been in Newcastle – a memory of a huge pair of rust-coloured wings unfurled and spread within, steel wings on the Angel of the North statue I had visited during that trip, gazing up at the enormous wings slightly stretched forward in an embrace.

I looked at a digital map to better find my bearings then walked on through the streets, relieved at being able to stand and stretch my limbs, to put one foot in front of the other. That morning on Hope Street seemed lifetimes ago, but I felt hope surge through me again as I walked. Hunger hit me and I stopped to buy food, then headed for my hotel to leave my bag before continuing on to the event at which I was scheduled to speak – I felt strongly that I could not pull out, that in true northern spirit the show must go on. I had a renewed sense, too, of just what an important tool the voice is, of those times it becomes imperative to communicate. I went ahead with both events I was programmed for; that evening's bookshop event and the New Writing North writers' conference the next day, at both reading from my piece in the *Common People* anthology.

It was strange being in Newcastle city centre and reading about being a child rising up into the glory of mountains and lakes for the first time, walking in nature and seeing all manner of wildlife, getting lost on the way back home on the trans-Pennine motorway, the highest in the country. I put my whole heart into both readings, shaken by what had happened, but opening my mouth anyway and putting one word after the other. I felt a strong pang to return to those mountains and lakes, not just glimpsing green from a train window or imaginatively returning, but walking through the wilderness, losing myself in that landscape. As I read, I felt how landscape as well as language has helped me to bear when life felt most unbearable.

As I took the train back from Newcastle, I received an email from the police constable assigned to my case, who had first taken my statement at Darlington, confirming that the man who racially abused me had been arrested and charged for the offence of section (4)(A) racially aggravated public order and would be appearing in court at the end of the month. The constable also said that Victim Support had been requested for me.

In an essay in the *New York Times* Margaret Atwood wrote about 'the literature of witness',[7] about the core use of words as ways of bearing witness. Her novel *The Testaments* is structured around a series of testimonies, and the fact that Offred records her story at all, says Atwood, is an act of hope since it implies a future reader. My experience on the train and thereafter showed me quite literally this use of language as a tool of bearing witness. Yet the stories of black and brown people have so often been overlooked, as reams of whitewashed history books and shelves of literature testify. Having our stories borne witness to is an important part of the healing process to centuries of racial injustice. Now is the time – as it should always have been the time – to bear witness to the stories of people of colour, to include our stories in all forms of documentation that end up forming a part of history – from curricula to libraries to bookshops, as well as actively listening in everyday conversations, not defensively silencing through discomfiture. Maya Angelou wrote of the 'agony' of bearing an untold story inside ourselves; likewise, when your story is not borne witness to, there is pain and anger, that pain when we speak but are not heard or are deliberately silenced – and systemic racism seeks to silence. Bearing witness to someone else's story creates empathy, a recognition of the existence of others' thoughts and feelings and their validity. I experienced empathy that day of the hate crime: on the station platform in Newcastle, I had seen the train manager who had sat with me and I thanked him again – he said he understood now why I chose not to move from my seat, and it was moving to hear him say this. A simple sentence: I understand now. Empathy can move us from 'I' to 'us' to 'we'.

It was having been gaslit about previous experiences of abuse that finally prompted me to report and bear witness to this one. Such gaslighting – the attempt to manipulate the truth by invalidating someone's experience and presenting a false version of reality – is prevalent in both the personal and political domain. The term originates from the 1938 play *Gas Light* and is now in more common parlance as it has become increasingly apparent that we are living in an age in which attempts to stop us from seeing clearly and bearing witness are rife – that we are being systemically gaslit. There are dangerous attempts to gaslight us into thinking climate change isn't happening, that global warming is a hoax, that habitats aren't being destroyed, that sea levels aren't rising, that rivers aren't polluted and rainforests burning, that what we see with our own eyes isn't real. Trump – who has a pro-fossil fuels agenda – attempted to gaslight the findings of a report by leading scientists warning of the devastating effects of climate change. 'I don't believe it,' he said, a classic phrase of the gaslighter presented

with facts. It is crucial that we recognise such gaslighting
for what it is, for it can impede us from bearing witness,
and from action being taken to save the world, make it a
safe and just place for all to exist.

What do we spend our lives watching? And what is
watching us? How much do we really hear and listen,
and what is listening to us? Those dragonflies' eyes, those
starfish eyes, those honeycomb moth ears and dolphin
ears, what is it they can see and hear of humans and how
we are hurting each other, the world and its wildlife? For
nature too is bearing witness. I remembered the sensation
of that sip of water in the police station, how it had so
revived me and enabled me to give my testimony at all,
to survive, yet how humans are decimating the world's
water supplies, its lifeblood.

As the train rumbled on through the country, I felt a
strong need to fully bear witness to what had happened,
commit it to pen and paper in a way the world could
see, and to continue my journey through the North, my
home, asserting my right to travel through it – bearing
witness to what I saw along the way through the writing
of this book, laying bare all the pain and hope, the
brutality and beauty, of this existence.

SKIN

Wanted: A Long Green Trail

3

If Your Nerve Deny You,
Go Above Your Nerve

Humans have long hungered for footpaths, and so too that summer did I. Paths, tracks, waterways, songlines all run through both human and natural history, from those man-made – train tracks and footpaths and canals – to those found and forged in the natural world: the course of rivers, the migratory routes of birds, and the astonishing ways all manner of wildlife great and small are variously led by magnetic fields and imprinted memories and meteorology. There is music in such movement. I think of the songlines with which I've been enchanted since traversing the Australian outback, songlines (also called a 'dreaming track') being a path across the land and sometimes the sky which some Indigenous Australians believe were travelled during the Dreamtime. Ancestors walked the world and sang the world into being.

That summer following the hate crime, I was filled with longing for a long journey in which I could explore my sense of belonging. I pined for Britain's oldest long-distance footpath, the Pennine Way. I read up about the trails which inspired it – the John Muir Trail through the Sierra Nevada mountain range including Yosemite in California and the Appalachian Trail between Sprinter Mountain, Georgia and Mount Katahdin, Maine – as well as others including the Pacific Crest Trail which follows the same footpath as the John Muir Trail for 260 kilometres, and upon which Cheryl Strayed walked, chronicling her journey in *Wild*. Learning about such trails seemed to expand the world and I yearned to walk upon some of them, to lose myself in the wildernesses along the way.

The Pennine Way wound its way through my dreams. It was the rambler Tom Stephenson's phrase 'Wanted: A Long Green Trail' that made me want to one day make a modern-day pilgrimage through the Pennines. I devoured all the information I could including from the National Trails' website and one day called up a Trail officer, Nick, who offered helpful guidance such as how to break up the Way into achievable daily walking segments, and perhaps select part of it to complete rather than the whole thing. He advised on the best gear to bring, including a headtorch, proper walking shoes, and warned me that in several places there would be no phone signal so I would not be able to rely upon Google maps and should consider bringing a compass, one which would give me my exact bearings. He also said storms had made most of the area dangerous to traverse, that it would be wise not to set out walking yet, but to keep an eye on the weather. The walk remained a pipedream for the time being. The early part of summer was filled with prior obligations anyway, adding to which I did not quite have the courage of my convictions to make such a journey, I did not yet have the nerve.

My anxiety grew as I waited to hear back about how the man who racially abused me would plead. The dread hung like a persistent grey cloud, and throughout me spread a searing sense of unease. My tweets had gone viral and I had received thousands of supportive messages, yet those days after the attack were some of my loneliest, showing the paradoxical nature of internet communications and exacerbating my isolation. I was feeling profoundly unmoored. I had been commended on my calmness during that journey, yet in the days that followed I felt an intense, searing rage that flooded my head as if with a hot dark liquid and curdled through my veins. I felt furious. While I had not expressed my anger directly to the man who racially abused me, instead ensuring he was dealt with appropriately by the authorities, it did not mean that I felt no anger.

The first week of June brought the news that my abuser had pleaded guilty. I was relieved that I would not have to relive the ordeal in court. I felt a strong solidarity towards not only those who speak out and get justice but to those who don't. It is rare to get a conviction for a race hate crime; they are often unreported and often insufficient evidence exists. My experience has deepened my empathy towards all who have suffered injustice and violation, and those striving for a fairer world. Although my experience was technically resolved and in the past, I knew that was not the case for so many others who will suffer what I did, incidents happening on a daily basis the world over.

Despite the successful outcome, I found that a generalised anxiety and depression had gnawed its way into both my body and mind, into my mouth and legs and hands and skin.

Then a sudden bereavement ruptured the summer and tore a hole through the world. I felt winded in shock, the oxygen drained from my brain, the solidity of objects blurring and the light fading when I heard the news. A vivid memory rose in me of the last time I had seen my friend and I felt the hug she had given me before we parted ways, promising to meet again soon, the kind of embrace that made you feel as if you could face anything with grace, as if everything in the world would be well. We had a coffee planned in just a couple of weeks' time. Instead of meeting again, I was attending her funeral. Sophie was twenty-eight years old when she died.

It was a day of sunlight so bright, glinting the world so golden, when I took the train to the funeral; that intense light seemed to hold in it something of her spirit. Through the train window I glimpsed red words on the side of a building reading TAKE COURAGE. I have no idea what the building was, but the words felt like a message from her – everything seems to take on a strange kind of symbolism when grieving. I walked through the greenery of Kemnal Park cemetery and ceremonial park set in acres of ancient woodland, where an abundance of wildlife, flora and fauna makes its home, a startle of brilliantly coloured flowers meeting the eyes, a bird soaring overhead. The leaves of the trees glowed from inside out. In the distance I saw mourners dressed in bright colours. Then I saw her face, huge and smiling and forever stilled in a giant photograph.

Standing there in the crematorium, the cold hard fact of her passing hit me. I felt faint with horror that she was dead, the sudden shift in tense from 'is' to 'was'. I felt raw with the tragedy of her loss, the burning injustice of it, how such a truly good person could be taken from this earth while others more cruel remain. Here was a human being who so loved life, who so belonged to life. The stark reality of a human being hugging me, the warmth and presence and sheer aliveness and energy, and then not long after a pile of ashes, shocked me to the core.

Even though I have experienced the death of loved ones before, the age-old questions about death rose within, childish questions that even an adult can scream silently into the void – why did she have to die? Where is she now? We know death as a fact for all of us, but it is still a struggle to grasp its enormity.

Death has long been figured as a journey and place – the final journey, as Shakespeare put it, to the 'undiscovered country from whose bourn no travellers return'. We live life with a hubristic sense of immortality, punctured by flashes of realisation that not only us but every living thing will one day perish, that our days on earth are finite; beneath that hubris is a primal fear, perhaps the greatest terror: losing those we love. Yet the funeral ended up a celebration of her life, reminding us of ways she will remain and live on and urging us to take what was best of her into our own lives, to make the most of our fleeting time on earth, to make the world brighter and more full of joy, to lead beautiful, kind and brilliant lives in tribute to her. I was awed by the courage of her family, partner and friends who put their grief into words through speeches, her younger sister reminiscing on their childhood and sharing the advice Sophie gave her, including powerful words from the poet Emily Dickinson: 'If your nerve deny you, go above your nerve.'

Sophie's handwriting in curling blue ink had been propped up on my bookshelf for months – she had sent me a handwritten thank-you card on the cover of which were the silver words 'A Little Card Full of Magic and Joy', and I often look at her handwriting and the miracle of language living on long after a person has passed away. That ink captures her thoughtfulness and kindness of spirit, a part of her still there, words both unmoveable and moving. We had become friends after she got in touch asking me to do an on-stage interview with one of the authors she worked with, Markus Zusak, author of *The Book Thief*, and she had sent me that card thanking me for the interview. It had slipped through my letterbox the bleak, cold winter before and had lifted my spirits, those inky words had warmed me, and we had developed a friendship bonding over breakfast and books and our shared love of walking, places and people. I was attempting to establish a life in London at the time and being a Northerner trying to make my way down South could feel lonely as hell – I often felt isolated and like an outsider, and my friend was one of few people who made me feel comfortable, as if I belonged. I looked at the beautiful blue handwriting and felt a renewed sense of the importance and primacy of words; not only can they be a vessel of abuse but also one of magic and joy – I looked at the handwriting and felt how language can triumph, in some way, over loss.

It was Chaucer's great poem of journeying and pilgrimage, *The Canterbury Tales*, that inspired the five-day walk I made along the southernmost tip of the country in early July, through the South Downs and along the English coast from Brighton to Hastings, walking with a group of refugees, asylum seekers and migrants formerly held in indefinite detention. At each stop-off there would be an evening of storytelling and music. I had been invited by The Refugee Tales to host the Eastbourne event and it was suggested I also do the whole walk, along the way fundraising for the charity the Gatwick Detainees Welfare Group of which The Refugee Tales is a part, each footstep aiming to walk towards a better future.

Like Chaucer's characters, millions of people of many faiths and backgrounds have undertaken pilgrimages throughout the ages, forging 'pilgrim ways', from the Camino de Santiago (a network of ancient pilgrim routes stretching across Europe), to the pilgrimage to Lumbini (the birthplace of the Buddha), and those to Jerusalem and Mecca. A pilgrimage does not have to have a religious purpose but can also mean a journey undertaken as a quest for meaning or insight into the self, others, nature, or to pay homage.

My sense of claustrophobia was by now intense and I was grateful to be on the train to Brighton as the sun set, and then to spend the following days walking by coast and cliff, through meadows and moorlands. On the morning we set off on our walk, we were welcomed by Caroline Lucas MP, co-leader of the Green Party: 'We need to continue pressuring the government to end the hostile environment,' she said. 'It's a scandal that in the twenty-first century we treat human beings in that way.' She spoke of visiting Yarl's Wood immigration removal centre, where people endure 'psychological torture' not knowing how long they will be held there. She encouraged the walkers: 'What you're doing today is a vital part of spreading a different message, a message of welcome, of compassion, of love.'

Our group of modern-day pilgrims left Brighton on a bright, hot morning and we journeyed to the city's edge, past wildflowers growing on the roadside, before the city gave way to countryside. Uphill we walked into the South Downs, the sun beating fiercely, but after some time a breeze cooled the skin and we stepped into fields filled with poppies. Our walk also followed a route along the muddy banks of the River Ouse where we stopped to admire egrets, herons and gulls, before continuing towards Charleston and Alfriston – some of the most quintessentially 'English' places. Onwards we walked all the way to Seven Sisters cliffs and beyond to Eastbourne, Bexhill-on-Sea, reaching our final destination on a day of sunshine sparkling the blue sea.

It was impossible to witness such beauty and not remember the horrors that have happened here at the border. Those with whom I walked had felt the worst of discrimination and the hostile environment and our walk through the English countryside was one of reclamation, breaking down barriers of race and place. I walked with people who have made journeys for desperate reasons of survival. As the sun turned the long maize golden, I walked and talked with a former detainee, R, who told me how he left war-torn Sudan aged nineteen and had a treacherous journey to the UK. I did not want to probe him further about his traumatic past and so I let him enjoy the walk, but at one of the evening events he spoke more about his journey from the Sudanese mountains, about leaving his family behind, then his voice broke into a great wave of grief. He took a breath and continued, shaping that grief into words, sharing how he grew up on a farm where he would help his father, about the last day he saw his family and home. He told of how he escaped from militia and ran and kept running through the night, until he reached a village and asked if he could send a message to his family as he would not be going back again. He crossed the Sahara Desert, and when he got to the border of Libya he kept saying to himself how lucky he was, but then he was arrested and put in a container for twenty days and had no money to be released. He was told if he had no money, he would have to die there. He managed to escape, but life in Libya was harder than Sudan: when you woke up you didn't know if you'd sleep again; if you walked on the street you didn't know if you would reach your destination; if you were going to work for someone you did not get paid. He decided to cross the sea to Italy but there were about 900 people including children and families crammed together for the passage. He remembers people pulling him from the sea, then he doesn't remember anything until he woke from unconsciousness in hospital and was told he was in Italy. He lost friends during the journey who drowned. In England he was arrested and taken to an immigration removal centre, where he said conditions were awful, that life in detention is not really life at all.

Other migrants I walked and talked with include M from Sudan, who also had a heartbreakingly horrific journey: one of three boats that set off from Libya sank, killing 200 people on board. I also walked with Ridy, who is using art to channel the intense anger he has felt.

The people I walked with have been connected with the Gatwick Detainees Welfare Group, whose volunteers visit detainees, offering friendship, practical and emotional support, unconditional acceptance and welcome, providing a backbone to some of the most vulnerable in Britain. The UK is the only country in Europe that

detains people indefinitely; 24,000 people a year are
detained in eleven immigration removal centres. The
people I walked with shared their pain at both being torn
apart from their home and prevented from making a new
home elsewhere. I walked with people who have had
severe restrictions of movement placed on them by the
state and also financially through destitution, literally not
being able to afford to get a train, which The Refugee
Tales helps with. They have experienced extreme isolation
and walking together creates a sense of community and
family, of belonging.

How did it feel to be walking now? As we walked
through the English countryside, we discussed how
painful it feels to be excluded from places, but how
joyful it was to be walking now despite some stares from
locals in predominantly white English villages. R told
me how much he loves being out in nature, how he feels
he can forget everything for a while, and how it makes
him feel at home. He told me more about his childhood
immersed in nature, inner landscapes of memory rising
as we walked – how the village he was born in is
surrounded by the Marrah Mountains of Darfur, where
water flows from the mountains to make lakes. As we
walked, he asked me about the mountains in Britain and
I told him about the Peak District and Lake District and
how the North has the finest mountains.

Walking for so many is an act of necessity – to escape
danger, to flee home and seek a safer life. Our walk led
us to imagine a world where walking could be an act of
joy. As we walked, each footstep felt one of hope. As the
writer Ali Smith, patron of The Refugee Tales, said when
she welcomed us near the end of our journey: 'How fine

your feet are in the world, you're walking towards the better imagined.'

This five-day walk had made me hungry for further epic walks and also shown me the power of making a journey of reclamation. A meaning of the word 'reclamation' is reasserting a right – in this case the right to roam freely and without fear in places where we belong, yet places where minority groups are in myriad ways made to feel as if we do not belong. The etymology of the word 'reclamation' is from the late fifteenth-century Old French *réclamacion* and directly from Latin *reclamationem,* 'a cry of "no", a shout of disapproval', a noun of action from the past-participle stem of *reclamare* meaning 'cry out against, protest'. The notion of protest is at the heart of a journey of reclamation, and walking is a powerful form of protest, as we have seen both in the UK and globally, with millions participating in marches.

In the past few years, I have been on more protest walks than ever before, using my feet to 'cry out against' human, political and environmental injustice, from Women's Marches to Global Climate Strikes and Black Lives Matter protests, feeling a palpable hunger for change as we marched through the streets of Westminster and beyond, along the pathways of power. Marches were also important in the civil rights movement, Martin Luther King describing the five-day march from Selma to Montgomery in March 1965 as a 'pilgrimage'[8] involving thousands of non-violent demonstrators, a 'mighty walk' through hills and deserted valleys, on highways and rocky byways. Walking had become symbolic since the Bus Boycott when feet replaced buses as the main mode of travel. At his speech in Montgomery

at the end of the journey, King commemorated Rosa
Parks and also told of how an elderly lady, Mother
Pollard, was asked while walking if she wanted to ride
and she declined and kept walking, saying: 'My feets is
tired, but my soul is rested.' King paid his last visit to the
UK two years after that march, visiting Newcastle where
he received an honorary doctorate. He was assassinated a
year later by a bullet that struck him in his jaw and
severed his spinal cord. The day before his death he gave
his prophetic last speech, 'I've Been to the Mountaintop'.
Days after his death, Congress passed the Civil Rights
Act of 1968.

The largest anti-racism protests since the civil rights
movement happened fifty-two years later with the Black
Lives Matter protests following the brutal murder of
George Floyd in May 2020, protests which showed how
walking is still a powerful form of activism. I walked
alongside thousands with rage and hope in our hearts
and breath still left in our bodies, many bearing banners
of his harrowing last words, repeated twenty times to
police officers: 'I can't breathe.' We walked in the
knowledge that urgent systemic change is necessary that
will ultimately help others to keep breathing for longer.

When I returned from the South Downs, I felt a sense of
crushing claustrophobia and the city hemming me in
again, and I longed for vast open spaces, for cliffs and
mountains, to breathe deeply in the great outdoors.
My hunger had intensified to walk through the natural
landscapes of the North, for when we are far from home
is when we often most yearn for it. And how could I not

use my own freedom as much as possible? Despite the racial abuse I have experienced, I exist in the country without the threat of deportation that looms over some of the courageous people with whom I walked along the South coast.

As summer deepened, I had such a strong pull to explore the nature of the North, as strong as a magnetic force drawing me to the region, and anywhere else I felt unsettled. I was hungry for the perspective that walking brings, to reflect on my experience and the issues around it, about hate and love, place and race, belonging and the longing to move around in the world freely and without fear.

I still felt strangely unmoored from the world, lonely and homesick. I was seeing Sophie's face everywhere, double-taking at someone who looked like her and turned out to be a stranger, and I saw her face etched in the limestone cliffs and in the shapes of the waves. I felt a persistent nausea, a sense of homesickness for our friendship, a friendship in which we had conversations about things and she had understood and shown insight where others hadn't – for people as well as places can make us feel at home. I felt her loss like an ache in my bones.

Along with grief, the rage I had felt at being questioned about my right to exist in a place on account of my race was still coursing through me, and rage at systemic injustice and inequality about which I was feeling a heightened awareness. I sensed a new level of fury too. I was furious at the fact that my friend had died, the injustice of it. I knew that to stop the anger consuming me, corroding me, I had to channel it, and I felt that putting one foot in front of the other in my own form of protest was a powerful way I could do so. Walking was not only a way of alleviating anxiety but anger too, of channelling and managing such emotions if not eradicating them. The fact of my abuser's conviction also fuelled my own conviction to try and keep going, to not give in to despair. The smoggy weight of depression, anxiety and grief was threatening to keep me paralysed and pinned into inertia, but I had to fight against it. I had to let the clarity of hope win out. I had to keep walking through the world.

4

You Make Your Own Path
as You Walk

I walk over a bridge across the River Aire, a river that
twists and winds through Yorkshire, beginning its journey
high up at Malham Tarn where I am heading, and
emptying into the River Ouse at a place called Airmyn
('myn' being an Old English word for 'river mouth').

I stop for a moment, elated to see the blue–black water
rushing beneath, letting the song of the river soothe.
Gazing out at the glittering water, I see trees reflecting on
its surface, even a surface so dark. How eerie those tree
branches look, reaching deep down into the depths of
the river. The origin of this river's name is thought to
come from Common Brittonic *Isarā* ('the strong one'),
so it literally means 'strong river'.

An abundance of rivers run through the backbone
of Britain including the Tyne, Eden, Lune, Tees, Ribble,
Aire, Humber and Trent. I loved looking at these inky
blue squiggles on the map while dreaming of making
this journey and yearned to see them in actuality. Even
looking at the colour blue calmed me. I planned my
journey to follow by foot the course of four of those
rivers, the Aire, Ribble, Tees and Tyne whose birthplace
is high up in the North Pennines, as well as riding some
of the local historic railways along the way. My plan,
though, was far from rigid, being open to the splendours
of spontaneity.

I've long been haunted by a line from the Spanish poet Antonio Machado, 'you make your own path as you walk' – the Pennine range of hills and mountains is not confined to the Way and I was keen not to restrict my journey to the pre-established footpath but to do it my way, to feel my way through places and let my gut as well as map guide me. The terms 'desire paths' and 'desire lines' refer to improvised routes and unofficial paths forged by the way the walker wishes to travel, and I was open to the possibilities of these too.[9] Above all, I wanted to transform that desire to make a journey through wilderness into action.

I wanted to strip life down to the bare essentials, to unburden, and packed only a few belongings for my journey in search of belonging. My intense workload ahead of the trip had left me barely any time to pack or plan, so I had left it to the last minute, buying a large black and red rucksack the day before I was due to set off. Panic rose as I gazed at my portable home splayed on the floor – how on earth would I fit anything in that and survive? I was about to go wayfaring but how would I fare upon the Way? I had not got round to purchasing much of what the trail officer had recommended, including a head torch, compass and specialist walking shoes. I could not afford such kit, and hoped the comfy black boots I already had would serve me well. They would have to. I lay inert for hours, crushed by a weight of anxiety, until I mustered the energy to begin packing. Soon my rucksack looked like a plump ladybird, ready to spread its wings.

Now I walk on over the bridge across that 'strong river', the Aire, with my belongings on my back. I pause to look back at the gateway which delivered me here in Gargrave on the southern tip of the Yorkshire Dales. 'Our gates to the glorious and unknown' is how E.M. Forster described railway termini. 'Through them we pass out into adventure and sunshine.'[10] I agreed with Forster when I first saw the idyllic station, countryside gleaming green through its elegant stone archway, great gatherings of grey clouds parting, turning the sky briefly and blissfully blue. The Pennine Way crosses the railway to the west of the station, which was opened in 1849, the train-tracks seeming to disappear into the hills.

As the grey clouds gather again, I am not feeling as optimistic as Forster about the perpetuity of sunshine. I am walking most of my journey along the backbone of Britain alone, but for this 15-kilometre section I am accompanied by a photographer friend, George, who was keen to join me in the hope of taking some pictures for a piece, as well as for the adventure itself. Highly attuned to the play of light and shadow, he pauses to capture a particularly powerful ray of light when it emerges. I'm reminded of Rick the photographer in the book *Tracks*, who accompanied its author Robyn Davidson during some of her epic journey through the Australian outback on assignment for *National Geographic*, and I vaguely wonder if, as with Rick and Robyn, there will be any hint of romance.

I had been alone in the Hope Valley, Kinder and Edale, and will be alone again after this stretch, and it is fascinating to compare the experience to walking with someone else, having another lens, quite literally, through which to view the world. Yet I'm looking forward to the time I'll be alone again, able to lose myself completely in the landscape. I wonder too how the way I am perceived by other people as I walk through this non-multicultural village and out into the countryside will be affected by the fact that I am with a man who looks white and whether I will be more accepted than if I had been walking alone as a brown woman. My companion tells me that although he is mixed-race, because he looks white he is not a 'visible minority' and not regarded so, which complicates his sense of identity further.

We leave the river behind and I miss it already. I miss the river more as we walk further into the village and the first thing to catch my eye are white and red St George's Cross flags on an ivy-covered tearoom. The flags quell my excitement and send a chill down my spine with their associations of racism and nationalism since being adopted as a far-right symbol, including by the English Defence League and BNP, flown at racist rallies and tattooed onto the skulls of far-right skinheads. I'd seen the flag being waved recently when I walked past such a rally in Manchester city centre. Of course not everyone who flies this flag has such views, yet since its appropriation by far-right groups it seems a chilling symbol. I have asked other brown and black people about their views on the flag and they said it seems hostile. In terms of 'reclamation', there is an argument that people of colour could reclaim the flag, assert it as our symbol too, of our own belonging in England.

Heavy rain is forecast, and we are keen to complete as much of the walk as possible before the clouds burst, but decide to step into a pub to look at the map of the journey ahead and properly plan our walking route. In such weather it would be better to know the way than being out in the landscape and losing our bearings. As I step inside, some stare at me with surprise – a quick look round shows I am the only person there who is not white. Others smile and I get chatting to some locals who advise me to do the Cumbria Way walk one day and take the scenic Cumbrian Coast line train. I look at the downloaded Ordnance Survey map on my phone, the first time I've had it on there, and the world opens out as I figure out how to navigate with it. I begin to feel more moored having such a map at my fingertips showing places in intricate detail and enabling me to plot out a route of my own as well as follow pre-established paths. I love looking at the Pennine Way marked on the map but am also intrigued by the unmarked landscape surrounding it and what might be found there, thrilled by the possibilities of forging a path of my own. I see two blue lines, one curving and snaking, the River Aire, and the other straight as a ruler, the Leeds and Liverpool Canal. I read the map, reading the landscape through which I will soon be walking, trying to imprint it within me, since taking out maps or phones will be difficult if it starts raining as it is sure to do. It will be far better to know the markings of the map by heart.

I am soon walking again, fortified by sweet tea, and see a signpost with arrows pointing towards the Leeds and Liverpool Canal and the Pennine Way / Sustrans 68, also known as the Pennine Cycleway. This first sight of a sign marking the Way fills me with delight, even though the clouds are growing more ominously grey. I am actually here. After all the pipedream of the project, alone in my bedroom and imagining walking through this landscape, I am here. In undertaking this long walk I faced obstacles

even before setting off, from practical issues such as the
ferocious storms earlier in the summer to the psychological
issues of fortifying myself to actually do it and believe in
my power to do it, to gain the courage of my convictions,
the nerve, to be walking here, to believe I belong here.
Curled up in bed, and all but paralysed with the inertia
that anxiety can bring, it had felt like a very big mountain
to climb.

Yet here I am now, trekking one step at a time upon
the Pennine Way which stretches through a diverse array
of natural landscapes, through mountains and meadows,
by caves and collapsed caverns, fells and forces (the local
word for 'waterfall'). Opened in 1965, the Pennine Way
was the first of sixteen National Trails that transformed
modern-day wayfaring and criss-cross the country, north
to south, east to west, the other trails including the
South West Coast Path that snakes through *The Salt Path*
by Raynor Winn and The Ridgeway that winds through
part of *The Old Ways* by Robert Macfarlane. The
Ridgeway was officially designated a Long-Distance
Footpath (as National Trails were then known) in 1973,
although it is an ancient trackway that travellers have
used for thousands of years. It meets the Icknield Way,
which the poet and writer Edward Thomas walked in
1911 during a bout of deep depression. There is a long
history of writers with depression seeking solace in
walking; looking deeper into history, the writer-walker
George Borrow would do so too, and I feel a strong
companionship with them as I seek to walk off – or
walk through – my own depression and anxiety.

We walk on, near another expanse of water, the Leeds
and Liverpool Canal that flows through the Pennines,

some of it along the same route as the TransPennine Express train journey I was on that day. I watch the water for a while and shiver to think of it flowing the same route, and of how I am now forging a new journey of hope through the Pennines. The canal was built between 1770 and 1816 to connect the rapidly growing industrial areas on either side of the Pennines and the most important cargo shipped across it was coal; over a million tonnes per year would be delivered to Liverpool in the 1860s. It is the longest in Britain built as a single waterway, stretching 204 kilometres from Merseyside to West Yorkshire, passing through cities, towns, villages and Pennine countryside. It was built with broad locks that avoided tunnelling beneath the hills, and it competed with railways as a mode of transportation throughout the nineteenth century. I have become increasingly fascinated with how routes through places – whether train lines, waterways, paths well-trodden or those less taken – first came to be forged, and the possibilities of forging new ones.

The canal often suffers from a lack of water because the reservoirs that supply it rely on rainfall during the summer and in recent years there have been droughts. There have been several summers when locks have been closed nightly in an effort to save water, since every time a lock is operated, 200,000 litres of water are used. A few years ago, almost half the canal closed due to the need to save water in drought conditions, including the section running from Manchester to Gargrave. Water supplies from the seven reservoirs that feed into the canal were cut off during the closure. A recent report by the Environment Agency warned that England could run short of water within twenty-five years unless drastic action is taken. Data from the Environment Agency published in September 2020 also revealed that every river in the country is polluted, with a mere 14 per cent of rivers being rated ecologically healthy.

The natural world is bearing witness to how humans have been treating it, in such dried-up reservoirs, polluted air and waterways, damaged landscapes, species decline. I remember again how the few sips of water in the police station revived me, and the miracle of those sphagnum moss plants on the Peak District moorlands, absorbing and conserving water. I think of how urgent it is that we learn to care both for each other and for the places through which we move, how sheer ignorance about the interconnectedness of people and places leads to careless damage, how learning more can ensure carefulness and true respect. Those healing sphagnum moss plants are themselves threatened due to the impact of climate change on habitats, causing declining biodiversity. The climate crisis is causing so much habitat loss, wildlife losing their homes, the places where they belong.

5

Walking as a Woman of Colour

Soon I see another sign for the Pennine Way and am stepping out into open fields, the village quickly falling away to leave countryside completely empty of any human. I will now be walking 15 kilometres uphill through this landscape to reach Malham, following paths, tracks and that strong river, and also navigating areas where there are not such well-worn paths at all. As I walk up the valley, what is supposed to be a gentle section of the Way, I am already feeling the strain, a night of sleeplessness not helping. Despite having brought the bare minimum of belongings, soon pain spreads seemingly to my very backbone. I think of creatures who carry their homes on their backs – turtles, tortoises, crabs, snails – and wish I could bear mine with such ease. My companion assures me I will get used to the weight, that my stamina will increase. I want to walk upwards, to rise through the Pennines, but there is physical and emotional pain involved in pushing past your limits. Every footstep feels arduous.

My companion asks me how it feels to be a woman of colour walking through such a village as the one earlier where I stuck out like a sore brown thumb – the differences between our skin colours seemed pronounced. But I tell him I don't want to talk, that every calorie of energy needs to go into walking. As my shoulders strain, I wonder if I will end up writing How Not to Walk the Pennine Way, but then the uphill section flattens out into meadowland, filling my field of vision, a sheer beauty of greenness, many shades from the dark copse to the luminous grass, the brightest green I have seen.

I walk deeper into the openness and it seems to embrace me. Then we stop for a breather and I lay down my bag and savour the weight off my shoulders. I stretch out my arms and feel my muscles relax and the hurt lessen in intensity. This is why it is worth it, for this wonderful sense of the world opening out. I breathe in and the fresh smell of the grass fills me, so potent it is almost as if I can taste it too.

Above all I love looking at the grass, which stretches like a green skin over the surface of the earth, covering whatever lies within its body. It is easy here, surrounded by the glorious green skin of the earth, to become blissfully oblivious of my own skin, unlike while walking through the village, unlike while walking through so much of the world. Whilst I was walking through the streets of Nottingham a fortnight before the train incident, en route to speak at a bookshop event, two young white women racially abused me in a mock Indian accent. When I told my fellow panellist about what happened approximately three minutes before, her reaction was 'Are you sure?', which made me burn with rage: of course I was sure. So often experiences of racism are gaslighted like this which exacerbates the trauma. The fact that it had been two white women who racially abused me that day, and a white woman who gaslit me, also shows the limits of white feminism and why we need a more intersectional approach to exploring the experience of being in the world, place and belonging.

I ponder the term 'woman of colour'– how language can imprison or liberate, and how and why it needs to be reclaimed by those it has historically been used to define and suppress. It was not so long ago that the term 'coloured person' was widely used and has since become offensive, and I wonder if that will also happen to the phrase 'person of colour' or 'woman of colour'. Likewise, the term 'BAME' can feel reductive – such labels can feel burdensome, one of the invisible burdens weighing on the shoulders. It is exhausting to be pigeon-holed, people not seeing beyond skin colour and making incorrect assumptions based on limited knowledge. I don't fit neatly in any box, and my heritage – encompassing Asia, Africa, the Caribbean, and South America – is often not understood, which long made me feel as if I don't quite belong anywhere. There is much failure to understand the huge nuances and diversity within the term 'BAME'. The term can also overlook issues specific to racial groups such as anti-black racism. Perhaps worst is the term 'non-white', defining a person by what they are not rather than by what they are – and linguistically positing white to be superior.

At present, working within the limits of language, I use the term 'woman of colour' to describe myself. I am also a woman who loves colour: walking upon the skin of the earth, I drink up the sight of greenness, the colour created by chlorophyll which captures the sun's rays and turns it into energy. I feel calm just looking at the colour. I also keep an eye out for other colours. Looking down, I notice bright hot spots of thistle growing out of the grass like beauty spots on the earth's skin, and observe the protective prickles surrounding its purple. I gaze at yellow-gold strands of grass amidst the green. I see flecks of brown mud on the dock leaves.

I consider the colours of creatures in the natural world –
bright green parakeets, kingfisher blue, golden tigers,
raven black. In such context you see how foolish colour
discrimination is. Does the purple thistle tease the grass
about its greenness? I look down again at the grass. Can
you imagine a blade of grass having low self-esteem,
being made to hate its colour or shape? Despite being so
literally trodden upon, it is so sure of itself, so confident
in its skin. *Be more like grass growing*, I think.

Bamboo, barley, bluegrass, foxtail, goldentap, hare's-tail
grass, Indian grass, love grass, quackgrass, sugarcane,
velvet grass, and wheatgrass. These are just some of the
different species of grass. Grass thrives in its diversity –
there are around 10,000 different species of Poaceae or
Gramineae, the 'true grasses'.[11] Grass – including sedges
and rushes and cereal grasses, those of natural grasslands
and cultivated lawns – is so vital yet we take it for
granted. Grasses are an important member of the plant
family, a source of fuel and food, nourishing animals,
humans and the earth itself. It is the world's single most
important source of food. Every step of my walk through
the natural landscapes of the North shows just how
crucial biodiversity is to the planet, in turn sustaining
humans in all our diversity.

Grass, the skin of the earth – walking upon it and
considering its value, I tread softly.

As for human skin, we rarely consider its actual role in
our bodies, why we have skin at all. Skin is like a landscape
in itself, home to incredibly diverse communities of
microorganisms.[12] The soft outer tissue covering vertebrates serves the main function of protection and is also
important for thermoregulation, sensation, storage of

water, absorption of oxygen and other roles. It protects the underlying bones, muscles, ligaments and internal organs. That for people of colour our skin – whose role is to protect – can often make us feel exposed and vulnerable and lead to us not being protected but attacked is a horrible irony. An eight-year-old child was relating my experience on the train and said in a simple but potent sentence: 'The man on the train was horrible to her because of her skin colour.' The epidermis, the outermost of three layers that make up the skin, provides a barrier to infection from environmental pathogens, but skin is still porous and can absorb harmful pollutants; the skin of those in highly polluted areas suffers most.[13] Structural inequalities literally affect the skin we're in.

I reach down and touch the grass and delight in its cold wet skin upon mine, rooting me. I stroke the grass with the back of my palm and my skin feels such pleasure. I gently touch one of the gold grasses and the texture makes my skin tingle. I wince as a plant prickles me. As well as playing a protective role, our skin is sensory, full of nerves – the nerve endings in the epidermis respond to pain and pleasure, touch, light and temperature variations. Sensation including pain is relayed from skin to brain by the dermatome nerves in the skin supplied by a spinal nerve.[14]

For a long time, I felt uncomfortable in my own skin. I would squirm in my skin, having been bullied as a child about its colour. It's high time we appreciate just how amazing skin is, whatever its colour. *Grow a thick skin*, we can be told or *don't be so thin-skinned*. I've always been extremely sensitive to touch, excruciatingly so and torturously ticklish (tickling has been used as a form of actual torture). Yet, as well as being supersensitive, skin is also paradoxically pretty tough stuff; indeed, the epidermis is composed of cells made of keratin – such a hard substance that it is also found in nails, the shells of turtles, hooves, claws, and in the spines of porcupines (yes skin is a backbone for these amazing creatures). The fact that environmental pollutants still manage to penetrate the skin shows just how dangerously potent they are.

Melanin is found in most organisms and is the main determinant of skin colour. As well as being found in skin, the pigment is also in hair, eyes, feathers, scales and some internal membranes such as the inner ear, and neuro-melanin exists in the brain.[15] Melanin makes up the ink used by cephalopods. That found in chestnut shells can be used as an antioxidant, and some moth species use melanin to increase thermoregulation. It is an effective absorbent of light and so protects the skin from damaging rays in sunlight. The earliest humans evolved to have dark skin as an adaptation to the loss of body hair that increased harmful effects of ultraviolet radiation. Migration to places where the sun is less intense contributed to the range of skin colours found today. Melanin also allows for greater visual acuity since it limits the beams of light entering the eye and absorbs scattered light within the eyeball. The dark feathers of desert-dwelling birds contain melanin as a protection since it provides resistance to abrasion. Melanin is nothing short of magnificent.

Skin makes up about 16 per cent of our body weight and we have around 1.6 trillion skin cells, about 30–40,000 of which fall off every hour. Over a twenty-four-hour period we lose almost a million skin cells. But for all that loss, skin regenerates itself, growing new, fresher cells.

As I walk, skin is shedding. Walking deeper and higher into the hills, the present moment sheds a layer and I am again a girl visiting the hills and mountains for the first time with my mother, on a journey that would show how nature can help us feel at home in our own skins, can be a home in itself. Mum had got a weekend stay in a bungalow and for ages beforehand I'd been singing about soon going to the Lake District. The nurses at her work had to sign up if they wanted to go, and finally Mum's turn had come up. I wonder if I would even have had this one early experience of the countryside had it not been for that nurse's subsidy.

My earliest memories of nature were visiting the local park in my hometown of Manchester, which had felt like a safe space before I heard that guns belonging to gangs were rumoured to be buried beneath the trees. My childhood home was just three kilometres from the city centre in the M16 postcode that criss-crosses Old Trafford, Moss Side and Whalley Range, and at the time my hometown had acquired the nickname 'Gunchester'. It seemed worlds away from the Lake District. There were some trips to parks further afield, to Lyme Park and Dunham Massey park, and a photograph captures my first memorable encounter with a wild creature, gazing deep into the eyes of a deer. On some occasions, my father took us to Blackpool, where I first remember seeing the sea, sensing its wild power, saving a shell from its shore and marvelling that the sound of the sea was stored within that shell's heart. I wished to be like that shell, hard on the surface, able to withstand the batterings of the waves without breaking yet storing that strong song of the sea within like a secret, a talisman.

For the most part, growing up in a single-parent family with a mother who worked multiple jobs, there was not much time or money for many trips away. But one day we did leave the city behind and venture beyond it, higher up in the world than I'd ever been before. We drove up through the hills, up and up and up, the roads growing thin and steep and windy, and I looked out of the window and gasped as the grey fell away into an astonishment of green and blue and gold. Then the car swooped down and we were heading towards a lake, a pinprick of blue that grew larger until it swamped the whole vision. I fixed my eyes on the water shimmering with jewels cast by the sunlight and it seemed as if I was flying towards the lake, flying into the blue. It was as if a surface had been stripped off the world to reveal its colours beneath. It was a shock to step out of the car and breathe in, for the air was so much clearer, the light so lucid, the sky so vast and reflected in the lake. I breathed more deeply than I ever had done before and, for the first time I could remember, it was a joy to breathe and feel the oxygen flowing through my lungs, around my body, lifting my heart, clearing my head. I walked through the grass which tickled my bare brown legs. Being tickled by a blade of glass, you sense the sheer sensitivity as well as toughness of skin.

I played outside, picking flowers and watching an elderly couple in the garden next to the bungalow. 'You don't see many brown folks out here in the countryside,' mumbled the man as he paused to gaze at me, frowning, then going back to his gardening.

One morning I went for a walk with Mum through the mountains, watching how the great expanse of green gave way to water and watching the wide-open spaces.

We walked and walked through this new world, stopping to inspect flowers and plants and birds and butterflies. We walked through a place filled with so many species I had never known existed. We stopped near a huge tree and I stretched out all my limbs so I was standing firm and proud like the bark of that tree. For the first time I remember, it felt right to be. I felt strong as if, like that tree, I would be able to withstand any fierce gale that may come battering. My heart was opening, growing, becoming as vast and deep as those lakes, as wide as those woods. I walked and walked through the world and the grass brushed my skin and the sweet scents of flowers filled my lungs and a bright purple butterfly fluttered by so quickly that my heart leapt and I walked and walked and forgot about myself entirely as the world flooded in and all the bad feelings drained away into the hills and Mum's rage seeped away into the lakes where it was swallowed up and washed away. I walked and walked and walked and the skin was renewing itself, each cell opening up and welcoming in the light, the skin was shedding itself, the bruised skin, the hurt skin, the thickened sore skin shed as the self renewed and strengthened and healed and new skin began to grow.

One day soon after our trip, Mum brought the world home for us. 'Close your eyes,' she said. She switched off the lights and when we opened our eyes the world was glowing in a corner of the room. Then she switched the world off – the globe was only to be lit on special occasions. She brought another world back with her too, a flatter, rectangular world. She stuck the map on the wall with BluTack and drew some circles on it in blue biro, lines marking significant places, as if to remember them even though we were far away. Every now and then the world's edges curled precariously, defying their flatness, and it slipped onto the floor. When it remained on the wall, I gazed at it and imagined the landscapes through which I would one day walk.

We all carry inner mappings of memory, places that trace their contours within, and as I walk such memory-maps every now and then unfurl. A journey is not just linear but takes us inwards – as the naturalist John Muir said: 'I only went out for a walk and finally concluded to stay out till sundown, for going out was really going in.'

I can't remember going to the Lakes after that; Mum mustn't have got another subsidised place through the nursing association. In fact I can't remember going to the countryside after that. I think of the map on the wall and consider how we move through the world, how social mobility and class mean certain places are inaccessible to certain classes, and how important it is to break down such barriers of place. It's vital that children of all classes and cultural backgrounds have ready access to nature, wildlife and the countryside. Even from my one trip to the mountains and lakes, that landscape lived inside me. My heart had opened huge enough to be filled with those deep lakes and high mountains; my heart had opened up and fallen in love with the world all over again.

Walking Through Wilderness as a Woman of Colour

There are no well-worn paths here at all now as we press on towards Malham, and the grassy fields show no signs of having been trodden by human feet. It is a relief for even the small village to have fallen away and to walk through a place where there are no sudden markers of national identity such as a flag. I push on and feel myself no longer flagging but instead my energies pick up as I watch the world through which I walk. I feel the world seeping into my skin, pouring into its pores, this wilderness becoming a part of me and I a part of the wild.

I relish even the moody and mercurial clouds threatening rain at any moment, for so vast are they that they add to the sense of the great outdoors' immensity, making me feel tiny in the landscape, my worries washing away. Along the way, the great clouds burst intermittently into sudden flashes of rainfall, which I revel in the feel of when it falls on my skin. My gaze moves between the earth's green skin and the deep grey clouds that are creating some of the most dramatic skies I've seen. Then a ray of light pierces through a cloud and the colours brighten and the horizons broaden. How the landscape changes with the shifting light, and yet of course doesn't change at all.

At the far end of the meadow I go through a gate and enter a copse that opens out to a view of Kirkby Fell in the distance. I pass through stiles and gates and my companion helps me to clamber over, reaching out a hand for me to grasp as I haul myself up and jump down. Walking with someone else, it is easy to become reliant on them, and I remember that I will soon be walking entirely alone again and will need to rely solely upon myself and perhaps the kindness of strangers. My companion encourages me along the way too, such as telling me to keep going despite the pain, and I know that when I am walking alone again I will have to trust in myself, be my own encourager. I will need all my nerve.

A dark brown bird suddenly swoops close by and soars away so sure of its direction, and I remember how birds have an internal magnetic compass making them excellent navigators, able to see the earth's magnetic field and having magnetite in their beaks. Having not been able to afford a snazzy compass myself, when my companion leaves and I'm in areas with no internet signal, I'm hoping whatever inner compass I have will guide me – after all, so strong was the magnetism drawing me to make my journey north.

The grass here is not a texture I've seen before. It is thick and plastered to the earth by the rain; close up in some areas it looks like great strands of long green hair layered over that skin. I stop now and then to admire it, gently touch it.

Although there are no other human beings in sight, the walk is nevertheless teeming with life. I walk among huge brown cows grazing and white sheep and see rabbits leap nearby and vanish again, entirely oblivious to me. I stop to admire wildlife along the way, much of which I as an urbanite cannot name beyond the red berries, although I learn to identify more, such as the bright white cow parsley and abundant rowan trees that some believe protect against witches.[16]

I hear the river before I see it, and the sound makes my heart surge as all remaining weariness drains away. Even the sound of it is energising, massaging my mind. I am lifted sky-high by the sight, and its wild energy washes away a skein of grimy anxiety. Anxiety and depression can work in much the same way as a gaslighter, skewing the perception, literally – when I have been in the grip of an anxiety attack the vision blurs, the world spins, whilst depression attempts to turn the whole world grey and convince me I am worthless. Paying close attention can be a powerful tool against such thought-attacks which have a physiological effect too. Watching the world and focusing on your immediate surroundings, on what you can see, hear, feel, taste, and touch, your sensory experiences bring you back to this moment. As I walk, I learn to use my body as the sensory tool that it is – full of 'sensory nerves' – and even after a matter of miles can feel how being immersed in sensing nature is ameliorative for the mind. A cool breeze suddenly blows through the grass and ripples the river and sends enlivening sensations through my skin.

We walk along the River Aire for much of the rest of the way as it follows a course all the way to Airton and on to Malham and up to its source at Malham Tarn. Otters and water voles are known to inhabit the river and I love imagining what lives beneath its depths.

I reach a footbridge across the River Aire and look down at it there, so strong, so forceful. It is a good place to stop a while for rest and reflection. I take off my backpack and feel the sweet relief of a weight lifted. I look down at the surface of the water, the river's skin, teeming with reflections. The footbridge is the first sign of human construction I have seen for a while. I walk along the bridge and think of how we are living at a time when we need to build bridges not walls, not only across rivers but also cultural divides. I listen to the rhythm of the river, reminding me of the ancient songlines, then speckles of rain start falling upon my skin.

6

On Race and Place

On being a brown-skinned Brit

As I stand on the footbridge an image of the St George's flag sears into my mind. What does it mean to be English? In Hope Hotel the morning of the hate crime, I had filled myself with a 'full English' breakfast – yet some have questioned whether I am fully English, whether English can be a term for people of colour from England or only ethnically white people. This brings itself to bear on how people treat me as belonging or not belonging in places regarded as quintessentially English such as the countryside and natural landscapes, when ethnic minorities are more associated with urban areas. To be brown or black in green landscapes is seen by some to be incompatible – it is chilling that in summer 2020 as protests raged throughout the world crying out for racial equality a giant 'White Lives Matter' banner was unfurled on the top of Mam Tor (meaning 'mother hill') in the Peak District by a white supremacist group.[17]

What does it mean to be British? 'Do you have a British passport?' – the first words the abusive man said to me. One of the many ironies of my experience is that I *did* have my British passport on me. That burgundy-coloured piece of identity, also stating European Union on its cover, had journeyed with me thousands of miles from the former British colony of Guyana where my mother was born, to a train travelling through northern England.

I look out over the River Aire, contemplating how it empties into the River Ouse at Airmyn and flows through northern cities and towns before joining the River Trent at Trent Falls to form the Humber Estuary, how the Humber flows until it meets the North Sea, which is part of the Atlantic Ocean – that same ocean bordering Guyana and into which the Berbice River runs, nearby which my mother grew up. Looking out over the river, I feel strongly the interconnectedness of natural formations and human beings. As John Muir said: 'When we try to pick out anything by itself, we find it hitched to everything else in the universe.'

As I look at the river, I reflect on the many hidden histories of both human and natural worlds, and how we need to get beneath the surface and understand them.

Speaking out about what happened to me on that train journey through the North also means speaking out about the true horrors of Empire and the failure of the UK government to ensure adequate education about it in the curriculum, which has led to the kind of ignorance that breeds racism. While growing up, I knew little about the migration stories in my history. I learned about Henry VIII's six wives in meticulous detail and vividly remember colouring in their fine costumes, but I don't remember being taught the stories of England's colonial history. I don't remember being taught anything about why I – a brown-skinned girl – was sitting in a classroom in northern England. I remember singing at school 'Rule Britannia, Britannia rules the waves', but I don't remember being taught about the effects of so-called Britannia's epic journeys to rule the waves. Every day I walked down the so-called 'Curry Mile' in

Rusholme, but I don't remember the school syllabus explaining how there came to be such a vast array of cultures and cuisines in our city, about the part of British history that resulted in so many journeys across the waves. I don't remember being taught much about those waves themselves either, about natural history – and how us humans are inextricably a part of it, how for far too long the world's waterways have been viewed as means to conquer, exploit and have themselves been ravaged. Calls to decolonise the curriculum have coincided with calls for greater study of the natural world, including a proposed new GCSE in Natural History, and it is important to see how these are related. There urgently needs to be greater understanding of how racial and environmental justice are connected – the climate crisis disproportionately impacting poorer places including many former colonies, and in Britain impacting black and brown communities the most. Instead of ruling the waves, now is the time to learn about, love and save them.

My identity is often interrogated with the question 'Where are you from?' To this, I have a short response: 'Manchester'. 'No, but where are you originally from?', 'Old Trafford, which is part of Stretford, Manchester,' I answer, cutting a long story short. The question wrapped inside that question is: why are you here? How did you come to be here? (And, from some right-wing nationalists: shouldn't you leave and go home?) So why am I here? Here's the reason, in a nutshell: Once upon a time, in the nineteenth century, indentured labourers (known as 'Gladstone's coolies') were brought from British India to British Guiana to toil for the Empire as it exploited the world's natural resources on plantations. My maternal ancestors made this journey. The British Empire shipped two million indentured workers to nineteen different colonies – what is now known as the Commonwealth – where they were kept in horrific and abusive conditions. Let me spell it out: it is nature that is at the heart of these journeys – the misplaced belief that nature belonged to the British Empire and that they had a right to exploit it using brown and black people as cheap labour to do so. Aged twenty-one, my mother migrated to England alone after gaining a nurse traineeship. She remembers the shock of arriving in the winter, the trees stripped bare of blossom. Once upon a time, Kenya was ruled by the British and that is where my father was born, his parents having journeyed from India to Nairobi. Following Kenyan independence from Britain, my father, aged nineteen, migrated to the UK. He and my mother met in England and married in Manchester – where I was born, a result of multiple migrations.

The rest, as they say, is history. But this is not only my history but also part of Britain's history (why I was born in Britain – why I'm here – is a direct result of Britain having colonised India, the Caribbean and Kenya – of Britain once being there). We need to become more educated about *all* parts of British history both human and natural, to make them part of the narrative of the country and not forgotten footnotes.

Everybody has their once-upon-a-time. And there are not effects without causes. As for new waves of immigrants, it's crucial we understand why they are here too, and Britain's part in that, and how war and

political and environmental catastrophe have led to
the worst refugee crisis in modern times, with more
displaced people than since the Second World War.
I find it alarming when some of immigrant histories
themselves turn against new waves of immigrants,
forgetting that they or their ancestors were once in the
position of making a new home elsewhere. (When it
comes to some brown politicians such as Priti Patel and
their hostile immigration policies, I am reminded of
the observation from Zora Neale Hurston: 'All my
skin folk ain't my kinfolk.') It's vitally important to
remember the once-upon-a-time of Europe too, with
European integration since the Second World War
being a concept based on peace not war, an alternative
to the destructive, extreme nationalism that seems more
rampant than ever.

Immigrants have become even more demonised with
animosity stoked by Theresa May's 'Go Home' vans and
UKIP's notorious 'Breaking Point' poster, forgetting
how much immigrants have done not to break but make
the country, and that this *is* home. I look at my map and
notice how close we are to the Yorkshire village where
MP Jo Cox was shot and stabbed multiple times in broad
daylight the same month of the EU Referendum by
Thomas Mair, a man holding far-right views who, when
asked to confirm his name in court, said: 'My name is
death to traitors, freedom for Britain.' Jo Cox had been
vocal in her support for a multicultural society in which
all regardless of skin colour belong, in her maiden speech
to parliament saying: 'Our communities have been
deeply enhanced by immigration' and that 'we have
more in common than that which divides us.' The judge

said the true 'patriot' was Cox not Mair and prosecutors jailing Mair for life said he was 'motivated by hate'.

'Those who cannot remember the past are condemned to repeat it,' warned George Santayana, but many in power still insist on forgetting. We urgently need to open up conversation instead of fatally forgetting. We should be bringing into the raw light of day hidden histories of people and place, the wealth of buried stories about who people are and how they came to be here and how nature is at the heart of that. There's a whole world of untold stories that deserve to be shared to better understand the Britain we live in today. The sharing of untold stories has the power to create empathy, transforming hate into love – love of not only humans but the natural world, which in turn ensures we save it.

It is walking that is giving me perspective; walking through this landscape frees my mind to reflect on my place in the world and on how deep systemic unbelonging is.

Government cruelty cutting to the core of identity and belonging has continued long after Empire officially ended. The Windrush scandal revealed shameful government attempts to forcibly deport some British people who were also variously sacked from their jobs, evicted from their homes or denied healthcare. Despite having been granted citizenship, they were wrongly told that they don't belong here. My mother was one of almost half a million people who made the journey to the UK from Caribbean countries between 1948 and 1971, termed the 'Windrush generation',[18] encouraged here by the UK government to fill labour shortages after the war. The British Nationality Act of 1948 conferred

British citizen status on all colonial subjects. But under Theresa May's 'hostile environment' policy, some British citizens from Commonwealth countries were demanded by the Home Office to show paperwork to prove and evidence their identity and belonging in Britain such as passports, settled status letters, and landing cards.[19] The Home Office, however, had themselves lost or destroyed records yet attempted to illegalise and criminalise people rightfully belonging here – an example of systemic gaslighting.[20] Paulette Wilson was a British grandmother locked up in Yarl's Wood detention centre where her belongings were confiscated because she could not prove she was British. Her decision to speak out was instrumental in exposing the scandal.[21] She died in 2020, the same year a report into the scandal described 'institutional ignorance and thoughtlessness' towards race, 'consistent with some definitions of institutional racism'.[22]

I have been questioned about my Britishness – explicitly or implicitly – many times, from a racist during a rail journey, to royalty. I was asked that question 'Where are you from?' by the future heir to the throne and my open letter to him in response was first published in the *Guardian* on 20 April 2018, the same month in which the Windrush scandal was revealed:

> *Dear Prince Charles, do you think my brown skin makes me unBritish?*
> I met Prince Charles this week at the Common-
> wealth People's Forum at which I was a speaker (on
> a day whose itinerary was entitled 'Politics of Hope:
> Taking on Injustice in the Commonwealth'), part of

the Commonwealth Heads of Government Meeting at the Queen Elizabeth II Centre, the major summit gathering leaders of 53 countries, representing over 2 billion human beings.

I shook the Prince's hand with my right hand. In my other hand I was holding a copy of an anthology *We Mark Your Memory: Writing From the Descendants of Indenture* in which I have an essay published from which I would later be giving a reading in that same room. I told him how my mother was born in Guyana and that the anthology collects hidden histories of indenture.

'And where are you from?' asked the Prince.

'Manchester, UK,' I said.

'Well, you don't look like it!' he said and laughed. He was then ushered to the next person.

Although I have experienced such off-the-cuff, supposedly humorous comments before, I was stunned by the gaffe.

Prince Charles was on 19 April endorsed by the Queen, in her opening speech to heads of government, to be the future head of the Commonwealth: it's her 'sincere wish' that he become so. That the mooted next leader of an organisation that represents one-third of the people on the planet commented that I, a brown woman, did not look as if I was from a city in the UK is shocking. This is exactly why people urgently need a history lesson about immigration, the British Empire, the Commonwealth and colonialism. Because I do look like I'm from Manchester, actually – a city into which many people of colour have been born and bred.

Whatever the Prince meant or didn't mean in our fleeting encounter, since it happened I've been through all the feelings – from shock to humiliation to rage. Most of all, I feel angry that there could be such casual ignorance in the corridors of power, an ignorance that also permeates society – not least as some British people of colour invited here have been threatened with deportation. They don't look like they are from here, according to some.

So what does a British person look like? A British person can look like me. A British person can have black or brown, not only white, skin and still be just as British (this shouldn't need to be spelled out in black and white). I could have proven that I was born in Manchester and that I am British, as I had my passport in my handbag – I'd needed it to get through the venue's security.

Yet I can't tell Prince Charles exactly where I am from originally, that old chestnut. Why? Because the British destroyed much of the evidence that my ancestors were shipped over from India in the nineteenth century to toil for the Empire as indentured labourers on sugar colonies in the Caribbean. I've been back to the National Archives in Georgetown, Guyana, to search for my ancestral history and stared down at a gaping hole where records of lives should have been.[23] The British destroyed so much that could properly explain and evidence our identities.

Of course, allegations of racism are not new for the royal family. The Duke of Edinburgh has made numerous contentious comments; and Princess

Michael of Kent wore a blackamoor brooch while meeting Meghan Markle.

I have a message for Prince Charles. Your Royal Highness, you asked me: 'Where are you from?' To adapt a phrase from the late writer and Director of the Institute of Race Relations, Ambalavaner Sivanandan: I am here because you were there.

My open letter to the Prince went viral internationally. Among the slew of racist, abusive hate mail I received, there were many heart-warming messages from strangers around the world about how my experience resonated, people sharing their own stories of identity and discrimination or simply sending love and solidarity, from an eighty-year-old couple in Manchester ('I wish thee well, Manchester lass'), to Guyana ('I hope a ray of Guyanese sunshine for you in your English life') to a seventy-year-old descendant of a freed Virgin Island's slave who welcomes a voice 'speaking up'. Such messages give me the courage to continue to hold power to account.

As for the racist and nationalistic trolls, I checked my emails: the subject headline was 'tea-bag complexion' and the email read: 'You don't look like a Brit STUPID'. (Dear troll: I'm actually happy to have a 'tea-bag complexion', tea being such a glorious substance from the natural world.) Other comments ranged from 'paper doesn't replace blood' to 'she has to go back'. I opened my Facebook account to find a message suggesting that as I am 'not English' I can't call out racism. One troll actually likened me, as a person of colour, to an alien. If anything succeeds in 'alienating' people, it's this toxic thinking – to be told that I do not actually belong on planet earth. In such hate speech, I've experienced just how hostile the 'hostile environment' is, how deeply ingrained racism is. I hope that writing this will expose some of the toxic thinking, how wrong it is, and why we need a national and international conversation to root out such ignorance.

I received an astonishing tirade, which included: 'We are in control, NOT YOU, and you should be thanking us for welcoming your family into Britain, because were it not for us, you would still be living in huts. We have given you everything. Say thank you.' A while later a follow-up message from the same troll appeared in my account, saying how 'ungrateful' I was for 'what the British have done' for me: 'We basically made you. Without us British, you'd be nothing and nowhere.' This shows how wrong the narrative around immigration is and how we need to rewrite it by speaking out. (The price for speaking up can be hate mail but it is worth remembering that sending abusive communications via the internet is now illegal.)

It's a deeply misplaced belief that people of colour should be grateful to be here, for it suggests that we do not really, fully belong. It is also part of the toxic 'white saviour' narrative. I have as much right to be here as a white person. Why should I, a person of colour, be saying thank you to white people for welcoming me into a country (where I was actually born) and where I fully belong? People of colour helped to rebuild this country after the ravages of the Second World War and, before that, toiled on plantations to help build a strong Empire. Where is the thank-you to the generation of immigrants who worked as cheap labour and then had to fight not to be

booted out of the country, who were used and discarded?
The government should not only be apologising but also
saying thank you. During the pandemic, those who had
been regarded as 'menial'– many ethnic minorities doing
low-paid frontline jobs – were finally accorded more
respect as 'essential workers'. But the pandemic also
showed how vulnerable they are due to the intersection
of socioeconomics and race, literally more exposed to
death. It should not take dying in a pandemic for people
to be respected and such respect should be permanent
and deep, not fleeting and superficial. Heartbreakingly,
there were also reports of racism directed to frontline
'BAME' staff, showing there is a long way to go for all to
be equally valued and regarded as fully belonging.

I walk further on from the footbridge, continuing along
the River Aire as it pulses and flows, making a music all
of its own. I sit down for a while in wide open pasture
by the river, my feet dangling over its edge, delighting in
being so close to the wild energy of the water. I think of
all of the miles I have walked and all those still to go.
I spot bright yellow ragwort nearby my knee and wonder
at how beautiful this wild weed looks.

Walking on, I hear a great plunging sound of water
that is not the river and see an astonishing water
formation rushing down the dale. I wish I could name
what it is, whether it is indeed a rapid, as my companion
suggests. Human and natural histories are inextricably
comingled – my ancestors historically had a strong
connection with nature, and my mother grew up in a

rural village in a country known as the 'land of many waters' due to its abundance of waterfalls, filled with enormous water lilies and all manner of wildlife, indeed home to the Amazon rainforest. I ended up being born in a city due to the fact that most immigrants arrived in cities for work. Having grown up in an inner-city, my inability to name some of the nature I see is at times frustrating and yet there is in me a yearning for nature and to learn more (indeed, the etymology of 'learn' is 'to follow or find the track') and so I am yearning and learning my way through the Pennines.

While walking through the remote wilderness, I spy a hiker doing the Pennine Way – the first human I've seen for hours – and we chat for a while about how there are fewer people than we expected on the trail and fewer worn tracks. The Way continues to follow the river before joining the road at Hanlith, a hamlet of around just forty people. I see a jet-black crow perched in a tree and the Ted Hughes poem-sequence featuring 'Crow' flits through my mind in which Crow wanders the universe in search of their creator. Then both actual and poetical crow soar away.

Walking as the last of the light fades, I see how the river splits into two tributaries, Malham Beck and Gordale Beck. There is a steep uphill walk into Malham, which I am almost not able to make as the weight of my backpack overwhelms me, those few belongings suddenly becoming so heavy there in their temporary home. My companion adjusts the pack and shows me how to wear it so its weight is more evenly spread, and I almost enjoy the sensation of it there, my portable home hugging me. I'm gradually growing to feel more at home both with my few belongings and sense of belonging. Soon the Pennine Way delivers us at our destination for the night, a bunk barn, where we dry off before going for fish and chips in the local pub, tomorrow aiming to walk high up into the limestone formations of the backbone of Britain.

A brief history of 'banana boats'

All night long the song of the river resounds, and I lie awake listening to it swelling and the rain pounding until it seems the world is washing away. I rise early the next morning, hungry to walk alone by the riverbank. While I walk, I devour a banana for breakfast and, biting into the delicious fruit, the words of my abuser echo in my mind, telling me to 'get back on the banana boat', and bemoaning 'these paki people who come over here on banana boats, strange people' – not only a racist but geographically inaccurate statement. I've been intrigued to research this fruit and how it has journeyed throughout the world – it's too frequently forgotten that food not least fruit is a part of nature and in turn becomes a part of us. My own journey has inspired me to explore journeys intrinsically interwoven – journeys of slavery, indenture, and freedom.

I walk alone along the riverbank and remember the voyage of those banana boats and the plight of both the natural world and humans, exploited due to power-hungry, greedy businessmen. Theirs is a history showing how the exploitation of humans and natural resources is connected. Who does nature belong to? In the history of this fruit alone we can see how an elite have attempted to own and monopolise nature, in turn ravaging it. To build banana plantations, United Fruit Company caused devastation to nature and wildlife, clearing out forests and draining marshlands, destroying ecosystems and biodiversity.[24] They used slave labour to build a railway through a jungle to get bananas to the port.[25] Here is just one example of colonialism's damaging effect on landscape and nature. Shipping the delicious fruit from tropical-growing areas in Central America and the Caribbean became lucrative for British and American businessmen from the late nineteenth century.[26] The first steamships of Elders & Fyffes were refitted in Newcastle-upon-Tyne and installed with a cooling system to help preserve the bananas during long sea voyages. The exploitative practices of imperialist fruit companies – exploiting both natural resources and human labour – is captured in the term 'banana republic' and satirised in Pablo Neruda's poem 'La United Fruit Co' and by writers including Gabriel García Márquez. When United Fruit Company workers went on strike for dignified working conditions, as punishment they were brutally killed with machine guns in what became known as 'the Banana Massacre'.

So how did the term 'banana boat' become so offensive? At the heart of it is how humans have travelled on the world's waterways, seeking survival. West Indian immigrants travelled to provide cheap labour to build the Panama canal and railways in Costa Rica and Mexico,[27] following which a wave of West Indian immigrants booked passage to the US on banana boats.[28] During the Second World War the UK government imposed a ban on bananas, and the only fruit that could be imported were oranges, but after the war, trade booked again and the banana boats began also carrying passengers including the West Indies cricket team and migrants from the Caribbean recruited to fill low-wage jobs and help rebuild the country. The phrase that someone was 'fresh off the boat' or 'fresh off a banana boat' was – and still is – hurled as a racist insult. '"The banana boat's coming for you" – Spike in racist incidents post-Brexit' is the title of a *Northern Echo* article of 30 June 2016.[29] It reported that a man outside a nursery in Sunderland hurled those words at a child and I think with horror of the child's shock, confusion and fear, having their right to exist in what should be a safe place so callously attacked. The report told how police linked several racist attacks in the area to the EU referendum result, after which there was a far-right, anti-immigration 'Victory March' in Newcastle.[30] In another incident a man sent an email to Wolverhampton MP Eleanor Smith, calling for her to be put on 'the first banana boat' to the 'jungle clearing you came from' – he was given a suspended jail sentence in 2018 and admitted sending grossly offensive messages,[31] including one warning MP David Lammy to 'remember what happened to Jo Cox'.

Contemporary controversies concerning the banana boat and racism include a revelation that Canadian Prime Minister Justin Trudeau wore blackface in high school while singing Harry Belafonte's song 'Day-O The Banana Boat Song', a folksong told from the perspective of dock workers working the nightshift loading bananas onto ships, seeing daylight coming and wanting to go home. There is a long history of racist mockery, using humour to dehumanise, from minstrel shows to the modern day

persistence of 'black face' and 'brown face', reducing
human beings to one-dimensional caricatures (the one
dimension being the skin). Growing up, it seemed
standard that people should not stand up to racism but
laugh it off, that those who resisted 'couldn't take a joke'
or were too uptight. I've experienced racist mockery in
incidents throughout my life and still feel a vein of it so
palpable in the present. Racism is about the skin, with no
regard of the human heart beating within.

Route-mapping and root-mapping: A potted history of the word 'paki'

I walk further alone along the riverbank which is filled
with sycamore trees whose barks are covered with
glowing green moss, whose branches reach high into the
sky forming a protective shade and whose roots stretch
out into the path I'm on, looking like giant webbed feet.
I remember seeing exposed tree-roots for the first time
during a walk in Wandlebury Woods and being in
wonderment at how wide-spreading these support
structures are. Today as I walk, I wonder where those
roots end up, the ways in which they are entangled, and
remember how trees communicate with each other from
beneath the soil and share nutrients. I look at the map to
inspect the route I'm walking. I have been drawn to
explore the roots of the term 'paki' and how it became
offensive. My journey of reclamation is one of prose as
well as place, of both routes and roots, route-mapping
and root-mapping.

Racism is rooted in language; the first way in which
we often experience it is through words, which is why

I feel impelled to use language as a tool of power, to write against the growing tide of hate. Language matters and can be a weapon for inflicting emotional violence, causing invisible wounds. 'Sticks and stones can break your bones, but word will never harm you,' the saying goes. Yet words can hurt the most, can bruise your self-esteem and break your spirit. The law acknowledges the distress, alarm and damage that words as well as behaviour can cause. My abuser was convicted under a section of the Crime and Disorder Act 1998 that recognises this and specifically mentions 'verbal abuse' as a crime – something that many I have met do not realise, since there is not enough education about this from the earliest years.

The word 'paki' contains within it a history of hurt, hate and hostility. During the 1960s the word became a weapon used against immigrants who were demonised by overtly racist tabloid media and culture, views that seeped into society. Enoch Powell made his notorious anti-immigration 'Rivers of Blood' speech in 1968, stoking further hostility. In it he quoted Virgil's *Aeneid*: 'As I look ahead, I am filled with foreboding; like the Roman, I seem to see the River Tiber foaming with much blood.'

I walk by the River Aire and look at the map again and notice how close we are to Nelson in Lancashire. It was to Nelson that my grandfather first moved in 1965 following the decolonisation of Kenya. My father settled in Manchester and his mother ran a corner shop that she lived above following the death of my grandfather. I remember the hostility during my 1990s childhood, and related terms such as 'paki shop', the 'PAKIS OUT' graffiti scrawled on walls, and the hours and energy

needed to scrub it off. Those words were saying: you
don't have a right to exist in this place on account of
your race; you don't belong here. My grandmother's
corner shop curved around a corner of Stretford not far
from the Lancashire cricket ground where from a white
sign blooms a blood-red rose, the sign of the county of
Lancashire. I was a Lancashire lass through and through,
born and bred there, yet othered through the offensive
term. There is a thin line between words and action, and
language can incite violence. 'Paki-bashing' – vicious
assaults on immigrants – increased with the rise of the
National Front from the 1970s onwards.

The word stung when I heard it, uttered even by
so-called friends. I was aged twelve, sitting in the
classroom, when the word again wounded. A classmate
was passing a joke around, and told it to me: 'Why did
the Romans build straight roads?' The punchline: 'So
pakis couldn't build corner shops.' Yet I was much
younger when I was first called that slur. I must have
been a toddler, playing on the pavement outside home.
On match day the pavement would be swarming with
football fans from the nearby Manchester United ground.
Drunk and aggressive fans hurled the word at me: 'Clear
off, paki!' Like many brown-skinned British children, I
feared the word and the prickles of shame that spread
over my skin. Like many children, I internalised the hate
directed towards me, so it became self-hate. That word
punctured the confidence and I grew up squirming in
my skin. It took years to build a sense of belonging in
my own body, a sense of self-worth in my mind.

As I walk, I notice how the river is not blue as it is
depicted on the map but here it is brown, tree-barks

beneath the moss are also brown, how this colour of skin has been so demeaned yet how it is part of the natural world and needs to be reclaimed as beautiful. I pause and press my ear against a tree-bark and shiver as the body of the tree touches mine, at the cool damp moss on my skin. I wonder what these trees might be talking to each other about. I walk on and on and my heart beating inside my brown-skinned body tells me that I too am a real person who belongs here.

Hostility has intensified in our contemporary age. We're living in an era in which politicians are getting away with racially abusive language; it must be condemned to prevent it becoming normalised. We must call out hate speech in the highest corridors of power. Who decides what words are offensive? I was invited onto the BBC's *Victoria Derbyshire* show on the day statistics were released revealing a 10 per cent rise in hate crime, with a 75 per cent rise in race hate crime. Shortly before going live on air, I was briefed by the producer that, while I could say 'paki' on air, I could not say the words 'fuck' or 'cunt' and had to say 'the f-word' and 'the c-word' in place of these, as if 'paki' were somehow more palatable – the fact that this is deemed so is outrageous and shows the ways in which language endorsed by the media permeates and shapes society.

The racial slur has been used at all societal levels – Prince Harry was caught on video calling one of his fellow army recruits 'our little paki friend' while on military duty in 2006 and when the video surfaced in 2009 he was sent on a sensitivity training course by the British Army and issued an apology.[32] I've also been called this slur by other minority ethnicities, though I believe inter-racial racism was stoked by white rulers during the British Empire under a 'divide-and-rule' policy, as was religious hatred and the caste system.

Words wound, but words can also heal. Language divides but can also unite. If I could journey back through time, I would tell my younger self not to internalise the voices telling me I was worthless and didn't belong, wanting to erase me and my place in the world. By speaking out, writing back, by finding and using our voice, we can break the poisonous grip of the past. Now I can finally say enough is enough: I belong in my own skin, in my mind, in the world.

Reclaiming 'cunt' – Walking through Wilderness as a Woman of Colour

What is it like walking alone as a woman through the wilderness? I savour these moments alone as I press on along the sycamore tree-lined path by the swollen river listening to its strong, wild power. I look down and see those moss-filled trees reflected in enormous puddles on the path. I savour being able to stop and linger whenever I wish and do so to marvel at the moss and drink in its green glow. I try and navigate using the natural world, and moss is an excellent natural tool of navigation – it tends to grow on the north side which is, in the northern hemisphere, shadier and damper. Moss grows and thrives on any surface moist enough, from trees and roots to rocks and concrete and cars, needing wetness to survive and reproduce. Moss is home to a world of microscopic organisms which can't be seen but are crucial in ensuring biodiversity. Walking alone here, without another person in sight, wholly absorbed in watching the natural world, the sliver of fear I felt earlier to be alone slips away.

After being racially abused, I was sent a personal alarm by Victim Support, a small silver rectangular shape, the second such alarm I've had, having been given a rape alarm aged 13 and remember its high-pitched screeching. I was taught not to walk alone, even in broad daylight, in areas where, if you were attacked and screamed for help, you would not be heard – so that ruled out natural landscapes and wildernesses. Oh to be safe while walking. Oh to be free of the misogynistic microaggressions experienced journeying through the world. Oh for women to be considered as belonging out walking in the wilderness. On arriving in Malham a man had looked at me and my male companion and said to me: 'Are you the support driver?' – the suggestion that a woman would be a mere accessory to a man's adventure rather than making an adventure herself infuriated me.

The attack I experienced was misogynistic as well as racist – called 'paki cunt' – and I feel the intersectionality of being a woman of colour walking through the world. I can't reclaim the word 'paki' without reclaiming 'cunt'. My journey has become one of tracing not only the origins of people and places but prose, for words define us. I remember learning swear words at an early age. I knew the word 'cunt' was loaded, including being loaded with shame, and wondered why we should feel ashamed of something that was a part of our bodies. Language has contributed to such misogynistic shaming of women – for so long, since the fifth century, has this word been used to degrade, objectify and control women. The *Oxford Learner's Dictionary* defines the word 'cunt' as

meaning 1. 'A woman's vagina and outer sexual organs' 2.
'A very offensive word used to insult somebody and to
show anger or dislike. *You stupid cunt!*' Internationally the
word is derogatory, too, the *Macquarie Dictionary of
Australian English* describing one of its meanings as 'a
contemptible person'.

'A nasty name for a nasty thing' is how the
lexicographer Francis Grose demeaned this part of the
body in his 1785 dictionary – there written as 'C★★T'
and 'belonging to the class of vulgarisms'. By the
seventeenth century to print the word in full rendered
one liable to prosecution – the word appeared in the
1960 trial of *Lady Chatterley's Lover*. The *OED* did not
list the term until 1972 but in the most updated edition
also includes derivatives; in 2014 it announced that it
was adding *cunty, cuntish, cunted* and *cunting*. In works of
literature, the word has several outings in Chaucer's great
poem of journeying *The Canterbury Tales* and Shakespeare
uses it in wordplay.

My journey is one of reclaiming both language and
landscape – and I've learnt just how much landscape
there is in language. Whilst the word is often cited with
its earliest known use in the place-name 'Gropecunt
Lane' (a brothel area of Cheapside, London, circa 1230),
the updated *OED* states that the word was applied to
topographical features, many from the natural world
such as a cleft in a small hill or mound (e.g. *Cuntelowe*,
Warwickshire, (1221), a wooded gulley or valley (e.g.
Kuntecliue, Lancashire, 1246), a cleft with a stream
running through it (e.g. *Cuntebecsic*), and 'cuntan heale', a
place in Hampshire where two small streams meet at an
elongated field.[33] There are also roots in the Latin *cunnus*,

from which the contemporary word 'cunnilingus' is derived and whose etymology could be Proto-Indo-European, evolved from 'gash' and 'slit', and *cuniculus*, an underground passageway, tunnel or hole.

Reclaiming language can help eradicate deep-rooted shame, for language is a form of power and consequently, crucially, affects how we take up space and our freedom to move through the world. Taboo around the word speaks of fear of women's power, women as active agents with control over ourself, living beings who feel pleasure and are not merely passive, reproductive objects. We have been conditioned to be ashamed of something which is a part of us, embarrassed to feel pleasure, joy, have desires. Such shaming speaks of the fact that for far too long women's bodies have been regarded as belonging to men, and reclaiming the word is a way of saying: I belong in my own body and my body belongs to me. I can choose how I use my body and where I take it, how I move through the world.

The movement among feminists to reclaim the word includes Eve Ensler's *The Vagina Monologues* (1996) and its section 'Reclaiming Cunt', and *Cunt: A Declaration of Independence* (1998) by Inga Muscio. Such reclamations recognise a long history of demeaning words for women such as 'bitch', 'whore' and 'slut'. In 1979 the feminist Andrea Dworkin wrote: 'cunt: our essence ... our offence.' Our cunt is not a 'nasty thing', to have one should not be an 'offence', and it should not be shamed but celebrated. Often used as a catch-all term, the word vagina actually refers to the internal muscular canal extending from vulva to cervix, vulva referring to the external female sex organs including the protective folds of skin, the labia (Latin for 'lips') – but the word 'cunt' refers to both inner and outer places. The naming of some parts corresponds with nature: vestibular and clitoral 'bulbs', stimulation of which can lead to orgasm (all female mammals and some female birds have a clitoris, the word deriving from a Greek word meaning 'little hill'; that a part of the anatomy which provides intense pleasure is particularly taboo is telling). Understanding its formation shows just how we are not apart from but a part of the natural world. Vaginal 'flora' are millions of microorganisms – unseen microbial life – that live in the vagina. It's estimated that humans are inhabited by ten times as many non-human cells than human cells – we are literally a part of nature. In a world where Female Genital Mutilation (FGM) and sexual violence are rife, it is important to speak out and share understanding about areas of being alive still shrouded in silence, shame and stigma.

Other terms for female genitalia range from formal to slang and include, of course, pussy – a word also meaning cat, also meaning coward, and suggesting women as tamed and domesticated creatures rather than wild and powerful and brave beings. The word pussy was pelted out of the mouth of the man who would become President: 'Grab them by the pussy,' he said in a taped recording publicly revealed the month before he was elected. Trump downplayed this as 'locker-room banter', as if this were acceptable communication, as if words themselves don't carry power. A year later the #MeToo movement began spreading, calling out sexual assault and harassment. It is important to remember that MeToo has its roots with the activist Tarana Burke, who began using the phrase on MySpace to encourage 'empowerment and empathy' among women of colour who have been sexually abused. Burke has told how the phrase came about as a result of being unable to respond to a thirteen-year-old girl who confided to her that she had been sexually assaulted, here an instance of language growing out of an initial silence, that lump in the throat.[34]

Oh to walk through the world as a woman freely and without fear. Women's lives are still constricted by harassment and intimidation in public spaces including the great outdoors – and I among many other women use walking partly as a way of reclaiming such spaces, as a way of saying: we belong here. The word pussy has since been seen on placards the world over during Women's Marches. I saw many such banners at the Women's March the same weekend Trump was inaugurated one cold winter's day in 2017. A memorable one was 'PUSSIES AGAINST PATRIARCHY' – words held aloft in a clear blue sky with silhouetted bare branches, a day that seemed full of hope and defiance as thousands marched through the streets. It was a powerful instance of a word being reclaimed. Social media memes included a #PussyGrabsBack hashtag and imagery of a snarling cat. In the years since that Women's March I have felt more than ever how language has become weaponised and abused by those in power, filtering through to all societal levels. More than ever have I felt those words also being reclaimed – and how words have been combined with walking as a way to do this. I have felt palpably and powerfully how putting one foot in front of the other can be a form of protest. I think of walking and words, and an unpleasant memory surfaces of a word hurled at me on the street by a stranger: 'Leave.' The incident was only a syllable and second long but stayed with me. Language itself has been hijacked by toxic political discourse – little words with enormous significance like 'leave', 'immigrant' and 'real'. Some phonetically lovely words have taken on sinister meanings.

Walking and reclaiming words can be acts of defiance and hope. Walking and words together – walking through the streets with words held aloft on banners, words painted and drawn and felt-tipped in all manner of colours, on paper and cardboard placards, and onto skin, black skin, brown skin, white skin.

Dehumanising language is designed to cause despair, but I will not leave the pathways I walk upon, this place I call home. I will not give in to fear and despair. Instead, I walk even further, even deeper, into this place where I belong.

BACKBONE

Malham Cove and Limestone Country

7

Protected Characteristics

Beneath the skin, the bone. I am walking through a landscape that has been scraped bare to the bone, a landscape of limestone. Once upon a time, the North of England was awash with tropical seas. Beneath the seas, limestone beds were formed of the shells of marine organisms.

I am walking amid skeletal fragments of those marine organisms, foraminifera and molluscs, coral, and crinoids that are part of the class Crinoidea, one of the Echinodermata that also includes sea urchins, sea cucumbers, brittle stars and starfish. Crinoids attached to the seabed by a stalk are called sea lilies while those without a stalk are called feather stars.[35] Such organisms secrete shells made of calcite or argonite (different crystal forms of calcium carbonate), shells that are left behind when they die. It is deeply haunting and eerie to think of such fossil remains all around, composing the limestone.[36]

What is the North made of? How long ago was it made? How did it make me? Such questions drive me to walk higher and deeper into the landscape, to walk all the way back to three hundred million years ago and the Carboniferous period. Today I will see some of the answers with my own eyes.

Although limestone is a hard rock, it is also partially soluble, porous and permeable, so water not only moves over it but through it, passing through its joints, cracks,

faults and fissures.[37] Rainwater containing carbon dioxide
slowly dissolves and erodes the limestone to produce
many of the magical landscape features – vast cave systems,
limestone pavements, sudden cliff faces and scars, sinkholes
and springs – that I encounter throughout my journey.

This place is called a karst landscape, created from that
contact between acidic water and soluble bedrock such as
limestone or dolomite, causing karstification, the process
by which these landscape formations come into being.
This place shares its features with other karst landscapes
around the world: Australia's Nullarbor Plain (the
world's largest limestone karst), the Yucatán Peninsula and
Chiapas in Mexico, the Tham Luang Nang Non karstic
cave system in northern Thailand from where a junior
football team were rescued after becoming stranded
in 2018, the South China Karst, the Lijiang River in
Guangxi, China, Hạ Long Bay in Vietnam, the Burren in
County Clare, Ireland, El Torcal de Antequera nature
reserve in the Sierra del Torcal mountains in Spain's
Andalusia, the Dinaric Alps and Karst Plateau extending
across the border of Slovenia and Italy.[38] Karst landscapes
are full of 'karst fensters' or 'karst windows', underground
streams and rivers that emerge onto the surface between
layers of rock, cascade and flow for a while, disappear
back down often into a sinkhole, and resurface elsewhere
sometimes under a different name. Such rivers include
the Popo Agie River in Wyoming and the Ljubljanica
River in Slovenia, which is known to have seven names.

The Pennines – like many limestone landscapes – is
also an area full of 'faults', cracks in the earth's surface
where the rock has divided into two parts that move
against each other. Indeed it has a zone of faulting called

the Pennine Fault System.[39] I walk close to the fault-lines of the Craven Faults,[40] major crustal fractures that run across the Pennines caused by the shifting of tectonic forces, and walk higher into the limestone uplands. Here is a place that wears its faults with pride; here is a place where brokenness has become a kind of bleak beauty.

While walking along I'm stunned by the sight of an enormous heart-shaped limestone cliff face dug into the earth, surrounded by bright green hills and fells. It is the first time I have laid eyes on so much limestone. It truly does look as if a surface of the earth has been scraped away to reveal the world beneath, as it has been over the years. Such is the power of glacial ice that it scraped away the soil covering the limestone, leaving it so barebone. Upon the path there is a stepping stone situated as if calling for passers-by to stand upon it and, although I am eager to reach Malham Cove and the Tarn that lies beyond it, I stop and stand upon the stone for a while, and it is a wonderful viewpoint. I look out at the silver-grey rock marked with streaks of black, surrounded by greenness, and get a sense of how huge the cliff is by seeing that the trees beneath look tiny.

Great grey clouds are gathered, looming above the limestone, matching its colour, and looking more ominously full to burst by the minute. It is already a remarkable day of walking the Pennine Way and we have not yet even reached the ancient natural wonder of Malham Cove.

Walking along the Way, my heart is lifted by the sound of the swollen River Aire, by hearing the wildness of water on a windy day. The river is full after three inches of rain fell overnight as I had been reliably informed by

the man who works in the village shop where we
stopped for supplies before venturing to the Cove.
Ronald was born in 1927 and the shop has been through
three generations of his family. He truly is a backbone of
the small community. His shop is hung with tea towels
celebrating Yorkshire Pudding and Yorkshire Dales, filled
with sweets laid out in the way of a traditional sweetie
shop – liquorice laces, fudge, whippy vanilla cones, sticks
of rock, and shelves lined with toys: flying missiles,
unicorn eggs, frogs, barrels of slime, and playing cards.
On the wall an aerial panoramic map shows tantalising
miniature markings of mountains and hills in various
shades of grey. The image made me hungry to continue
my journey along the Way towards the Cove and Tarn,
to step into those markings on the map and have them
come to life in all the glory of their colour and scale.

I continue to walk along the River Aire. The sheer
force and energy of it swirling there has the effect of
washing the mind free from worries; the churning is
outside instead of the churning anxiety within. The
sound silences noisy thoughts as I instead wonder about
the river, how long it has been there, how deep it might
be. The swollen river, so strong and sure of itself and its
direction, also becomes a subterranean stream somewhere
near here at a place called 'Water Sinks', and I wonder
what it is like, inside the earth.

Then I see ahead an enormous, vertical limestone
formation, like a giant cathedral or amphitheatre but
made entirely by nature itself rather than any human
hand. The sight stops me in my tracks, and I catch my
breath before walking on towards the natural wonder.
This is Malham Cove, a curved crag of carboniferous

limestone formed by a waterfall carrying meltwater from glaciers during an ice age. Once thought to be around 12,000 years old, a stalagmite discovered in a flooded cave dated it as being at least 50,000 years old. Standing beneath it and looking up and understanding that it has existed for so long, and that the processes leading to its formation began over three hundred million years ago, my sense of self changes as I see my existence in such a scale. I see how fleeting my own lifespan is compared to these natural landscapes. The priest and antiquary Thomas West described the Cove in 1779:'This beautiful rock is like the age-tinted wall of a prodigious castle; the stone is very white, and from the ledges hang various shrubs and vegetables, which with the tints given it by the bog water. &c. gives it a variety that I never before saw so pleasing in a plain rock.'[41]

From the top of the Cove it is often possible to see peregrines, an acquaintance has told me. I've longed to see in real life those powerful birds since reading *The Peregrine* by J.A. Baker, and dreamed of the great, blue-grey falcons beloved of rocky cliffs and upland areas. I start to keep an eye on the birds that soar past, seeing if I can spot any identifying features of peregrines such as the dark crown of its head, black moustache-like markings, muscular legs, or long, broad, pointed wings. Peregrine chicks have this year hatched high on the Cove, according to the Malham Peregrine Project, and the adult birds have been spotted carrying food to nesting sites.[42] I ponder the lifespans of peregrines, usually ten years, the oldest known wild peregrine having lived seventeen years – a mere heartbeat compared to those millions of years ago of the Carboniferous era.

The name 'peregrine' is a translation of Latin literally meaning 'pilgrim falcon', and originally meant 'foreign'. Medieval falconers found peregrines difficult to capture in their high-up nests and tried to do so while they were making their first flights or airborne pilgrimages. As a result the word 'peregrine' has evolved to mean wandering, travelling or migrating, and 'peregrination' a long journey.

Near the cliffs, silvered now by a ray of sun, an abundance of trees grow – old, gnarled and magnificent trees, such an intriguing confluence of elements of the natural world here in sight. Before walking up the Cove I spend some time among the branches hanging low to arm level and stretching around me, their green leaves seeming to glow. A breeze rustles through the trees so they really do sound like they are talking to each other. Gazing up into the trees' canopies has an amazing ability to calm me. Thousands more trees have recently been planted in Malham by the National Trust to help create a healthy habitat including hawthorn, hazel and holly. A walking adventure – a peregrination, such as the one I am endeavouring to make – requires a balance of staying to admire places and moving on, and so it is upwards, on and into the Cove.

The steps up to the very top – all 400 of them, which look to have been carved from stone and rock – prove to be remarkably steep and I am soon out of breath but happy to be fuelled on by the chocolate supplies I bought from Ronald's village shop. I am also glad to be walking this particular bit of the Way with someone else, if only to have an arm to cling on to, to stop me slipping down or off the cliff. I've never felt my heart beat so intensely and rapidly as we climb. The steps seem interminable and at one point I almost feel like giving up. But we pass some people coming the other way who advise me to press on, to keep going, that it will be worth it. The summit of the cliffs opposite draw ever more parallel with the height we are, and I look down and gasp in terror and exhilaration at how high up we are, how far we have climbed up the Cove. There are still some steps to climb, though, and I press on, feeling my muscles straining and my heart beat rapidly as I walk ever closer to the clouds and away from the earth. A few speckles of rain have begun to fall, and I enjoy the feel of them on my skin.

After a while, I start to feel dizzy as the energy from those chocolate supplies leaks away. I wonder how many of the 400 steps we have ascended, but the thought of so many steps makes me nauseous and I concentrate on simply putting one foot in front of the other. A breeze sweeps over my skin, through my hair, then becomes so strong I think it might lift and topple me.

It has started to rain more relentlessly, and the rocks have become perilously slippery and my breathing ragged as I walk through the rugged landscape. I'm then startled by a shrieking sound – not quite human, perhaps the call of a peregrine – and feel the blood rush to my head as my foot slips slightly, but I regain my balance without falling.

Time seems to pass both glacially and in the blink of an eye as I put one foot in front of the other. Moments seem cavernous and filled with possibility, then the next moment contracts.

We finally reach the end of the steps, which give way to giant, silvery-grey and white-patched rocks, uneven blocks of limestone called clints. It is as if we are stepping onto the surface of the moon or another planet. Walking upon the rocks requires all my concentration not to slip and fall. This feels like the backbone of Britain, here upon this hard, harsh yet beautiful surface. Sprouting between the stones grow luminous green plantlife, what look like fern and species I cannot name. The great limestone clints stretch out all around, and even through the thick soles of my boots I can feel how hard they are, how strong. It was worth climbing all the way to walk upon this wonder.

A blue-grey bird suddenly swoops up from a rock and soars into the sky and I'm sure it is a peregrine. It is so swift, so agile and soon vanishes before I can spot its identifying features. After all, the peregrine falcon is the fastest member of the animal kingdom, soaring to great heights and diving at speeds of over 300 kilometres per hour. That blue-grey blur, whatever it was, has made me happy, made my heart lift to have seen even the possibility of a peregrine.

'Where flinty clints are scraped bone-bare / A whale's ribs glint in the sun' are words by poet Norman Nicholson on a sign I see on one of the huge rocks, framed in green, the only human intrusion in this landscape. The sign also has illustrations in green and purple of Baneberry, Dog's mercury, and Hart's-tongue fern. It reads:

> The glaciers that created Malham Cove also helped form the barren rocky landscape on top of it. The famous limestone pavement of the Yorkshire Dales National Park was scraped bare by the ice over 12,000 years ago.[43] Since then, slightly acidic rainwater has dissolved the rock away along faults and cracks.

The deep grykes, as they are known, now shelter a wonderful variety of plants, protected from overgrazing in their deep fissures. Today, these special pavements are protected by law. You can help protect this special habitat. Try not to damage the plants growing in the cracks and remember, never, ever buy waterworn limestone to use in your garden.

Protected by law. Words from that sign linger in my mind as I continue along the limestone pavement. I stoop down, wanting to inspect the grykes for their plantlife, but my companion calls me to hurry up so I continue clambering over the slippery clints in the rain.

This is such a haunted landscape. I think of all the creatures who have inhabited this place when warm seas washed through it, whose shells still remain forming sediment in layers of limestone. We shed some of the past like skin, but other experiences stay with us like sediment. What experiences settle in us like sediment? What experiences become fossils within us, shaping us? What are the fossil hauntings that live within you?

I think too of all that exists here that I cannot see, invisible to the human eye, creating another kind of haunting. I shiver to remember how our own bodies are haunted landscapes – right now billions of 'ghost particles', neutrinos, will be passing through your body. Our minds too, such haunted terrains.

The clints upon which I walk remind me of vertebrae, the thirty-three individual yet interlocking bones that form the spinal column running all the way to the coccyx or tailbone. We are able to walk due to the backbone, an astonishing landscape in itself that houses the spinal canal, which in turn protects and encloses the spinal cord. 'Let us worship the spine and its tingle,' wrote Nabokov who posited the seat of artistic delight as between the shoulder-blades. 'Let us be proud of being vertebrates, for we are vertebrates tipped at the head with a divine flame. The brain only continues the spine, the wick really runs through the whole length of the candle.' The spinal cord runs from the brainstem, and the brain and spinal cord make up the central nervous system. Information is relayed to the brain through spinal tracts, through the 'final common pathway' to the brain's thalamus region and cerebral cortex. Spinal nerves connect the spinal cord to skin, muscles and joints and allow for transmission of sensory and motor signals. Spinal interneurons make up neural circuits known as central pattern generators – responsible for rhythmic movements such as walking. How remarkable it is to be able to walk at all, and it is all too easy for the able-bodied to take it for granted.

We walk further out into the clints as they spread right to the very edge of the precipice, and I stretch out my arms and savour being so high up and the sweet sense of achievement for having made it up here. I let the rain run all over my face as I raise my head heavenwards. I am so close to the very edge here, mere footsteps from that massive plunge over the precipice.

I take another step forward and then am startled by a voice – my companion urging me to press on, if we are going to make it to the Tarn in time – and I stumble and trip suddenly, and do seem to see my life flash before me as I fall, a lifetime of images blurred into a millisecond. Then I hear the loud thud of a bone in my body against the limestone, and a searing pain shoots through me. It was my ankle bone that bore the brunt of the fall, my knee feels grazed, and another dull pain that seems weirdly dissociated from a specific location but spreading through my entire foot. The skin on my palms is also scraped and sore from where I put out my arms to break the fall, but not so much that they are bleeding more than a few speckles that I staunch with a tissue.

I haul myself up and continue on, walking through the pain and the rain. It feels as if I am soaked to the bone. I thought I had packed the most appropriate clothing for the trip – I had given myself a pat on the back for remembering to pack a rain mac at all and had thought the boots I would be wearing were perfect for all weathers – but I learn the hard way when the rainwater seeps into my boots and I feel it swell around my soles. I had not been able to afford expensive new walking boots and had hoped for the best that these would serve me well. The rain mac also fails to provide sufficient protection from the rain falling so ferociously that soon I am drenched, shivering, teeth clattering.

I had set my mind on reaching the Tarn. I have seen images of tarns and dreamed about them but cannot remember seeing one in actuality. I have encountered Malham Tarn imaginatively as it was the inspiration for Charles Kingsley's 1863 novel *The Water-Babies: A Fairy Tale for a Land Baby*, in which Tom the chimney sweep is transformed into a water-baby after drowning and journeys to the Other-end-of-Nowhere. Even though I had been so keen to reach the Tarn at the start of the walk – in my mind it glittered like a blue beacon – I do not know how much longer I can go on, how much more I can bear this relentless rain and the rocks beneath my feet now so hard to walk over, so slippery and dangerous, so easy here and now, as I have learnt, to lose the footing.

We pass some walkers coming the other way, and I ask the two teenage girls – huddled together, hoods up, maps in protective sealing strapped around their necks, shoulders hunched in the biting cold – if it is far to the Tarn. They nod and frown.

'Is it worth going?' I ask and they shake their heads and grimace.

'The ground has become ridiculously muddy because of the rain and the whole thing has literally turned into a massive bog,' one says.

'It's dangerous and impossible to walk through,' warns the other.

I am put off and want to call it a day. I had been longing to see the Tarn but going further feels unbearable.

'I'm going to go on,' says George.

I turn around and look at how far we have come. Through the lashing rain I see the giant limestone clints and beyond them the cliff falling eighty metres beneath. I think of the 400 stone steps there are to walk back down the Cove in this rain, which shows no sign of relenting. I decide to press on, hobbling over rocks in the rain. Despite my boots having a thick sole, soon I can feel the very bones in my feet.

I see some other people approaching and ask how far the Tarn is and an elderly man tells us forty minutes. My companion needs to be back at the bunkhouse by 3.30 p.m. as he will be heading home and I will be walking the rest of the way alone.

We walk further to a ledge that looks out over the cliffs and stand there in the rain, admiring the view, before deciding that this ledge will be a wonderful place to end this stage of the walk. On the way back, the rain lightens a little, and such is the relief to be heading back that the pain in my foot is more bearable too.

I am looking down, taking care of each step as I clamber over the great limestone pavement, when I glimpse a glory of bluebells growing in a gryke, along with an abundance of other plants and flowers flourishing between the fissures of the rocks. I pause to photograph them, risking the rain on my phone for I so want a memory of this life growing. Then I linger to look down properly into the microhabitat in those cracks, into glowingly bright white flowers that I cannot name and a multitude of other wild magic. Raindrops have gathered all over the petals of the bluebells, little diamond-mirrors reflecting the colours of the Cove. The contrast between the delicacy of such soft leaves against the huge, hard stones is striking. I see other wildlife in the grykes: wall-rue – a small fern growing exclusively on limestone rocks and crevices, a bright pink five-petalled flower named herb-robert, green spleenwort and wildflowers I can't name. I spot some silver thistles that haven't blossomed yet, tightly closed and protected in dark brown, cream-headed bodies. There is some wood sorrel with its gleaming white petals in citrus-green leaves. I see Sophie's face then, the smile she gave when we last met, her eyes bright and shining, and feel again the warm hug of our last parting. 'I left feeling really inspired,' she had emailed me afterwards, and now I sense that it is her inspiring me onwards.

Far from being lifeless up here, life has found a way of growing in the most unexpected of places, through

cracks and fissures and breakage. It seems miraculous to
see, uplifting and hopeful.

On our way walking back I see another sign, covered
in raindrops:

SAMARITANS. Talk to us, we'll listen.
Whatever you're going through, you don't have to
    face it alone.
Call free day or night on 116 123.

The colourful sign in three shades of green is filled with
teardrop-shaped rain and fitted into a wall built from
harsh and uneven dark grey stone. I point out the sign to
my companion and he tells me about his acquaintance, a
man whose portrait he had photographed who had
tragically taken his own life by jumping off a cliff.
Another acquaintance had also attempted suicide by
jumping in front of a train but survived. She lost her feet
in the process, but has since become an activist, speaking
out on the topic of mental health.

Earlier in the year, I had made a call to the Samaritans
for the first time. I had found myself on the edge. 'Call
someone close to you and tell them how you are feeling,'
a friend I thought I was close to had emailed when
I told them how I was feeling. I think of those structures
of support that have been set up in society to help those
feeling at their most vulnerable, to hold them back from
the edge, and how crucial they are. There should be no
shame and stigma in using such support systems, in
realising we are all connected – and that recognising
such connection and reaching out can be crucial and
lifesaving.

We walk back down beside the cliff face, down those 400 stone steps, relieved to be soon drying off from the rain. Along the way I look out into the startling drop below, think how plunging down it would doubtless lead to instant death, and about what it is that keeps us going at all, putting one foot in front of the other, what keeps despair at bay, how we move from feeling we don't belong in the world enough to want to leave it, to a sense of belonging. More than ever I want to stay alive to tell this story, to help others who may have been through a similar situation and internalised feelings of worthlessness and despair that being violated can incite, and to help do all I can to stop what happened to me happening to anyone else.

The steps are so slippery but we manage to make our way down all 400 and are back by the River Aire, its water even more swollen and roaring ferociously, its sound again soothing away all care and discomfort, making me forget about the pain or the cold that has burrowed its way into my bones. The sight of it makes me feel awe as it rushes and churns and we follow it all the way along until we are back on the Way and walking past the vast limestone cliff that we had stopped to look out at from a ledge.

In the village we head to the pub and devour fishfinger sandwiches and savour hot sweet tea. It's then I feel just how freezing cold I am. I take off my soaked mac and shiver non-stop. My boots are completely sodden inside and out and now stinking and the pain in my foot caused by falling is piercing. I go and stand near the roaring fire and chat to some people sitting on nearby armchairs, a group of men who are also walkers, also sheltering from the rain.

We make our way back to the bunk barn and my companion packs his possessions and it is time for him to leave. I feel a lurch of nerves at the thought of being alone and doing the rest of the journey alone. I feel how much I have relied on him to be the one reading the map and finding the way, across non-existent paths, over fields which looked as if no human feet had ever trodden before, and over those great limestone cliffs and clints. How will I manage, walking alone? How will I manage both physically, with no arm to clutch on to when it seems as if I will fall, but also emotionally, with no one to chat to or offer practical tips or encourage me, to tell me to keep going when I feel like giving up?

The night before, we had had something of a row over the difference between the terms 'fearlessly' and 'without fear' – he had recorded a short video of me at the river and said the only thing he would change was me saying 'fearlessly' and would instead say 'without fear'. I had said it was impossible to predict whether I would encounter a dangerous situation, that fear might be the natural and instinctive response, and that the word fearlessly acknowledged that – I may feel fear but despite it continue on. We had got on each other's nerves. But as he is about to leave, that drains away and I feel I will miss his presence. We hug at the door and I treasure the feeling of another human body holding mine, and feel, yes, a twinge of fear about the journey ahead.

The exhaustion then hits me and the cold seems to have crept into my very bones. I am tired and cold to the core, so exhausted I cannot summon the strength to shower, despite the rain, sweat, mud and blood that cling to me. Instead I curl into my sleeping bag, like a soft blue skin, and lie down for hours. I feel anxiety seeping back in despite my exhaustion, a sliver of it clutching at my neck, and yearn for sleep to bring some respite. The pain from my fall starts up again and I check the graze on my knee to see it is deep but, before I find strength to put on a plaster and bandage my foot, sweet sleep carries me away.

Later, I venture into the barn's living area and write notes on the day. Walking today has shifted my sense of landscape in terms of both place and time, being somewhere where the macro and micro are so contrasted and yet coexistent, the giant rocks and the tiny flowers, the millennia and the millisecond. William Blake famously wrote that it was possible to see the 'world in a grain of sand'. Today I seemed to see a universe in a gryke, the enormous existing not apart from but within the tiny, eternity existing not apart from but within the present moment. The eye and the mind become sharpened by walking and watching the world, seeing more. I remember the things too tiny to see that still exist, those 'ghost particles'.

I browse further about Malham Cove's history; it was interesting to have walked up without having researched much about it beforehand. Only now do I learn that *Harry Potter* was filmed there, and about the deaths that have occurred there, details of the suicides, accidents, and a murder. I wonder if it is bad to have found a place beautiful when such tragedy has happened there.

I glance outside the window and see the sky deepening into a darkness not known in the city. I then curl back into my blue skin of a sleeping bag and lie and listen to cows mooing and the wind howling until I fall asleep again. The river, full and swollen, rushes through my dreams, and I am again walking upon great slabs of limestone and looking down into their cracks and fissures, into their grykes and seeing all manner of life growing where life was least expected. I am again sensing my friend who died a few weeks ago, her spirit, so strong.

The words 'protected', 'protected by law' and 'protected characteristics' have been lingering in my mind since being racially abused. I remember the words I saw at the top of Malham Cove, stating that the limestone area is 'protected by law' and sharing how we can 'help protect this special habitat'. It is by understanding the protected characteristics of both people and places that the backbone of civilisation is kept from crumbling.

Many people I have spoken with are ignorant of the fact that there are 'protected characteristics' defined by law. The Equality Act 2010, section 4 states the following are protected: age; disability; gender reassignment; marriage and civil partnership; pregnancy and maternity; race; religion or belief; sex; sexual orientation.[44] Hate crime describes criminal behaviour where the perpetrator is motivated by hostility towards the victim's protected characteristics. Statistics show that attacks on the protected characteristics are increasing,[45] yet the Institute of Race Relations reveals that race hate crime is under-reported to the police.[46] Hate crimes are under-reported for various reasons: the fear of not being believed or taken seriously, being gaslighted, an awareness of systemic racism.

Even though the man who racially abused me on the train himself pleaded guilty, even though I had no less than six witnesses, even though I had recorded evidence, still my experience was gaslit by some.

It is important to understand why hate crime is different to a crime such as having your car stolen. Hate crime is an attack on the identity that cuts to the core of the self. It is about hatred of the other, of difference. It is an attack on the dignity. Hate crime is an assault on the sense of belonging. Hate crimes impact not only individuals but whole communities, sending out a signal that such groups are vulnerable to attack.[47]

The first modern-day hate crime laws were passed in the US in 1968 with the Civil Rights Act, a few days after Martin Luther King's assassination. In the UK, the Macpherson Report – initiated following the brutal murder of the black teenager Stephen Lawrence in 1993 – found that the Metropolitan Police were institutionally racist and made seventy recommendations for reform, covering criminal law and policing. It was instrumental in contemporary race hate-crime definitions. Before such terms as 'hate crime' and 'protected characteristics', there has of course been a long history of abuse of individuals and communities stemming from hatred of their identity; language and law has only relatively recently in the scale of human history defined this behaviour.

The police put me in contact with Victim Support, who in turn provided a list of contact numbers for organisations offering further support: anxiety helplines No Panic and Anxiety UK, and organisations a part of CATCH (Community Alliance to Combat Hate)[48] including The Monitoring Group. The Monitoring Group was established in Southall in the early 1980s by community campaigners and lawyers wishing to challenge

the growth of racism, for Black and Asian young people
were enduring daily racist encounters. They have become
a leading anti-racist organisation, helping those in distress
and promoting good race relations through education
and awareness-raising. Over the past forty years they have
led many campaigns to help families including those of
Kuldip Singh Sekon who was stabbed to death by a racist
in 1989, Stephen Lawrence who was stabbed to death in a
racist attack in 1993, Ricky Reel who was found dead in
the River Thames following a racist attack in 1997,
Michael Menson who was set on fire by racists in London
in 1997, and Zahid Mubarek who was killed by his racist
cellmate at Feltham Young Offenders Institution in 2000.
Some of these cases led to public judicial inquiries and
consequent changes in legislation, social policies and
practices. They have also supported the Joy Gardner
Memorial Campaign – five police officers from the Aliens
Deportation Group raided Joy Gardner's home in London
one early morning in 1993 with orders to 'detain and
remove' her and her five-year-old son. She was restrained
with handcuffs and leather straps and gagged with four
metres of adhesive tape wrapped around her head; unable
to breathe, she suffered brain damage due to asphyxia and
died following a cardiac arrest.

The founder and director of The Monitoring Group,
Suresh Grover, was born in Kenya and came to the UK
in 1966, growing up in Nelson, Lancashire to where my
own paternal family emigrated. Grover recalls being
stabbed by a racist while visiting the cinema to see the
latest Clint Eastwood movie. He reported it to police
but they never took a statement or followed up on
the attack.[49] One day in 1976, Grover, then aged

twenty-two, saw a pool of blood on the pavement and asked a nearby police officer what had happened; he was told that someone had died the previous night and 'it was just an Asian'. The blood belonged to eighteen-year-old student Gurdip Singh Chaggar who was murdered by racists. Following this, hundreds took to the streets in protest and Grover became one of the founders of the Southall Asian Youth Movement, galvanising youth to challenge racism and police response. Their slogan was 'Come what may, we are here to stay.'

I want to learn more and get in touch with Grover, who shares his experience of racism as a youngster: 'The paki-bashing was like a massive wave coming in front of you and you didn't know what hit you. You were surrounded and beaten up. What paralysed me was the fear. It was like a wave; the first punch that landed on my face I still remember like in slow motion; you don't feel the pain at first, then it comes.' The 'paki-bashing' occurred daily and made him frightened to go to school. 'You navigate your lives totally differently – you choose different paths in the streets.' Grover said he and his family and friends were trying to integrate and did not regard themselves as different ('We were into music like Marc Bolan and Slade and T. Rex and Eric Clapton, though he later made a racist speech'), 'But that world changes when you get beaten up – the people who should be protecting you don't care and that's simply because of the colour of your skin and it makes you angry. The teachers turned a blind eye. In a way, a level of violence was accepted as the state doesn't care what happens to the working-class. Emotionally I rebelled; I found music and left

Nelson. I thought if I stayed, I'd either kill someone or
get killed.' He says what really made him angry was
when the racists started picking on girls and spitting on
them. The racist harassment and violence changed his
life. 'The negligence of the police remained with me
and I came to distrust authority, like many who have
experienced racism. Little acts of solidarity were so
important and that's how the Monitoring Group came
about – helping people to not fear anymore.'

Many attacks on the protected characteristics have
been made while people have been travelling. I was
deeply affected to learn of the Portland, Oregon train
attack which also happened in broad daylight one day in
May, three years before the hate crime I suffered, and
which commentators cite as an example of the rise in
hate crime during Trump's presidency. A white nationalist
on the train uttered racial slurs to two teenage girls,
telling them to get out of 'his country', that they were
'nothing' and should kill themselves. Three people who
intervened were stabbed, two dying of their injuries, one
surviving serious wounds.[50] 'Tell everyone on this train
I love them,' one victim, Taliesin Namkai-Meche, said as
he lay dying. In a heartrending video, one of the teenagers
subjected to racial abuse, Destinee Mangum, thanks the
strangers who helped, and said what happened was
'haunting' her. The root cause of the problem needs to be
recognised – those nationalistic views that only white
people belonged on that train. For notions of belonging
can be toxic when they become extremist, excluding and
hating anybody who is perceived to belong to a different
group.[51] Other reported attacks include on a Sheffield
schoolgirl who survived being strangled with her own

hijab while travelling home on a bus. Less than a fortnight after I was racially abused on the train, two women suffered a homophobic and misogynistic attack on a London bus – Melania Geymonat posted a photograph on Facebook of herself and partner Chris covered in blood. Three teenage boys pleaded guilty. The judge included in the sentence diversity sessions, 'Which will make you think about hate crime, the protected characteristics and minority groups.'[52]

That society is not an equal playing field has been horrifyingly apparent in attacks on the protected characteristics in playing fields and public arenas themselves. After England players were racially abused during a Euro 2020 qualifying match, football's European governing body UEFA said it is committed to eliminating the 'disease' of racism and pointed to the rise of nationalism for fuelling hostility.[53] Football star Raheem Sterling has spoken out powerfully about the racist abuse he has suffered and is fronting a campaign, No Room for Racism.[54]

Weaponising the protected characteristic of race against someone in a recreational space happened in the 'Central Park birdwatching incident' of May 2020 – in a viral video, the white woman Amy Cooper called police on a black birdwatcher who had done no wrong, histrionically and falsely claiming he was threatening her life and specifically mentioning his race. The incident occurred on the same day George Floyd was murdered.

Protected characteristics should be taught at the earliest age, young people learning that it is not only wrong but illegal to abuse someone's identity, the core of who they are. While there are signs marking places that are 'protected by law', such as that limestone ledge on

Malham Cove, people should not have to wear signs saying that aspects of them are protected. Respect of others should be ingrained as basic civility.

Places have various degrees of protection, from those protected by law to those actually granted a form of legal personhood. Protected areas in the UK have laws to help ensure that nature and wildlife are not harmed or destroyed and include national parks and Areas of Outstanding Natural Beauty, Marine Conservation Zones, Sites of Special Scientific Interest, Special Areas of Conservation, Special Protection Areas and Ramsar wetland sites.[55]

A government-commissioned report into the future of Britain's protected landscapes (DEFRA Landscapes Review, Glover, 2019[56]) criticised national parks for not doing enough to make people from diverse sections of society feel welcome.[57] 'We are all paying for national landscapes through our taxes, and yet sometimes on our visits it has felt as if national parks are an exclusive, mainly white, mainly middle-class club.' The Review proposed systemic reform of National Park and AONB governing boards stating that only a 'tiny fraction' of board members are from black, Asian or minority ethnicities. Natural England posited the staggering statistic that only 1 per cent of visitors to national parks are from BAME backgrounds. Those with protected characteristics need to feel welcome in the UK's protected landscapes.

Places with a legal personhood around the world include all nature in Ecuador, a country that wrote the rights of Pachamama (Mother Nature) into its constitution in 2008,[58] currently the only constitution in the world where this kind of protection exists. Such a law makes damaging nature comparable to damaging a human being. It reflects that, thanks to the activism of indigenous communities, indigenous thinking is now ingrained in the constitution[59] including the Kichwa notion of 'Sumak Kawsay' or 'buen vivir', which means 'good living' in English and expresses the idea of harmonious, balanced living among people and nature.

There is a long, painful history of Maori communities of New Zealand being severed from their land in violating, violent practices during British colonialism: in the early 1860s, the parliament of New Zealand, then part of the British Empire, passed legislation for the confiscation (raupatu) of Maori land to punish tribes deemed to have 'engaged in open rebellion against Her Majesty's authority'.[60] It is heartening that in 2017 the Whanganui River in New Zealand was granted legal personhood in line with the Maori worldview that the river is a living entity – an ancient Maori proverb is 'I am the river, and the river is me.'[61] The Ganges and Yamuna rivers in India were also granted legal personhood status before this decision was later overturned[62] by India's supreme court.[63]

If you witnessed a human in distress would you look the other way or would you help them?

If you witnessed the natural world in distress, would you look the other way or would you call out for help? In *Braiding Sweetgrass*, Robin Wall Kimmerer uses the term 'more-than-human beings' for the natural world and points out the injustice of an economy that grants personhood to corporations but denies it to more-than-human beings.[64] 'People exploit what they have merely concluded to be of value, but they defend what they love, and to defend what we love we need a particularising language, for we love what we particularly know,' wrote essayist and farmer Wendell Berry.[65] That applies to both people and places, and both human history and natural history show how people of colour and other marginalised groups – both their labour and land – have been exploited and continue to be so.

'No one will protect what they don't care about; and no one will care about what they have never experienced,' said David Attenborough. Considering the protected characteristics of both place and people together helps us think about how humans and the environments we inhabit are inextricably connected, how we need to care about each other and the natural world. Such care, respect and empathy are the bedrock of civilisation and survival.

To empathise is to imagine yourself into and beneath the skin of another, into their mind and heart, and what it would be like walking in their shoes. We need greater empathy for both human beings and the natural world. Imagine yourself into and beneath the skin of the earth, to its core, to its backbone and bedrock. Imagine yourself into a tree and a river and a gryke and a flower. How can you possibly now cause these beings hurt?

8

On Strength, Courage and Trauma

I've long loved getting beneath the skin of words, to their very core, to understand the multiple meanings layered in them, as with the word 'backbone'. Walking upon such strong rock, which runs a rugged course through the North of England, seems a symbolic place to reflect upon those various definitions. The *Oxford English Dictionary* contains three definitions: 1. The spine. 2. The chief support of a system or organisation. 3. Strength of character.

The *Merriam Webster Dictionary* includes in its definition: 'something that resembles a backbone', such as 'a chief mountain ridge, range, or system', as well as 'the foundation or most substantial or sturdiest part of something' and 'the longest chain of atoms or groups of atoms in a usually long molecule (such as a polymer or protein)'.

The *Oxford Learner's Dictionary* spells out the third definition as 'the strength of character you need to do something difficult', while the *Cambridge Dictionary* uses the word 'courage' as well as 'strength' in that third definition.

What does it mean to have backbone? What does it mean to be 'strong', 'courageous' and 'brave'? I had thousands of strangers telling me that I had been so for speaking up. One of the messages read 'Strong hero', at which I laughed, for when I read that message on my phone I was curled up in bed in a quivering anxious state that felt far from conventional notions of 'strength'. I had ironically discussed the topic of braveness in life and literature on a panel at the Bloomsbury Institute that same week I fell victim to hate crime, and I've been led to further explore ideas of strength, braveness and courage throughout history, from the strong men of legends such as Hercules, to the present day and how such notions need to evolve.

I google 'strong hero' and my eyes are accosted with images of men's muscles, flexed, fists clenched. In the 'People also ask' panel, questions include: 'Who is the strongest superhero in the world?' and the answer is: 'Superman is the strongest superhero ever. If we're talking about the present, it's Franklin Richards' (a character in Marvel Comic books). 'Who is the greatest superhero of all time?' The top answer here is also Superman. I search for 'superhero' and it brings up related searches for 'Top 10 Most Popular Superheroes of All Time': Batman; Spider-Man; Iron Man; Superman; Wolverine; Captain America; The Hulk; Thor. There are few women in sight, though *Britannica* lists Batgirl, Batwoman and Catwoman.

Hercules, the Roman hero and god known as Heracles in Greek mythology, is of course who springs to mind and fingertip concerning notions of the strong hero in myth.[66] Hercules, whose strength was such that he strangled two snakes when still in his cradle, and aged eighteen killed the Lion of Cithaeron. Other heroes of Greek mythology include Achilles, who became invulnerable after his mother dipped him in the River Styx, except for a soft spot of vulnerability – the heel by which his mother held him. There is an idea of physical strength in the traditional notion of being strong, brave and heroic – think of those Herculean muscles. Several images of 'strength' and 'strong' also show the anatomy of the body and skeleton, or the back with a strong spine.

The definition of 'strongman' also refers to political leaders who exert power through authoritarian methods that may be violent, threatening or morally wrong. We have been living in an age of 'strongman politics', and in this world of so-called 'strong men', strength can be exploited to bully. Bullying is a repeated pattern of abuse of power designed to dominate those perceived as weaker, to make them feel as if they don't belong. Bullies love to chip away at an identity and can be worst in their belittling words. We need to recognise the signs and empower ourselves to deal with and prevent it. Bullying can happen in childhood or in adulthood, and is rife in politics – Trump, for example, former leader of the most powerful country on earth has used bullying to dominate and degrade his opponents.

Yet strength is not only about the physical, nor should it be about domineering use of power. There is strength of mind and spirit. There is strength of words and language.

I remember Virginia Woolf's words, 'For most of history, "Anonymous" was a woman,' and commend all the undersung female thinkers, explorers and scientists who showed strength. One pertinent here is the fossil

collector Mary Anning who would walk in the Jurassic
marine fossil beds in the cliffs along the English Channel.
One day, aged twelve, she discovered the skull of an
ichthyosaur, an ancient reptile, and a few months later
she found the remains of the skeleton and went on to
make other fossil discoveries that contributed to a sea-
change in thought about the origins of the earth. When
she made her first discovery, her father had not long
died, suffering from tuberculosis and injuries sustained
falling off a cliff. Stephen Jay Gould described her as:
'Probably the most important unsung (or inadequately
sung) collecting force in the history of paleontology.'[67]
Anning is the star of the children's book *Stone Girl Bone
Girl: The Story of Mary Anning* and inspired the tongue-
twister I would roll around my mouth as a child: 'She
sells sea shells by the seashore.'

Looking at the strongest substances in the natural
world also overturns stereotypes of strength. Long
thought to be the hardest natural substance are diamonds,
one of the 'superhard' materials. Strength and toughness
are not quite the same as hardness, though they are often
conflated. Two important properties that all physical
materials have are strength (how much force it can
withstand before it deforms) and toughness (how much
energy it takes to break or fracture it).[68] Spider silk is
stronger than steel.[69] It is the toughest material of the
natural world and was believed to be the strongest natural
material until researchers in 2015 found the teeth of
limpets, snail-like creatures with conical shells, to be
even stronger. Limpets use their super-strength teeth on
rock surfaces and to remove tough algae for feeding.[70]

Growing up in the North there was a pervasive idea of the need to be strong and tough, to be 'well 'ard'. There is a northern dialect term 'nesh', meaning susceptible to the cold; if so much as the slightest shiver escaped us while running around outside in nothing but gym knickers during a PE lesson in the middle of winter, the teacher would yell 'Don't be s'nesh!' Another frequent term I heard was 'Don't be s'soft.' I tried to be 'well 'ard', to harden myself against the cold, against racial slurs, against any blow that might come battering. I imagined myself with a carapace, a creature with a tough shell that nothing would break through. I remembered the hard shells I found on a beach in Blackpool. My mother, too, tried to turn herself into a stone: 'I should be tough like a stone, and not feel anything,' I remember her saying when I was a small child and my parents were in the midst of an acrimonious divorce. Of course, that doesn't work; although we have some elements of stone in our bodies, including our bones, we are also flesh and blood and water. We are also feeling creatures, who wound and are wounded. As well as being 'well 'ard', I now try and live by words in Charles Dickens's *Hard Times*: 'Have a heart that never hardens.'

My own carapace crumbled when at school we were learning about blood in science and I fainted; there was no hiding from the fact that I am squeamish. When I fainted at getting jabbed, there was no disguising that I have a low pain threshold. *Today at the doctor's I was brave as a lion,* reads the sticker with a cartoon lion on an old journal, given to me in young adulthood by the nurse who jabbed needles in my arm before I went abroad to places with risk of malaria and rabies, the same nurse who had also given me a smear test and grew to know what a low pain threshold I have. Even as an adult, I appreciated such a lion. I think back to my earliest memories of being called brave, and those stickers we'd be given. 'I was brave as a limpet' perhaps doesn't have the same ring to it, but I pay tribute to the many tiny but tough creatures in nature who show great strength.

It isn't pretending that we don't feel pain that makes us brave; it's instead finding ways to bear it – to know that, like a needle being jabbed in the arm to immunise us, sometimes pain might ultimately serve a purpose, might make us stronger and more resistant. Being brave is also not beating ourselves up for the times we struggled to bear pain at all, those times it overwhelmed us.

Like limestone we are porous, even the supposedly hardest and strongest of us. Life pours into us. Life slides into our skin and into our hearts and seeps into our minds. Sometimes it can be acidic, it can hurt and sting. We can carry that hurt within us. Some experiences roll over us, while others become like sediment, settling deeper within.

In the 1980s there was a Thatcherite notion prevalent that 'society was dead' and individual resilience was all. The classical notion of a strong person was one who acted individually and was reliant solely upon their own strength. Theresa May attempted to continue this with her much-derided 'strong and stable' slogan. Yet one of the definitions of backbone is: 'The part of something that provides strength or support' (*Cambridge Dictionary*) and 'the most important part of a system, an organization, etc. that gives it support and strength' (*Oxford Advanced*

Learners Dictionary). I think of those services that have
come into existence over the years that provide such
support. The NHS came to life following the Second
World War as a backbone to Britain, with the notion of
altruism and the common good at its heart – that good
healthcare should be available for all regardless of wealth.
It was initiated following the Beveridge Report, which
proposed reforms to address 'five giants on the road to
reconstruction – want, disease, ignorance, squalor, and
idleness'. During the pandemic inadequate funding
was starkly apparent in the lack of Personal Protective
Equipment (PPE).

Our mind as well as body can become ill, hurt, wounded
and need tending to; experiences can damage the mind
much in the way the body can become damaged, but so
too the mind can heal. I think of those in need of support
yet lacking it, the long, underfunded waiting lists with the
NHS for counselling and therapy, compounded by the
deep sense of shame and stigma that can still exist around
acknowledging the need for mental health help – such
stigma needs to be smashed.

Then there are organisations such as Victim Support,
offering free emotional support which I was provided
with soon after being racially abused. I remember the
miracle of my phone ringing and a human voice at
the end of the line, there to ask if I was OK and to
offer expert emotional support. I told the Victim
Support worker about the emotions I was experiencing,
about the anxiety and anger I felt. Although many
people I knew did, there had been a few who failed to
find the words to condemn what had happened, who
didn't know what to say, had not shown public

solidarity or understood the importance of doing so, which I found triggering.

Let's be clear: racism, and indeed all forms of systemic inequality and abuse, affects the mental health in myriad ways. I told my Victim Support counsellor how I had not taken my anger out on the person who deserved it but had instead ended up lashing out in angry messages to a couple of people who were, at heart, well-meaning. The simplest yet most helpful thing she said was: 'These feelings are completely normal after what you have been through.' Those words took a weight off my shoulders, recognising the shades of emotion we feel as humans. It was a relief to know I was not alone – anyone who has been abused has been violated and the consequent feeling can be rage. I look back and see how such an organisation provided a backbone of support when needed. I wish I had had such support when I desperately needed it during my youth, that more people are aware of the existence of such support and feel able to access it, and that more organisations are better funded and readily available to all suffering.

When I went to the police station to give a Victim Impact Statement, I spoke of the emotions I had experienced as a result of being racially abused. It is important to state that the law itself acknowledges our vulnerability as humans, the 'impact' of having our humanity violated, the emotional damage it can cause.

My experience has shown me that being brave and strong also paradoxically means allowing yourself to reveal your vulnerabilities – that if you have experienced abuse you are likely to be traumatised thereafter or feel a turbulence of emotion. Being open about those emotions, about how we have been hurt, will help others draw from the strength of showing vulnerability. There is no shame in acknowledging that no person is an island; there is strength in doing so.

We all need to know how better to support each other, for example how best to respond to someone who has been racially abused, to find the words to condemn what happened, to acknowledge the strength it takes to speak out. We should be able to discuss such matters, since people's responses can be even more traumatising than the actual incident. Best is to listen to people, to ask how you can support them, and to realise we are all ultimately connected and the strength of one person is going to impact upon our own.

The fault-lines

Trauma can manifest like a great dark wave of deep-seated panic and fear, crashing over the mind – and can be created or exacerbated when we don't have that backbone of support when it's needed, by being caught in the fault-lines. It can cause fissures, those places of pain becoming deepened and more susceptible. Time doesn't always heal; it can do quite the opposite. And like those rivers and springs in a karst landscape, trauma can rise up suddenly and engulf us. But through acknowledging that, we can begin to look trauma in the eye, to look into the cracks and fissures, and thereby begin the process of understanding that enables healing. When we look into our pain it might ultimately offer up gifts, like the gifts

I saw in the grykes of a limestone pavement at the top of Malham Cove, a place battered and seemingly barren and yet teeming with life; we can see that new growth is possible.

Look upon a limestone landscape and you will see its many 'faults', deepened by time. There is a certain strength in letting go of guilt over the times we thought we failed or fell short, those times we took wrong turnings and found ourselves lost, those times we teetered on the brink and almost broke, or those times we did break and had to remake ourselves, reconfigure ourselves.

There is a freedom in realising that something we have been beating ourselves up about wasn't our fault. Far too often when a victim speaks out, they are gaslighted into thinking the experience was their fault – we see this in the misogynistic notion of 'slut shaming', that women were 'asking for it'. This is victim-blaming. I would like to say to all victims of abuse: *it was not your fault*. Gaslighting has a corrosive effect on the self-esteem and mental health, wearing us down like that acid wearing down limestone. The sufferer can then be gaslit and excluded further, branded as 'mad', have mental illness weaponised against them, asserting that what they are saying is not true but a symptom of their illness, in an attempt to invalidate reality. Depression, anxiety and other mental health illnesses are also too often described as character faults, sufferers as 'weak people' – I would like to say: *this is not your fault*.

What is often not considered and acknowledged as even existing is the wider landscape, its fault-lines and their effects. What happened to me on the train exposed fault-lines in our society, a mixture of racism and misogyny.

Austerity has also created huge economic inequalities and resentment has been wrongly directed towards the scapegoated, immigrants, stoked by certain political groups and media.

Fault-lines can be exposed by events in individual lives or major crises such as the coronavirus pandemic through which fault-lines in society became glaring, revealing deep structural inequalities: disproportionate numbers of people of colour dying, huge inequalities in living conditions and access to nature. Becoming caught in the fault-lines is deeply traumatic and will affect the mental health – the lack of adequate support due to underfunded mental healthcare systems can further exacerbate and compound suffering. We cannot see these fault-lines and stay silent – we must speak out and demand a fairer, more equal world.

As I walk upon the fault-lines in the earth, I think of why potentially good people do bad things, whether through some deep-seated pain of their own, through sheer ignorance or hate, or through lacking backbone of whatever kind. Walking through such a complex set of fractures as the Pennine faults has deepened my understanding of fault-lines.

I forgive the man who racially abused me on the train. I forgive those who wronged me before him too. Forgiveness is not to condone the fault in behaviour. Forgiveness is to see the ignorance at its root, to not let the feelings of hurt and anger corrode us, to be able to walk on and move forward. There is strength in forgiveness, a deepening of empathy, extending empathy even to so-called 'enemies' or those who have hurt us.

These days I don't try and steel myself but spider-silk myself. The web I weave, though, is made from words. In my own moments of weakness, it has been picking up my pen that has saved me. It has been stringing words across the page to try and make sense and shape some order out of my experiences. As I type this up, watching the words form lines, they remind me of tiny bones strung together to form something of a backbone, that of language – and language is a uniquely strong substance. Language can survive the greatest loss, and when we put our pain into prose, language can in turn help us – and perhaps others who read it – to survive. Language is stronger than death, words like fossils, holding within them a memory and haunting of life.

9

Going Viral

One of the dictionary definitions of 'backbone' is 'the primary high-speed hardware and transmission lines of a telecommunications network (such as the Internet)'. I love the nuances and variety of meanings in the word – from the actual (mountain range) through to the virtual (cyberspace) – and how they are all at the heart of my experience.

It was that 'backbone' of transmission lines in cyberspace that allowed me to communicate my experience as it was happening on the train, tweets that went viral and racked up millions of views and engagements. It is a democratising form of communication, allowing instant connection with a world of strangers. Sending a tweet can be a powerful way of connecting people globally. This became more apparent than ever as lockdown saw us relying on the virtual as our backbone: offices replaced by Zoom meetings; events by virtual festivals, concerts, launches; actual travel by virtual travel.

Yet the internet and social media can paradoxically both enhance connection and create a sense of isolation. In the days and weeks after I went viral, I felt strangely disassociated. My life at the time meant I would go days without interacting with another human being or even hearing the sound of my own voice. I'd pass days without being touched. It was as if my mind and body had separated, the anxious whir of thoughts intensified, as if I was not fully inhabiting myself. The bleeping notifications of my

phone would make me jump out of my skin, however
soothing a ringtone I chose. And like so many women of
colour, I'm susceptible to being on the receiving end of
the more toxic side of the internet – misogynistic, racist
and abusive trolling and gaslighting – and how vicious and
vindictive the veil of anonymity makes trolls, although I'll
never let trolls silence me.

That 'backbone' of the internet is also highly addictive;
soon enough it's our instinctive response to refresh
the email, to check for notifications, receiving a hit
of dopamine with a 'like' or positive message. Its constant
distraction can interfere with deep concentration. The
desire to get likes on an Instagram post of a place can for
some surpass actual engagement with the place itself.

After days of communicating with headshots and gifs
rather than 'real' human beings, it's easy to become
weirded out. The virtual realm makes 'absent presences'
of us – there yet not there, disembodied, creating an
eeriness to the experience. Strange things happen to time
in cyberspace – it can seem to disappear down a vortex,
be rapidly devoured. I wanted the glorious slowing-down
of time that being fully in the present moment allows.
Strange things happen to the sense of place as well as
time. Cyberspace is a 'space' in itself and yet not a 'place' –
our minds can be there but our bodies can't, beyond the
tapping of fingers on a keypad. I longed to immerse
myself in actual place, to free myself from the tyranny of
too much time online. I wanted my mind and body to
re-engage with landscape, which in turn might return
me to myself, enable me to inhabit myself more fully.
I needed to alter my way of being in the world.

LIFEBLOOD

Upwards: A Pennine Journey

10

Settlements

'Thousands of tired, nerve-shaken, over-civilized
people are beginning to find out that going to the
mountains is going home; that wildness is a necessity'

–John Muir, Our National Parks

What is it like walking in someone else's shoes? I would
not wish my worst enemy to be walking in my shoes
today, an extremely unpleasant experience since my black
boots lined with thick wool have proven to be inappropriate
footwear, having soaked up the rain during my walk
through Malham, and now soaking up the intense heat as
the sun sears down. I am profoundly unsettled as I arrive in
Settle, the next stage of my Pennine journey.

I am walking alone now and feeling acutely the
absence of my companion. Having not slept well last
night, I am exhausted and struggling to navigate with the
OS map. My belongings are straining down on my back
and I have not got the energy to readjust my portable
home to make the weight more bearable. The pain in my
foot from when I slipped over on Malham Cove has
flared up again. And how I long to take off my hot, heavy
boots, fling them over an abyss and walk barefoot.

But as soon as I see the train station something in me
settles. It was built in the nineteenth century and is filled
with relics such as large Victorian-style luggage trunks.

With all its curiosities, it seems like a museum in itself. I have a look around and see a piano, framed images of the landscape, and a large picture reading 'A JOURNEY THROUGH HISTORY ON THE SETTLE–CARLISLE LINE' depicting a red steam train chugging out smoke. There is a kind of hushed peace to the place, so different from my recent association with fraught train journeys. I see another picture of the Settle to Carlisle railway journey, declaring it to be 'one of the world's greatest railway journeys'. I look again at the route, which spans 115 kilometres through the North, and the place names along the way have a soothing symphony: Settle, Horton-in-Ribblesdale, Ribblehead, Dent, Garsdale, Kirby Stephen, Appleby, Langwathby, Lazonby & Kirkoswald, Armathwaite, Carlisle. I hum the words to myself and hope to make it to those places.

I look out over the train tracks at the sign reading SETTLE, and on the platforms either side of the tracks are two maroon benches with cream-coloured words reading 'SETTLE DOWN' and 'SETTLE UP'. I've often been told by well-meaning but annoying people to 'settle down' (dictionary definition: 'to adopt a more steady and secure life'); to buy a house, get a stable job, get married and have kids – all the stereotypical elements that comprise the act of 'settling down'. As if it were as simple as that. Due to socioeconomic factors and structural inequalities, many struggle to become settled. I struggled to find a foothold in London and often felt at risk of falling through the fault-lines of the North–South divide, of regional and class inequalities and the housing crisis.

Home creates a sense of belonging but if you don't have a stable one, life becomes beset with a sense of temporariness, impermanence, unsettlement, moving from room to rented room. Living conditions can be temporary and precarious and having two feet perennially off the ladder a stark reality – I've lived in twenty rented rooms in the UK alone. How can you feel settled when your landlord warns you not to vote – attempts to take away your constitutional rights, rights which are crucial to a sense of belonging – as your room is a sublet and they don't want you to show up on the system? How can you feel settled with the risk of being evicted and losing your home on one month's notice? How can you feel settled while worrying how to pay the rent for a place smaller than a shoebox? How can you feel settled if, unable to pay full rent during a pandemic, your landlord ignores pleas for compassion, warns you that you have no legal rights, are trespassing if you stay any longer, and makes clear that even the small room you have been renting does not really belong to you?

I would build my sense of belonging somewhere then experience the pain of having it severed.

There's not only the home we're born into but also the home we create for ourselves, and the latter has left a generation unmoored.

On a global scale, we are living in an age of unsettlement and displacement, with reports indicating that the number of people forced to flee their homes due to environmental or political catastrophe has exceeded 50 million for the first time since the Second World War.[71] Life is structurally insecure for so many. Since the pandemic, the world feels more unsettled than ever before. Is it any wonder you might develop a sense of personal insecurity if your life is beset with structural

insecurity? 'Stay at home' was the coronavirus command,
but glaring inequalities of home have become more
pronounced than ever, with many either trapped in
substandard, precarious housing or with no home at all.
Of course, such a state of unsettlement will affect the
mental health, not having a stable home and being more
at risk of losing one's place in the world, one's foothold,
and falling through the fault-lines. Of its nuanced
meanings, to feel settled is to feel 'calm' – a mighty
achievement in unsettled circumstances.

How can you feel settled in your own skin if you're at
risk of racism? Racism can also affect finding a home at
all, with racial profiling on room rents still insidious.
How can you feel settled in the present moment if
you're besieged by very real anxieties about surviving
beyond it and having a future at all? How can you feel
settled in your own life if you're threatened with losing
your home, your place in the world? If you've never
been able to create a settled life at all?

Adding to my existing sense of unsettlement, I realise
just how unsettling my experience on the train was. That
summer I decided not to try and settle down but to
'settle up' geographically by walking up, following my
unsettled feeling upwards into the hills and seeing what
I might discover. Alongside a primal need for home is a
need for freedom and adventure, a longing for somewhere
that lets the spirit soar. I use this time to explore and
challenge the notions of what it means to be and feel
settled. This summer, as the song lyric goes, wherever
I lay my hat that would be my home.

I enter one of the stone-built waiting rooms to shelter from the heat, and see a large map reading A PENNINE JOURNEY and a plaque to Wainwright who walked that journey, beginning right here at Settle station. The circular plaque in a midnight blue colour reads: 'On 25th September 1938 Alfred Wainwright left here on his Pennine Journey and returned on 5th October having walked a distance of around 210 miles.' I had never even heard of the place Settle before, but here it is, a gateway to such a historical journey made before my own. It is one of many times I feel spine-tingles that I am doing the right thing by making this journey.

A poster on the wall from the Wainwright Society tells me:

In the autumn of 1938, with Britain on the brink of war, Alfred Wainwright escaped the pervasive fear and gloom by playing truant in the Pennines. He set out on a long walk from Settle to the Roman Wall and back. The manuscript of the book he wrote about the journey lay in a drawer for almost 50 years. In it there's a portrait of the young, Jack-the-Lad Wainwright, vibrant, humorous, in search of adventure. When it was published in 1986, a reviewer described it as 'A marvellous account of a solitary journey by a man with a profound, even spiritual love of the hills.'

A map of his Pennine Journey shows that it is distinct from the Pennine Way in its circularity rather than linearity. I take my temporary home off and settle down on the bench to rest and read up on the Pennine Journey. Wainwright walked through some of the most bleakly beautiful parts of the North. He walked a route that had not yet been taken, he found and forged his own way before the creation of the Pennine Way. The route has now been put on the OS map and the Wainwright Society has made an official guidebook, but it is only relatively recently that his epic walk has been rediscovered. It was only when Wainwright needed to raise funds for his animal rescue charity that he decided to publish *A Pennine Journey*. By then he was acclaimed for his Lake District writing, and the Pennine Way had been created with Wainwright writing a guidebook to it.

After taking a train from the mill town of Blackburn, Lancashire, where he was born and brought up, to Settle at the bottom edge of the Yorkshire Dales, thirty-one-year-old Wainwright set off by foot with the aim of walking to Hadrian's Wall, around 175 kilometres to the north. He would follow the eastern edge of the Pennines and, to return to Settle, he would follow the western edge, through valleys, vast dales, and high, wild moorland. The first days pass through limestone landscape, which Wainwright described in his pictorial guide 'Walks in Limestone Country'. After passing the immense Hull Pot – the largest hole in England below the slopes of Pen-y-Ghent, one of the Three Peaks – the route arrives at Buckden-in-Wharfedale. The route passes through Bowes with its ruined castle, and from Middleton-in-Teesdale there is a walk along the River Tees, followed by crossing over into Weardale before reaching the medieval village of Blanchland. Then, by way of Hexham, Hadrian's Wall is reached, before circling back down towards Settle.

On my phone I have a look at the opening pages of *A Pennine Journey*: its foreword describes a situation in

September 1938 in which events were moving to a crisis and 'fear and apprehension prevailed throughout the country' with war seeming imminent and the press and wireless giving 'no respite, no peace of mind'. He describes that 'everybody felt sick, upset, nervous. Nobody smiled any more'. Wainwright compares Hitler with Alexander the Great – empire-builders who sought to invade every corner of the worlds they knew. There seemed to be no escape from the atmosphere of gloom and despondency, at home, at work or in the streets, but he had a fortnight's holiday due from his job as clerk to the borough treasury of Blackburn, and in the wild Pennine hills he found some peace.

The parallels with our anxious, crisis-ridden contemporary situation seem pronounced. The summer I set off on my journey, a prime minister had been elected who was known for using racial and homophobic slurs, and there seemed no escape from the fraught atmosphere either, with both actual and virtual worlds afrenzy with anger, fear, tension – and a general sense of unsettlement. Wainwright tells of how the effect of newspaper headlines was 'To stun you so that you read on in a state of torpor, which in turn gave way to extreme nervous debility.' In our contemporary times this anxiety can be exacerbated by the intensity of social media.

I longed to breathe deeply, for tranquillity and quietude, for deep silence, a yearning intensified by the fact I'd been renting a room on a busy road on a cramped council estate where the roar and screech and shriek of traffic was so loud it shattered any sense of peace and was affecting my mental health. Globally too, the summer

I set off there was anxiety in the air with the rise of the far-right and hostility towards minorities. One morning, I had opened my Twitter feed to see a sickening video of a Trump rally that had horrifying echoes of Nazi rallies, with crowds chanting 'send her back, send her back', referring to Ilhan Omar, a Muslim senator and one of what Trump termed 'the squad'. In response Omar tweeted lines from a Maya Angelou poem 'Still I Rise', which chime with my own experience.

It was – and still is – a time of political and environmental crisis. In Malham, I had read the news for the first time in twenty-four hours, having been offline while out walking, and saw the horrifying images of wildfires destroying huge swathes of the Amazon rainforest, the lungs of the world. The world seemed like a gaping wound, with people destroying each other and the planet.

The world was in a state of great woundedness when Wainwright returned from his journey, and he found some solace not only in having made the journey but also in the months writing it up thereafter, chronicling both the places he travelled through and the people he met along the way, also capturing the psyche of a nation and a world in crisis.

With the world still in a state of woundedness, and in the crisis of the coronavirus pandemic, it is deeply poignant looking back at the freedom of roaming through the hills.

Learning about how Wainwright forged his own route, I felt even more liberated from following the rigid path of the Pennine Way, and eager to continue plotting my own way along the backbone of Britain, incorporating elements of pre-established routes but also very much doing it my way along 'desire paths'.

Browsing around another of the Victorian stone-built waiting rooms, under another picture of 'one of the world's greatest train journeys', I sit down to rest for a while and get chatting to someone called Alison with strawberry-blonde hair who tells me she is travelling alone. We talk about being lone lady travellers and the liberation we feel. She spent her birthday here in Settle and it was her first trip alone. She tells me how she has walked near the River Ribble and we discuss our shared love of water.

'The sound of it cleans the mind,' she says.

She asks me about my journey so I tell her my story in a nutshell, and she congratulates me: 'You've inspired me. And I hope I've inspired you too, to keep going,' she says. 'We were meant to meet like this.' I am heartened by her encouragement and the warmth, kindness and openness of a stranger, into continuing.

Walking back out into a bright hot day, I pass a large sign saying 'Welcome to the Settle – Carlisle Railway: 72 Miles of Scenic Splendour' – and vow to savour that splendour one day soon. I walk past Settle Coal Co. Ltd, a sign for the Settle Flowerpot Festival, and on past a red-framed cafe called The Settle Down Cafe, Records & Relics, laughing aloud to see a place called Ye Olde Naked Man Cafe. I walk past the huge limestone rock of Castleberg, which towers over Settle and was once a giant sundial; an eighteenth-century sketch shows the hours marked into slabs of stone running down the hill.

I visit the Folly museum and browse an exhibition on the human settlements of the area, and the first human beings to penetrate this place at the end of the Ice Age around 12,000 BC – the nomadic Stone Age people. I learn how, after the Ice Age, forest spread over Craven and hunters set up camp on the moors. It is what they left behind that endured and provides the evidence of existence – the stone axes, pottery, and of course bones both animal and human.

The notion of human settlements is fascinating and it is instructive to remember that the first humans were nomadic: walkers and wanderers, hunter-gatherers who did not have contemporary notions of belonging – they did not own belongings nor did any land belong to anyone.[72] Only relatively recently in the scale of time, around 12,000 years ago, did humans begin settling, putting down boundaries and building walls. Humans have for so long been a migratory species. Travelling from place to place on foot, the earliest humans respected the natural world and wildlife, seeking shelter and sustenance from forests and woods and rivers. I shiver to think that the wayfaring journey I am on is such an ancient one and I realise that in this state of being unsettled there is wisdom to be found, another way of being in the world.

Our contemporary notions of settlement have taken us further from the wild – we've bricked it off, fenced away the natural world, paved over the power of wilderness in our quest to be settled. But within our bricks and mortar dwellings, we have lost so much, along the way plundering and destroying wildlife and their habitats, their homes – a destruction that will ultimately lead to our own since we are interdependent with the healthy existence of the natural world. Can we actually gain a profounder sense of settlement through being closer to nature, in a more mutually respectful relationship with wilderness? And will this ameliorate the other unsettlements of our age?

My sense of belonging in the world had been shaken to the core. I could not build my entire sense of belonging in a manmade world. But as I walk, I wonder if I can recover a deeper, more primal sense of belonging in nature. I dwell on what it means to dwell well, and whether I can find some sense of home in the wild.

I walk down a route to find the River Ribble, desperate for some shade on what has become a sweltering day. I am heartened to hear its rippling and I cross a bridge over its dark waters and to the other side which takes me right beside the riverbanks. I stroll along, loving its great rushing and swelling, and look out over an abundance of bright green dock leaves and other plants I cannot name, their shades set off against the treacle-coloured river.

Walking along, I see some rectangular-shaped stones covered in moss between two trees whose branches are also layered in luminous green mosses. It seems the perfect perch to sit for a while with the tree branches stretching their arms over me, making a protective shade. I watch the swirling water, which has an incantatory and meditative effect of bringing me entirely into the present moment. The sunlight is filtering over the water, which now gleams a dazzling copper colour, and I want to stare at the colour all day. The sunlight dapples through the branches and over the mosses, which seem to glow green. The whole natural landscape around me seems to be glowing with life. Sitting there near the river, I feel a sudden sense of belonging.

I'm letting my stress drain away into the churning river when an old man with robin-egg blue eyes passes and says hello. He tells me how the Settle–Carlisle railway journey is one of the most beautiful in the world and passes through places including the highest train station in the country.

'What you want to do is sit one side of the train and see all the scenery that side, and then sit the other side on the way back. You'll see all the hills and the river. If you go in winter, you can see snow on the hills. I've been riding it for years.'

I ask him how old he is.

'I was born in the year we had three kings,' he replies. Although I have studied history, I cannot guess which year. '1936,' he says. 'King George V, Edward VIII and King George VI.'

'So you were just two years old when Wainwright set off from Settle station on his Pennine Journey. He walked this route, by the River Ribble…'

We walk and talk along the river for a while. He tells me how he often rides the train just for the view. He wells up as he says how his son has been a train driver on the Settle–Carlisle line for many years but is ill now and no longer drives. He asks me further about my plans and I tell him.

'I used to do a lot of walking,' he says, his watery eyes glinting, 'including all over the Lake District.' I tell him how I love the Lakes and was there earlier this year.

'That's why I'm still alive, I think,' he says, 'because of the walking. I'm eighty-three now.'

I look into his face and it looks like a map, with its lines and indentations, the markings of a well-lived life, and folds of grief too.

We part ways as he heads back down the route towards his home and I continue along the River Ribble, following its course. An information board I pass tells me that the Ribble flows 115 kilometres from its source near Ribblehead at the confluence of Gayle Beck and Cam Beck to enter the Irish Sea between Preston and Lytham St Annes. It is one of the longest rivers in the country to flow westwards rather than eastwards. I learn about the Settle Riverside Project, which has planted 150 trees, with a diversity of species to encourage different forms of wildlife. In the local conservation projects I encounter during my walk through the Pennines I've seen with my own eyes how biodiversity is crucial for the survival of the planet, and learned about the astonishing diversity of species, from those sphagnum moss plants in Kinder to the purposeful planting of a variety of trees in this project. I try to spot those tree species including rowan, silver birch, ash, wild cherry as well as holly, hazel, goat willow and quickthorn.

I follow the river as it flows through dramatic limestone landscape, winding its way past 'drumlins', round mounds in the landscape made of layers of clay and rock, created aeons ago by moving ice. As I walk on through pastures and wooded slopes, I notice how the anxiety that besieged me as I arrived in Settle seems to have washed away. My attention has been so focused on watching the world around me, listening to the river, breathing the fresh air. I walk and breathe, walk and breathe, walk and breathe.

I am the river, and the river is me – the Maori saying runs through my mind. The sound and sight of the river fills my head, swelling and rushing and flowing, and there is nothing else my attention is focused on but its waters. I forget about myself entirely, instead watching the sunlight reflecting upon it, rendering it a tease of colours, now an opaque coppery colour, now toffee-coloured, now translucent.

I am the river, and the river is me. I feel myself falling away, the shell between the self and world dissolving as I walk. I am unsettled from my burdensome mind and settle into the sound and sight and smell of the river and its wildlife. I see a grey heron standing and watching the river, perhaps waiting for prey. I see a swallow soar into the blue sky, and a grey wagtail with bright yellow in its tail. I see a sand martin, and a goosander.

I walk on through moorland, loving being alone now and not a bit lonely. Walking alone like this allows me to totally lose myself in the landscape, to watch and listen to it, breathe it in. On my journey I have not wanted to 'find myself' but lose myself, have the self dissolve into and perhaps be transformed by the landscape. Without the lens of my companion's camera or any other human eyes on me, I can be utterly unselfconscious. This is what it feels like, to think yourself into the natural world, to empathise with it. I want to empathise with the river, get beneath its skin and surface, to imagine what it would be like to be the river.

I decide to take off my boots, so uncomfortable in the heat, and walk barefoot with the bliss of the grass on my soles. I feel so much lighter with that weight off my feet, more alive with the touch of the earth on my skin. I remember how in Dreamtime, ancestors walked the world into being. There has been so much longing in my search for belonging, so much yearning, but by following 'desire paths' I have reached a place beyond desire, where for these moments, I want for nothing more than where I am, here, now. I have moved from longing to belonging. I have also, somewhat miraculously, reached a place beyond pain – for now at least. Here in the wild, I feel settled.

Then the river tumbles in peaty, tea-coloured cascades into the Stainforth Force, its sound swelling and crashing over limestone outcrops. I stop to look into its swirling waters for wild salmon, which I've heard are beloved of the river here though more frequently seen when they return with the rain each autumn on the 'salmon run'. Salmon are some of the most determined and persevering creatures in existence as they forge their way upstream while migrating back to their spawning grounds. They also have a strong urge to return to their first homes, to their birthplace, in what is known as 'natal homing'. I look into the foaming and bubbling water and see a silver flash and my heart leaps high, but then it's gone again and I can't be sure if it was a mere trick of the bright light. I think of the salmon out there, perhaps beginning their long watery pilgrimage home from the sea as I continue walking, further north. How do they know their way home? Navigational tools, scientists have posited, may include geomagnetic imprinting and olfactory clues.

I walk over a bridge and onwards, through miles of moorland, and see mountains rising in the distance that must be the Three Peaks. I'm nearing Horton-in-Ribblesdale, the next stop on my Pennine journey. I have walked miles along the River Ribble with my portable home on my back without even feeling its weight, or at least not as much as previously when it would cause such pain that I was barely aware of my surroundings and felt unable to put one more foot in front of the other. I realise that, throughout my walk, I have developed stamina. I have become stronger.

I see the summit of a mountain rising up ahead, a distinctive shape dominating the landscape. It is Pen-y-Ghent, a key landmark of both the Pennine Way and Pennine Journey.

I keep walking along the course of the river as it flows throughout the limestone landscape that flashes diamond bright in the sunshine. How strong and forceful the river is as it swells and flows, and yet how soft it is too. I think of how much of the earth's surface is made up of water, almost two-thirds, and how much of our body is made of water – up to 60 per cent of the human adult body being water, the brain and heart composed of 73 per cent, the lungs around 83 per cent and even the bones being 31 per cent water. In some organisms, their body weight is up to 90 per cent water.[73] Water has its home in the most astonishing places in our body, even within the seemingly solid; there is fluid to be found even within our backbone, cerebrospinal fluid, protecting the spinal cord and brain and supplying nutrients.

I walk on and look out into the river, drinking in the scene as I know we will soon be parting, and the river really does feel like a vein of the earth, like lifeblood.

I arrive into Horton as sunlight is gleaming over the summit of Pen-y-Ghent, which looms out proud and magnificent and looking very much alive, like a pale green humpback whale. By now, I am exhausted and cannot even imagine climbing a flight of stairs let alone a mountain – or rather 'fell'. (It is somewhat controversial whether Pen-y-Ghent classifies as a mountain, although digital maps describe it as such and I shall too.) I walk up a steep road following my OS map and then pass by The Crown pub and see the sign marking 'Pen-y-Ghent Cafe on the Pennine Way'. It is a sense of achievement to reach this. Before I set off on this journey, when it seemed to be merely a pipe dream, I had lain in bed with the inertia that anxiety and depression can bring, feeling as if I could barely move my fingertips, let alone walk hundreds of kilometres up footpaths and fells. I had looked up images of the Pennine Way and seen pictures of this sign's white and gold letters on a black background, so it is amazing to actually see it in real life, its letters glinting in the sun. I rest for a while, peeling off my portable home, and realise how parched I am. I make my way to the cafe, longing for a cold lemonade, but it is closed so I continue walking, looking for Horton Women's Holiday Centre, where I have been hoping for a bed. I know that if I don't get a proper night's sleep I won't be able to continue my journey.

I keep walking in the direction of Pen-y-Ghent itself, which looms ever closer, but I can see no sign of the women's centre even though my map shows a blue heartbeat telling me I am all but there. I see a small shop and buy a cold lemonade. I look at cards – one with a picture of a sheep reads: 'Ey-up Somebody Bleated It's Yer Baarthday!'; I gaze at one of bluebell woods at Cleatops near Settle, with deep purple fields – I want to step inside that picture and walk through those bluebell woods. I finally find my destination, marvelling at how close it is to the Pennine Way, right on its very doorstep. The deep emerald-coloured door is slightly ajar and I push it open and step inside, delighted to discover that they do have a spare bed and I can stay the night.

'Help yourself to tea and food,' says a lady who works there. We chat for a while and she asks me about my journey. She tells me about the history of the holiday centre, how it began as a place of refuge, the only place of its kind, established in 1980 as a co-operative by women involved in feminism and the women's liberation movement, and has made a difference to thousands of women from all walks of life who otherwise would not be able to afford a holiday, including many single-parent families. As the daughter of a single parent, I think of the few holidays I had as a child, and how my trip to the Lake District as a small child was made possible only by subsidised accommodation such as this. Our lives – like those of the women and children whom I meet over the coming couple of days – were in a state of unsettlement, the structure of the family shifting, reconfiguring. Here too, in Horton, in a place altruistically designed to

provide respite and rest for women, I have found
something of a backbone of Britain. My journey has
been along the actual backbone of the country, those
rugged limestone hills; it has also been one of discovering
the support systems and networks crucial to communities.
For individuals need the backbone of community, and
that needs to be acknowledged without shame.

I make a cup of tea and meet a family baking scones
in the kitchen: a mother and three children. The delicious
smell envelops the room. We chat for a while and I tell
them that I'm aiming to climb a mountain here, perhaps
Pen-y-Ghent, and twelve-year-old Rori says she'd love
to come with me. As I settle into the sofa back in
the reception room, about to write up my notes from
the day's journey, the young boy from the family bounds
up to me.

'Do you want to play UNO?' he asks, thrusting a set
of cards into my hands as his elder sister also joins us and,
before I know it, I'm playing UNO for the first time.

The smell of scones and jam wafts from the kitchen,
making my tummy rumble, and I realise how hungry
I am. A volunteer shows me to a large room I'll be sharing
with the family and says, 'You can have the double-bed
there.' I'm hugely relieved as I lie on the lower set of
bunkbeds and stretch out my legs. The volunteer laughs to
see my delight.

I am shown the living room, where a group of friends
are watching *Educating Rita*, a film I haven't seen for
years. An array of feminist books lines the shelves, and
I spy stacks of *Spare Rib* magazines and books ranging
from Mary Wollstonecraft's *Vindication of the Rights of
Women* to Angela Carter's backlist.

I reflect on how women take up space in the world – the places they can and can't occupy, here on account of both gender and class since accommodation is offered on a sliding scale. The history of this centre is one of creating a space for women who otherwise would not be able to occupy such a place. It is about saying: you belong here.

How do women occupy space and move through space, and what are the barriers to them doing so? How do women occupy place in writing about place? I think of how many books about moving through the world – or, to give it a genre label, 'travel writing' and 'nature writing' – are written by men. Of how in the history of the genre, the experiences of women – and in particular women of colour – as well as perspectives from working-class voices and other marginalised groups have been excluded until relatively recently. It is as if the industry has been saying: you don't belong here, in the pages of books about journeying through the world. A whole tranche of experience is going unseen and misunderstood. As a child devouring books, I would love to read stories of epic journeys and adventures, but it was overwhelmingly the white boys who got to have such adventures: *Robinson Crusoe*, *Gulliver's Travels*, and *Boy's Own Adventure Stories*. *Alice's Adventures in Wonderland* was the most famous example of a female having adventures and misadventures.

My gaze flicks back to *Educating Rita* on the screen, and I reflect on early education and how that shapes us and how much of it we need to unlearn. I read *The Water-Babies* in childhood and did so without being warned about what we might find beyond the wonder of the water-baby, for it is a book teeming with racial prejudices – and that is just one example. As I read more of *A Pennine Journey* I was alarmed by its misogyny. Of course, these writers were 'of their time' but prejudices can be internalised from reading books uncritically, and I wonder how much has been by people over the years. Discussion about this has been alarmingly absent, but in the wake of recent protests for racial equality there has been some re-evaluating: for example, *Gone with the Wind* was removed from HBO Max due to its 'racist depictions' and reintroduced with a disclaimer discussing its historical context.[74]

Some contemporary travel narratives by women I admire include *Tracks* by Robyn Davidson, about her epic walk through the desert with her camels; *The Living Mountain* by Nan Shepherd, which conveys a differing way of being in the world, a way of moving through the mountain rather than conquering it; *Wanderlust* by Rebecca Solnit, which shows how walking can be a form of activism in itself. There are narratives from indigenous perspectives I admire including Robin Wall Kimmerer's explorations in *Braiding Sweetgrass* and *Gathering Moss*, which provide a vital perspective on humans' relationship with nature. In a photographic series, the artist and photographer Ingrid Pollard, born in Georgetown, Guyana and living in the UK from an early age, challenged the notion that black British people only belong in urban settings. I also love the nature imagery in the writing of Guyanese poet Grace Nichols, although when I interviewed her she mentioned how such topics along with her stylistic merits can be overlooked as she and so many writers of colour are pigeonholed as writing solely about race.

While there are more voices from so-called marginalised backgrounds chronicling the experience of being in the natural world than there were a decade ago, they are still few and far between. It is still a greater struggle for these voices to be regarded as equal and as important as voices from the so-called 'centre', for them not to be pigeonholed, and for these stories to truly and fully belong here, on the bookshelves.

That night, I burrow my way into my bed early, after I have shared more delicious jam scones. I end up chatting with the family about divorce – the parents are going through a divorce – and I share my own experience growing up in a single-parent household and trying to forge a new sense of belonging within the shifting form of family. We talk about issues of race and place. The children are mixed-race and discuss their differing experiences on account of having varying shades of light and dark skin – from the younger daughter who looks white to the elder daughter who has the darkest skin and describes being bullied, called 'terrorist' and 'paki' at school. The family have also been branded 'sand people' while walking through the streets of their Lake District hometown. I ask if they are taught anything about the 'protected characteristics' at school and they aren't.

We talk long into the night, about their hopes and dreams, as well as the heartbreak of not belonging or being made to feel as if you don't belong in a place that is your home, and about the search for a sense of home itself, which can feel so elusive.

The next day I decide to ride the Settle–Carlisle railway and at least glimpse from the train those symphonic place names. I did not sleep much last night, and it is an effort to even pack my bag. A lady who slept in one of the bunkbeds in the shared room sees me struggling with my bag and tells me it reminds her of 'The Monster', the name Cheryl Strayed gave to her backpack in *Wild*. I finally manage to pack all my belongings and then I am on my way to the train station for that 'world's greatest train journey'.

It is bliss being on the train and watching the places rush by me in a blur, the idyllic landscape of hills and small villages beneath a day of blue skies, and the Ribble Viaduct, which featured in the Harry Potter films. I remember the man I met while sitting by the river, born in the year of the three kings and how his eyes welled up talking about his son who is now too ill to drive this route. I drift off to sleep for some of the journey but awake just in time to see the highest train station in England, Ais Gill, and the sign proudly announcing the fact that Ais Gill Summit sits 1,169 feet above sea level.

Back in Settle I decide to take the Sunday bus to Slaidburn but stepping out into the village I feel claustrophobic – perhaps on account of the heavy heat and my night of insomnia – and want to come straight back to Settle. I see a St George's flag hanging in the tiny village as I walk to find the YHA I have booked for £8. It is closed and the people in the post office opposite tell me it will not be opening until 5 p.m. On its stone side a deep green plaque reads:

This youth hostel is one of many both in this country and abroad where young people, regardless of race or creed, may

spend the night. The buildings are diverse in character but they
have a common purpose: to help all, especially young people of
limited means, to a greater knowledge, love and care of the
countryside' – YHA National Office, Trevelyan House.

I walk near the river for a while. It is a scorching-hot day,
though, and I have started to feel sick, exhaustion from
the sleepless night before hitting me hard, so I take
shelter for lunch in a cafe opposite where the bus is
scheduled in a couple of hours – I'm now yearning to
return to Settle. When the bus arrives I am so relieved at
the sight of it that I leap on and tell the driver how
pleased I am to see him, then I watch the hills and
meadows roll by all the way to Settle.

Walking through Settle, en route to Horton-in-
Ribblesdale, near the train station, I hear a voice calling
me and see an elderly man and lady sitting on a bench:
'Come and sit down for a while, you look exhausted!'

I must look like the shell of a human. It is a relief to sit
for a while. I tell them how I have been walking for days
and the man, named Bob, explains that he and Kathleen
have been good friends for thirty-five years.

'Kathleen's husband and family were farmers. Her
husband died of a brain tumour. Kathleen had a family
of three daughters. Unfortunately, we lost the youngest
daughter and we don't know why.'

'I'm so sorry. How old was she?'

'Twenty-five. She was out one night and we got a
phone call to say she'd collapsed. We went to the hospital
in Blackburn and she just looked like she was asleep. We
never found out why Jill died. We think she may have
had a massive epileptic fit. She had rosy cheeks. If anyone

looked like a farmer's wife, Jill did. It was twenty-two years ago when she collapsed in the pub. It was a big shock. Kath still can't talk about it and I struggle to…'

I express my sympathy and try and find words of comfort, saying how a lot of angels die young, how people never really leave us, and when an intense ray of light suddenly appears that she's there in the sunlight. Kathleen smiles and her face brightens.

'Do you have any family, my dear?' asks Bob.

I brush the question aside, not wanting to go into my unsettled life. I tell them about Sophie and how at the funeral we were encouraged to make the most of our lives in her memory, which inspired me to do this walk.

'Well, I pat you on the back. Because I had a stroke, I can't run and can only walk slowly. But I'm getting on a bit…'

He returns to the loss of Kathleen's daughter. 'After Jill died, one friend said it would be nice if she was buried in her wedding gown, so the undertakers made it so it was like she was asleep in her wedding gown.' Kathleen adds: 'She wasn't so well that week. She went to the pharmacy to get some headache pills.'

'She dropped like a stone in the pub,' says Bob. 'Her partner had gone to get some drinks. There was a doctor off-duty but he couldn't bring her round. So we lost Jill…'

He continues: 'We hope one day that you may find the right person… Somewhere along the line someone will guide you and look after you.'

'Another human being you mean?' I say.

'Maybe. I was brought up a Roman Catholic. I don't know if you have a religion or you don't; it doesn't matter to me. But if people believe that what they are doing is right then they should do it and you'll be guided.'

'I do follow my heart, and my heart was telling me to do this walk,' I say.

'I would say this to you: avoid walking on your own. There's too much going on out there that can be dangerous. I know you're an innocent girl and I don't want to see someone's attacked you and it come on TV, you know? I don't know your name and am not going to ask how old you are...'

'I'm Anita from Manchester,' I say, it striking me how we have talked about life and death without them even knowing my name.

'We haven't met anyone from Manchester before. I have noticed that you do seem to get the extra kilo of water there compared with the rest of the country,' he laughs.

I ask if in their lifetimes they have seen many changes in Britain, and Bob replies: 'I'm afraid so. There's far too much crime, knives, drugs. That's why I said when you go walking do your absolute best to go with someone. When I'm around and Kathleen is around you're safe. Life will come out just like that, like the pages of a book. Whatever's to be is to be... But be careful, try very hard for your future walking to travel with a friend. Kathleen, what do you think?'

'I think the same.'

'We've had a very welcome conversation,' says Bob. 'Do what we say – get something to eat, and rest and you'll benefit tomorrow.'

I say goodbye and look at their weathered faces textured with lines and markings that remind me of a limestone landscape. I smile and walk on, and think of those strangers, telling me to take care of myself, to eat and sleep properly, and am warmed not for the first time on my journey by the kindness of strangers.

I walk on and look out for the limestone moors and limestone reef knolls which formed in warm, shallow waters of ancient seas. I see the image of a young woman 'dropping like a stone' to her death, a young woman in her wedding gown seeming as if she is asleep but in reality being dead. I see again Sophie's face smiling at me the last time we saw each other and feel again the warm embrace before we parted.

That night I dream of Sophie's inky blue handwriting in the card she sent me. I dream of rivers running in blue ink, of sentences like veins through which time passes, inky veins filled with language, a lifeblood.

11

Scars

Definition of scar:

1. A mark left on the skin or within body tissue where a wound, burn, or sore has not healed completely and fibrous connective tissue has developed.

   'a faint scar ran the length of his left cheek'

   1.1 A lasting effect of grief, fear, or other emotion left on a person's character by an unpleasant experience.

      'the attack has left mental scars on Terry and his family'

   1.2 A mark left on something following damage of some kind.

      'Max could see scars of the blast'

   1.3 A mark left at the point of separation of a leaf, frond, or other part from a plant.

      'this fossil bark is typified by its lozenge-shaped leaf scars'

2. A steep high cliff or rock outcrop, especially of limestone.

   'high limestone scars bordered the road'

I can barely see the world at all when I awake the next day, so dense is the mist outside. I spent the night in a room of my own called PeaGreen at the women's centre in Horton-in-Ribblesdale, and so settled did I feel there and so well did I sleep – deeper than I have slept in a long time, a sleep that felt healing – that I was up not quite at the crack of dawn but soon after.

It is so misty this morning that it feels it will never be daylight.

I venture downstairs for a cup of tea to wake me from grogginess and twelve-year-old Rori is there in the kitchen, dressed and ready to go, smiling with relief at seeing me.

'I thought you'd gone without me!' she exclaims and I laugh that no, my bed was so comfy that I could not drag myself out of it.

'She really wants to climb up the mountain with you, she's so excited,' says her mum.

I gulp down the sweet tea, then dress and pack water and food supplies of chocolate bars.

Rori and I set off, stepping out into the cool, misty morning. We follow the arrows to the Pennine Way until the blue heartbeat of my map shows us, after just a couple of minutes, to be walking along the Way – we slept literally at its mouth. At the end of the short path we see a sign showing two diverging routes up the mountain, blue arrows pointing left via Horton Scar Lane, and red arrows pointing right, via Bracken Bottom. An arrow points to a circle in between the routes and words above it read YOU ARE HERE. I feel a rush of excitement to read those words, to actually be right here on the Pennine Way and about to climb a mountain. For a moment we are undecided which direction to take. A lady passes by while walking her dog and we ask her advice. She tells us she would definitely recommend the blue route, up Horton Scar.

We follow that route up the Scar, walking along a path shrouded in a mist, upon rocky pebbles, so rocky that soon the soles of my feet begin to ache. We pass an old grey crumbling shed straight out of a ghost story, and Rori pauses for a picture. A light rain begins falling,

and I worry at the prospect of our walk being a total
wash-out and having to turn back. But all worry vanishes
when I see spiderwebs in golden plants and strung out
wherever I look. I stop and peer at them and glimpse
gatherings of dew like silver tears in the astonishing
webs through which I also see a sky thick with grey
cloud. In the heart of one web I count ten teardrops of
dew clustered together like diamonds. It looks as if the
world has been weeping into these webs. So many webs
do I see, though not a single spider, for they must be
sheltering somewhere from the rain. *Be strong like spider
silk*, I think. *Don't steel yourself, spider-silk yourself.*

I check my OS map and the red arrow shows the
words 'A Pennine Journey' and my heartbeat quickens –
we are actually walking the same route Wainwright took
all those years ago. I had not intentionally planned to
follow his route, but it is nevertheless thrilling to see that
deep red arrow showing that we are right on the route
of the Pennine Journey, having followed the path all the
way past Brants Gill Head caving system. Over to our
left the map shows there to be Shake Holes and further
up Areas of Shake Holes, Harber Scar and Whitber
Pasture. To the right, parallel to where we are, is Limekiln
Pasture and beneath us to the right, though beyond view,
is Douk Ghyll Scar, a cave and waterfall. Where we are
walking now, the map shows, is Horton Scar and beyond,
another Area of Shake Holes.

Scar. What do I know about scars? I can see the word
three times on the map I'm looking at, and when I zoom
out, even more scars come into view. We are walking
through an area filled with scars. I had never known
before that the word scar means 'a steep high cliff or

rock outcrop, especially of limestone', as well as meaning, of course, 'a mark left on the skin where a wound has not healed', and 'a lasting effect of grief, fear, or other emotion left on a person's character by an unpleasant experience'. This natural landscape of the North, the Pennines, is filled with scars and I am walking upon them. I am walking through them, and into them. Along the way, I am also thinking about all those other meanings of the word. All through my journey the scar on my right hand, between my thumb and first finger has been itching. I'm embarrassed of the ugly-looking scar on my hand, which has been there for months ever since I burned myself but failed to treat it adequately at the time so that the skin did not heal properly. It still itches, itches, itches, though walking through such awesome landscape as this, it is easy to forget it, just as I have all but forgotten the throbbing pain in my foot from the Malham Cove fall. Those other scars, too, that 'lasting effect of grief, fear and other emotion left on a person's character by an unpleasant experience' – those scars I am thinking about, too.

What are marked on the OS map as 'shake holes' are also known as sinkholes, defined by the dictionary as 'a natural depression formed by the undermining or sudden collapse of the land surface, often as a result of groundwater enlarging cavities in underlying limestone or other easily soluble bedrock.' The second definition of 'sinkhole' is 'a place into which foul matter runs'. Such formations are also known as 'swallow holes' – 'a depression in the ground surface, esp. in limestone, where a surface stream disappears underground.' As well as shake holes, my OS map shows this to be an area full of pot holes, defined as 'deep natural underground caves formed by the erosion of rock, especially by water'. We walk along Horton Scar, past Skell Gill Pasture, up towards a sign for more Pot Holes.

The path upon which I walk is here and there suddenly filled with great wedge-like stepping-stone rocks. After clambering over some, we have a decision to make. I tell Rori about Hull Pot, the largest natural hole in England, and ask if she would like to try and find it first or go straight to Pen-y-Ghent. I still have signal on my phone and show her some images of Hull Pot, which she says looks amazing – the pictures show Hull Pot Beck plunging down a huge hole in the earth, the green grass giving way to an incredibly steep, circular, cliff-like drop. She says we should definitely try and find it. After walking a little while longer, we reach a signpost pointing the way to Pen-y-Ghent. Hull Pot itself is marked by no signpost at all and so we will be venturing into uncharted territory – no human marker here acknowledges its existence. This is the last chance to make the decision to brave our way out into unknown, unmarked landscape and try to find that largest hole in the country or to plough on up the mountain. We both want to try and find Hull Pot.

It is deeply haunting following the path away from the sign pointing to Pen-y-Ghent, a path rising into mist, and vanishing far ahead. Some men appear from the mist and are playing spooky music I can't identify, and fear floods me momentarily. Despite the fear, I ask the group of men about the way to Hull Pot and they gruffly say they have never heard of it before they walk on.

On we walk up the path shrouded in mist, which now seems completely deserted, not another soul in sight but us two. I check my OS map and find the app has frozen completely. My blood freezes too at the thought of being lost in these misty mountains, of sudden sinkholes swallowing us up. I feel a great responsibility towards Rori and ensuring her safety. The mist seems to close in around us, and I can sense those huge holes and gaping caves beneath our feet. I'm frightened to take even another footstep forward for fear of falling down a hole. I check the blue heartbeat of Google Maps, which has been fickle in working, and it shows that we have been straying away from Hull Pot, into a place where there are no paths at all. We are lost, lost, lost. The mist thickens and my heartbeat quickens. Then Rori suggests the one direction we have not yet taken. We try it out and soon that blue heartbeat shows we are walking towards Hull Pot and we both cheer.

I turn around and look back at the path, the oldest long-distance footpath in the country, and watch it wind its way through the mountain. The path curls behind us, weaving its way like a strand of silver hair in the mountains and then vanishing into the mist. It looks magical and we both have our photograph taken standing upon it, to forever have a memento of these moments. The path seems like a living thing. We want to stay and linger a little longer here, taking in the view of the path snaking its silver way through the mist, but we press on to Hull Pot.

I read out the history and geographical characteristics of Hull Pot and we are keener than ever to find it. Hull Pot measures 91 metres long by 18 metres wide and

18 metres deep. Hull Pot Beck rises on the western side of Plover Hill and flows into Hull Pot, after which the water flows under Horton Moor before reappearing just east of Horton-in-Ribblesdale at Brants Ghyll Beck, where it flows into the River Ribble. Hull Pot was formed by a collapsed cavern, and a guidebook published in the late eighteenth century called it 'Hulpit' and stated that it 'Would have appeared like the inside of an enormous old Gothic castle, the high ruinous walls of which were left standing after the roof was fallen in.'[75]

As we make our way towards that collapsed cavern, towards that sudden plunge in the earth, Rori says with a voice of steady certainty that she has a gut feeling we will find it. We walk over grass of such vivid green and no well-worn paths at all. This feels and looks so off the beaten track that I wonder if we will find it or be able to see it at all or whether it will be hidden from view by some other formation. I am more pessimistic than Rori, who is radiating a child-like optimism. It is now peaceful walking across grass beneath the feet instead of harsh pebbles, stones and rocks. We pass even more spiderwebs, this time strung over a deep toffee-coloured plant the name of which I, urbanite, have no idea.

I wonder what it is like inside a mountain. What are the innards of the earth like? I am hungry to look inside the great hole. 'A mountain has an inside,' said the writer Nan Shepherd, and today I might see such insides.

The mist has risen a little now it is mid-morning, and the sky has all of a sudden become more lucid.

Rori gasps and says: 'Listen.'

We both fall silent and listen to the landscape. It is so, so silent but then I discern the sound of plunging water.

We follow the sound until my heart lurches and my breath is sucked in as I lay eyes on an enormous hole in the earth and a sudden steep plunge down. I warn Rori to be careful, to keep away from the edge. The green earth gives away so suddenly to a vast vertical drop of limestone. There are no barriers around the edge, no signposts at all marking it. If it had not been for Rori's sharp ears hearing the water first, I dread to think how easy it could have been to walk over that edge without seeing the sudden drop into the gaping chasm.

From where we are standing, Hull Pot looks and sounds like a giant mouth made out of limestone, wide open, gasping and gurgling. We still can't see the water though we can hear it. We walk closer to the chasm, taking small steps nearer to the edge, and there it is: a waterfall far below, gushing out of a cave and flowing underground, to reappear elsewhere. It is the most astonishing sight I've seen.

Here we are, gazing down the largest natural hole in England. The proportions of the world shift, and the sense of self changes, so small in the face of such enormity.

We walk carefully towards a ledge and perch down and peer over at the plunging water, feeling the thrill of being here and seeing something extraordinary, the innards of the earth. We are looking at the insides of a mountain. I'm shocked that we can get so close and there are no perimeters holding us back. So close to the edge.

Rori suggests we walk up and around the chasm, and I worry that it is dangerous, but then see what looks like a safe ascent up along grass. We take care to watch the ground below us, for there may be sudden slippery patches. There may be unmarked pot holes or shake holes or sinkholes. But the ground beneath our feet feels firm.

As we climb above Hull Pot and look down upon it, we gasp again, for each footstep brings us to an even more magnificent view. To the right stretch fields and meadows, and hills of purple heather fill the horizon. The light breaks through ever more and we see blue sky for the first time all day. We approach giant flat slabs of rock that form a natural platform of varying shades of brown, dark black and bits of white limestone – a formation looking like a solid Viennetta ice cream that we walk upon to the edge.

We circle the hole, wondering if we will see the waterfall again after being teased with a small glimpse of it, and then it comes into view even more clearly from above. It was a great idea of Rori's to walk up here for this wonderful view of the whole hole.

I have a sudden realisation of how high up I am, of how far and deep the world is beneath, how far away is my life in that cramped rented room on a blaring road in London. From up here, I can look down on my life, see it from a clearer perspective instead of feeling engulfed by it.

Purple flowers spread out over the edge and we sit among them and discuss how it was so worth it to come off the beaten track, how amazing it is that such a wonder as this has no signposts marking the way towards it, that it truly is a hidden gem, and I remember the Spanish phrase *caminar es atesorar*, 'to walk is to gather treasure'.

We walk further around the hole, our eyes widening as we take in the whole of it, and notice two sheep venturing frighteningly close to the edge. One of the sheep moves far down the side and we worry for its safety and then it is lost from view.

'What if it's fallen over?' says Rori over and over again.

I try to reassure her, saying we would have heard it making a noise if it had fallen, so not to worry. The other sheep starts making anxious sounds that rise into a blood-curdling bleating as it starts moving towards us. There is nowhere for us to go. I tell Rori not to worry – though I myself am incredibly worried as the sheep closes in on us. An agonising few seconds later, we hear a different bleating and look towards the other side of Hull Pot where the sheep had disappeared, and see it scrambling back up the side and onto the grassy flatland. The sheep that had been heading towards us turns and starts making contented sounds as its fellow sheep appears and soon they are walking off together. We are both relieved after our horror at the thought that it had plunged to its death. Sheer terror too when the other sheep had been making its way towards us with that wounded sound.

'Look!' exclaims Rori and I look and can't see anything, but looking more closely at the landscape I make out some kind of black bird in the grass which then soars up into the sky and soon vanishes.

We spend some more time soaking up the sight of the hole, our pupils wide as we watch. How can I lay eyes on a sight as astonishing as this and not in my very sinews feel a seismic shift, knowing that such natural wonders exist in the world and that I have walked upon paths snaking silver through mountains to find them? I feel a shift in me, a sense of awe, a deepening. The landscape of my mind and heart is deepening with everything seen.

I close my eyes and there are new places in there, new spaces opening up within, new depths, a greater awareness of the earth.

Rori runs about on the grass for a while, as do I, enjoying the wide-open space around the hole and the gorgeous purple heather. It is incredible to see the collapsed cavern from different perspectives, and as we walk back to a point where we are no longer able to see the whole of the chasm, it looks like a great big knife gash in the earth. It looks radically different depending on where we are standing. Seeing it from such a range of viewpoints is a great lesson in perspective, that things depend on your position.

Rori tries to call her mother but the signal is patchy, so we keep walking back around Hull Pot until she picks up a signal and FaceTimes her mother.

'Look, Mama!' she exclaims, holding the phone out. I reassure her mother that I have been looking after her and keeping her away from the edge, and she laughs and asks if Rori has been keeping me away from the edge. I'm warmed by the simple and genuine trust of a stranger.

It is now late morning, and the sun has risen, brightening the world into purple and green and even the grey gleams. As Rori runs around the meadows, I sit down for a while and gaze at the landscape and breathe. I knew that journeying through the North had something to offer up to me. I felt it calling me. *Go back to where you're from.* This is where I'm from. I'm from the North. The glorious North.

We are all made of the same substance.
We are all bone.
We are all water.

We are all flesh,
life-blood,
matter and energy,
heart.
Earth to earth ashes to ashes dust to dust,
Go back to where you're from.

We're all from the same place, and will all end up reaching the same destination: death.

We all belong to the natural processes of life and death, and there are ways we do live on due to the first law of thermodynamics, which states that energy is never destroyed but converted, the atoms and energy of which we are made repurposed and changing state.[76]

As I look out over the largest natural hole in England, I feel the other holes in the world. I think of the gaping hole that was torn in the world with the sudden death of my friend earlier in the summer, a great tear ripped inside my heart too. I feel an aching sense of loss then, a deep grief, and an intimation of all the other losses over the course of a lifetime. I remember my childhood friend Orly who was truly the life and soul of a room, who died a few years ago from ovarian cancer, and how I learned about her death by logging into Facebook; I recall the sheer shock of it, as I learned about Sophie's death through the internet too, and how in those moments the world was ruptured. I remember seeing my grandmother's dead body in hospital and touching her feet in a mark of respect, after her lungs collapsed. I remember the last time I touched her when she was alive: a kiss on the forehead to which she made a sound of recognition. She was the only grandparent who lived during my lifetime, and the corner shop where she worked and above which she lived offered something of a refuge from my own warring parents and fracturing home, from bruises and bad words. The day of her funeral was the day of a GCSE exam and I was not permitted to sit the exam another day; I did not attend the funeral of my grandmother. I hid my grief away.

There was so much other loss that I had not grieved for; I never really grieved losses in all the stages that grief takes us through before reaching some kind of healing. We are not as a society encouraged to talk about death and loss and grief but to keep a stiff upper lip, to bury pain within the dark caverns within us and not speak of it. We don't talk about the sheer shock of someone we love going from being a living breathing being to a pile of ashes. Loss is, of course, difficult to talk about; it all but defies language, but find the words we must.

I think of animals known to grieve, such as elephants with their incredible memories. This mountain feels like it has a memory too, what happened in the past shaping it, literally.

We grieve not only literal death but all kinds of loss; we grieve the loss of people who still live but nevertheless leave our lives in some way. We grieve the loss of friendships, partners, relationships of all kinds, work, homes and homelands, a sense of safety and belonging, ways of life, time, nature and wildlife. We grieve lost connections to both people and places. Some say we can't miss what we have never had, but that's not true – we have basic needs, and if they're not met, we'll miss them, we'll grieve them; we'll feel the absence of a safe home, or a connection to the natural world, or love. We also grieve for what could have been but never was, the lost potentials and possible selves and lives, the ghostly other paths not taken, snaking away into hypothesis.

I look upon the innards of the earth. I look upon the innermost landscape of the heart and mind. I see how I have carried unprocessed grief within throughout my life, darkly coiled and clutching me, at times manifesting in anger, at times depression. Grief has burrowed its way into my body and the recesses of my mind. 'The lasting effect of grief' is one of the definitions of the word 'scar'. I let myself grieve then, to really feel the grief, how deep it is, bone-deep, mind-deep, heart-deep. I grieve for everything that was loved and lost. I grieve for everyone who died too soon due to someone else's hate.

I think of Rori's parents divorcing, and the sense of a hole being torn in the world when I was a young child, the palpable loss of my father, his presence slipping away as visits to his home became more sporadic. I realise how deeply I was affected by the break-up of a relationship some time ago, a grief my mind was not consciously aware of but that had seeped into my body and the depths of my being.

Those times I have looked back on all the losses too much and desperately tried to rewrite life in my mind so they never happened, I have felt sick with grief, I have felt myself falling falling falling as if off an edge such as this so that I have become stranded in a black hole of loss. For grief is vertiginous, it can feel like having the ground pulled from beneath us, a sudden caving in of all solidity and certainties.

Yet this great hole in the landscape I am gazing into is so magnificent.

A hole is not only an absence but also an opening, a possibility. I wonder if those metaphorical holes, those emotional holes, can also be alchemised as such, become part of the shape of our lives if we accept that allowing ourselves to fully grieve will deepen us in some way, that grieving shows us who and what we love. Is there anything that can be salvaged from the place of loss? Perhaps some wisdom about what it is we love, why what we loved was lost, and the fact that love is so much greater than loss and can power us on, move us forward.

I feel a caving in within myself as I gaze into the huge hole and hear the rushing of its hidden stream, hot tears welling. The music of the waterfall reminds me of the songlines.

I grieve, too, for the losses occurring in the natural world, for the trees that have existed for hundreds of years but are being burned to their deaths in the wildfires sweeping the Amazon rainforest as I sit here, for the dying of those lungs of the world. I grieve for the species that are being wiped off the planet due to humans' carelessness for the earth and the creatures who inhabit it, each of these deaths, even of the tiniest and seemingly most insignificant of creatures, leaving a void in the world.[77] That love of the natural world must power us on to care for it better, to help ensure no more of it is lost, to understand that its existence is inextricably bound up with our own.

Rori comes bounding back from the purple heather fields, marvelling about a bird she has seen. We would like to linger all day by Hull Pot but decide we must press on to Pen-y-Ghent, having told her mother we would be back by lunchtime, which is now only an hour away.

We walk away from Hull Pot and back along those untrodden stretches of grass with barely any sign that humans have made a way here. We near a signpost pointing to Pen-y-Ghent, three kilometres away. A group of people are gathered beneath it and Rori tells them about Hull Pot and how it is the largest natural hole in England, and that they should definitely make a detour there.

We find the path up the mountain and I start to feel the strain from the steep ascent. The view along the way alleviates the arduousness of the journey up and looking down at how far we have come is satisfying, watching the Way slither away into the grass.

The sky is gradually clearing, creating a drama of white cloud, grey and blue, purple heather, golden patches amid green, all in one sight. I let Rori walk on into the distance to take a picture of her with the path and the view and I feel again how alive that path seems to be.

As we climb higher, the clouds get more dramatic and the sky intermittently becomes a beautiful blue before being hidden again in mist. We take rest breaks along the way, stopping to nibble on chocolate and oat bars.

Soon we reach a steep climb to the summit. It is very misty, but people we chat to along the way tell us that up there it will be clear. Then the world suddenly turns grey. Our mood dampens as the light vanishes up here, and we see another ascent up a steep flight of stone stairs. It is

spooky here, surrounded by such vast dense greyness. It is
bleak all of a sudden. We have a good moan about how
steep it is, how long and seemingly endless the climb,
how exhausted we now are, and joke about how people
do this for actual fun when it now feels torturous. I am so
exhausted that we stop for another rest on the steps,
sipping water. I let my heartbeat slow and the oxygen
begin to flow again around my body.

This set of stone steps seems to go on and on for ever.
They seem less a stairway to heaven than to purgatory.
I feel I cannot go on a single step more. I glance down
and feel vertiginous at them falling away beneath me.
I cannot turn back either. Rori presses on ahead of me.
I'm on the verge of giving up but keep walking.

I walk and walk up, and let the mountain be my
mentor, thinking about reaching its summit.

Step by stone step we are ever closer to the summit.
Then the steps are giving way to flat land and I am
almost too exhausted to realise we have actually reached
the summit. But the mist is so thick up here, as if we are
actually in a cloud – we *are* actually in a cloud. Several
walkers along the way had told us the mist would clear
and leave lucid skies when we reached the top. We cannot
help but be disheartened, and I can see disappointment
etched on Rori's face. There is no disguising the emotions
of a child. I try to raise our spirits and say how cool it is
that we reached the top even though the thickest cloud
obscures our view. But neither of us can get rid of the
gulf between what we thought we would find and this
dense opaqueness.

The family we saw at the signpost pass by and march
back down the other side of the mountain, barely

stopping here at the top. We sit on the grass exhausted and eat oatcakes and sip ginger ale, which tastes like actual heaven and awakens me. We sit for a while in silence.

Soon the cloud begins to clear.

There is the faintest hint of blue in the sky and then, through the veil of cloud, I see faint greenness. More and more visibility. Then I see the curves of the mountains, as if they are being born all over again.

How does it feel to sit inside a cloud and watch it clear? One minute it is so opaque you cannot believe you will ever see through the cloud again, and then the light seeps through, the blue and green seep through. How marvellous are those first rays of light, that first sight of colour, brighter, brighter now, until the world is born again into colour.

We run and spread out our arms and marvel at the feeling of sunlight on our skin, laughing at the foolishness of those people who did not have the patience to pause, for if they had they too would have seen the cloud clear and reveal the view from the top in all its glory.

A great flock of crows soars into the blue sky in a flurry of beating wings. Butterflies flutter around us.

I lie down and feel the earth beneath me and enjoy the feeling of it there, its solidity and surety. Here I am, lying on the backbone of Britain. *You must not lose your backbone or courage,* I think. *You cannot give up now. You have come too far.* We had set off on a path and it was too late to turn back, and now I am so glad we did not turn back. It truly does feel like a lesson for life.

I love looking at the OS map and seeing the red arrow showing us right at the summit of the mountain.

The map also shows that there are many shake holes nearby, and to the right is marked Fawcett Moor Cave.

It is now way past lunchtime and Rori is being chased with a message from her mother to come back, so we decide to set off home, our temporary home. Rori leaps about in the new light that beams down, turning the top of the mountain gold.

It is easier on the way down and we are able to enjoy it more and watch out for wildlife. We stop to admire a white and black butterfly, more spiderwebs, silvered in the sunlight. I am doing it. I am actually walking the Way. Following paths and tracks and desire lines. Following the gut.

Then we see a clear spring in which Rori dips her hand. The water is so translucent we could have missed seeing it were it not for a ray of light sheening its surface. I wonder if it is one of the magical springs, peculiar to karst landscapes, that disappear underground and suddenly reappear elsewhere; it seems so. I dip my hand in the glistening water too and savour the coolness on my skin.

'Look,' Rori exclaims, pointing to something in the distance. It. That. There it is again from a different perspective. A scar in the earth, a mark, a beauty-spot often ignored. I can't believe we've been there and looked down it. That largest natural hole in the country, here re-appeared.

I look upon the formations of the natural world. How a collapsed cavern can cause something ultimately beautiful, how scars in the earth are formed. I think of how a human personality is formed and shaped.

Then the past is pushing close to the surface, rising up with all its force though buried deep within. I am Rori's

age again. I am about to turn thirteen and curled up in a
foetal position and being kicked in the ribs, being told to
curl up in a corner and die. I'm screaming in pain until
my voice is hoarse and then it catches and I have no
voice at all, it becomes a silence that sticks as a lump in
my throat that stays there for years.

Tears well, as if from a subterranean stream, and
I dwell for a moment on how tears well from a hurt
place. I am walking through wounds, wandering a
wounded landscape, what I call a 'wounderland' of sorts.
The etymology of 'trauma' is from Greek and literally
means 'wound'. A definition of scar is a wound that has
not healed. Trauma plays tricks on us; the wound is
not always localised but omnipresent within, springing
up suddenly.

The past has been imagined as a place – 'The past is a
foreign country,' as L.P. Hartley said – and walking
through this terrain now I feel how pain is a place too,
full of tough paths to tread, pot holes and sinkholes and
hidden streams. 'What's hurting you?' a friend had asked
when that welling happened quite unbidden one
evening. I could not say or name it or put a finger on it;
I could not see it for it was so buried and hidden. Hurt
can seep into the skin, the body, the mind and become
dissociated from its source.

That incident on the train is not the first time I have
been abused. Violence ruptured my childhood: the
searing sting of a slap, the foot kicking me, hands shoving
me into the blaring traffic of a busy road whilst calling
me 'Paki'.

The body has a remarkable ability to heal itself from a
wound, and so does the mind. But the body and mind

don't always heal fully from hurt, and so a scar remains. If the body became wounded we'd have no shame about seeking help, and it should be the same with the mind, yet stigma still remains, and treatment needs to be more inexpensively and abundantly available. When the self is violated it can have deep and damaging consequences if we don't get the necessary treatment, causing scarring of the mind, psychological trauma. Studies reveal that childhood bullying and abuse can be a major risk factor for poor mental health in adulthood, raising the risk of depression, anxiety, panic attacks, post-traumatic stress disorder, and suicidal thoughts. Research by the University of Montreal also suggests that bullying can change the structure surrounding a gene involved in regulating mood. Another study into the long-term ramifications revealed that bullying could lead to 'reduced adaptation to adult roles including forming lasting relationships, integrating into work and being economically independent'. Bullying and abuse – physical, mental, emotional or verbal – can steal a lot including our self-worth and sense of belonging. It can steal language, the ability to express what we have experienced. I think of how I never spoke out or even stood up for myself those other times; trauma had stolen my words.

Trauma can be corrosive, like acidic rainwater on limestone. In early adulthood I had not long been trying to make my way in London when I was sexually assaulted. I did not speak out about it; the rage and pain I felt was internalised, corroding further, reopening earlier wounds. I am inside the earth. Hands pushing me against a wall in the Underground. Then I can't breathe, my mouth full of a tongue not mine. I want to scream but silence. I am frozen. The mouth then a gaping wound. I want my body back. I want my mouth back. *Speak!*

I think of how I was affected by the experience, the erosion of trust in the world. I would be pulled into a vortex of fear as if down one of those sinkholes ('the lasting effect of fear', part of a definition of the word 'scar'); trauma was exerting a toxic power. The past is not dead and gone, it courses through the present. The past is comingled with the present, it formed it. I think about the scale of time as well as place. Some days can pale into insignificance; others become enormous within us. As Albert Einstein said: 'The distinction between past, present and future is only a stubbornly persistent illusion.' Knowledge about trauma is still evolving, including relatively recent studies about the inheritance of trauma, how it is passed down generations through 'epigenetics'.

I suffered from PTSD for a long time, which shifts the experience and scale of time further. Sufferers can experience flashbacks, like a replaying video or audio-recorder. Likewise, the mind replays incidents from the past, rendering time not so linear in our hearts. On other occasions there are no flashbacks, but the emotions of fear, pain and anger provoked by the traumatic experience remain.

Sometimes I still think on the past, the time I lost stranded in the sinkhole of depression and anxiety, and I feel winded with horror at the moments I let those 'lasting effects of grief, fear or other emotion' shape my decisions and took the wrong path, severing relationships I should have kept or staying in those I should have severed. But from here on high, walking on a scar itself,

I can look back upon my life and know that those supposed wrong-turnings, those times of flailing, were a result of how the mind formed from the effects of having literally been flailed – and that there is so much to learn from whatever path we're on.

Now I'm more skilled in avoiding tripping and falling into sinkholes – and scars are much better than sinkholes. There is a great freedom in accepting our scars as part of the landscape of our lives. Those scars might ultimately turn into something beautiful. We can even come to draw strength from them – and so can others. If you look into the wound and turn it into words, there is wonder to be found. I think of the shape of a life, and I don't feel regret and shame at my so-called scars, but am instead proud to have survived. I see myself no longer as just a victim but as a survivor.

Every human being has at least some scars. Scarring is part of the healing process and every wound results in some kind of scar. The moment the umbilical cord is cut it leaves our first scar – the navel or belly button, which is technically a scar, created by being born and the first severing, from our mother's body. All placental mammals have such a scar. Would you be ashamed of your belly button? (I make no apologies for this necessary moment of navel-gazing.)

There are some amazing wildlife that do not scar and can completely regenerate: salamander can regrow a lost tail to full length; starfish have regrowth powers through storing nutrients; sea cucumbers can regrow damaged parts and heal deep wounds in only a week. Us humans, though, while good healers, are more sensitive to scarring.

There are sayings such as 'etched in the mind' – language reveals how the mind becomes marked. We can see the landscape, body and their markings, but we cannot see the mind – where is it? We can try and locate the markings of the mind, those etches, in the shape of our lives, and the people and places with whom we've interacted. Our mind is in the world; we leave particles of energy wherever and with whoever we've interacted. What traces will we leave behind on the planet and other people? What traces will they leave on us?

Now I look forward and think of the markings I want to make in the world, the paths still to be trodden. Today I have walked through and beyond a wound. My journey today has been both wounderful and wonderful as I wandered through the wound, looked inside it, distilled from it some kind of understanding.

On the way back down Horton Scar we hear something that we cannot see: a grasshopper. We hear a magical sound of plunging water: a waterfall set in huge cliffs, and limestone formations not marked on the map. There is a forest near the waterfall and we talk about how one day we will return here and walk through the forest. I stop to admire that other meaning of 'scar' – 'a mark left at the point of separation of a leaf, frond, or other part from a plant' – and wonder at the intricacy of the marking left behind on the plant I peer at.

Walking further down the scar, we run into Rori's family, who have been walking up in the hope of meeting us along the way. We are delighted to see each other.

They have brought a picnic and are also with a friend of theirs who has come to take them back home to Cumbria. We do end up walking to that waterfall, via a shortcut. We picnic upon a scar, strangers become friends sharing a meal together, breaking bread in the English countryside. I have a piece of chocolate, savouring the sweetness in my mouth, and look out over the landscape, marvelling at how it is home to such magic. I one day hope to visit other scars in the Great Scar Limestone Group, the name given to the scars which formed in the Pennines and the Isle of Man during the Carboniferous era. After a while, we're walking again, along the scar and back to our temporary home, and bid farewell.

Scar. We can be shaped by those 'lasting effects of grief, fear, or other emotion left on a person's character', but we are resilient too and can be reformed; it is possible to move beyond traumatic emotions, to survive and thrive after them. Even walking this way through astonishing formations has re-formed my mind to some extent, so profound can be our relationship with place, deep as the earth, an experience reaching to the very core of the self. Trauma disrupts the body's natural equilibrium, leading to hyperarousal and fear, but rhythmic movement such as walking can free us from such a frozen, fearful state, burning off adrenalin, releasing endorphins and helping to repair the traumatised nervous system.

I've long been intrigued by 'muscle memory', with how time burrows into our bodies, as well as our minds, with the relationship between walking and time, and how walking can stir the buried sediment of memory. I am hungry for new experiences too, new ways of being in the world, and forging new muscle memories. Each footstep has not only been a looking back but a living now and a looking forward, forming new memories in both mind and body, and strengthening resilience.

Later, I walk alone through the wounded landscape. That collapsed cavern was formed by natural causes. But what scars are we leaving on the earth by our careless actions? The natural world bears witness to how we move through it, carrying traces of how we have treated it. We must stop wounding the earth. I remember the sphagnum moss, used as a wound dressing during the First World War and now being used to heal the wounds of the earth caused by humans, pollution having destroyed wildlife habitats such as moorlands. How heartbreaking that healing sphagnum is itself now threatened by climate change. If we act urgently it is possible to heal some of the wounds in the earth caused by humans, to tend to them and ensure no new ones are inflicted.

I walk alone along a Scar and look out over the landscape and there is nothing but walking and looking, walking and looking, there is nothing but now. Then I see a glint and it is another karst spring, its water totally clear and reflecting the world. I can only hope to hold on to these feelings of awe, this raw sense of being alive and alert and absolutely in the moment; a creature on earth.

FEET

The Way: North Pennines to Hadrian's Wall (via Manchester)

'Traveler, your footprints
are the only road, nothing else.
Traveler, there is no road;
you make your own path as you walk.
As you walk, you make your own road,
and when you look back
you see the path
you will never travel again.
Traveler, there is no road;
only a ship's wake on the sea.'

— Antonio Machado

12

Northern Nature

How do we find our feet in the world and what stops us from doing so?

I'm heading back to my hometown before beginning the next stage of my journey along the backbone of Britain. Stepping into the train carriage at Leeds, I see other brown and black faces, more than I have seen in weeks put together, and I immediately feel how racially segregated the countryside is from cities. I remember the train carriage in which I was racially abused, and I was the only person in it who was not white.

I'm delaying the next stage of my journey through the North Pennines for reasons including the physical. The injury I incurred falling on that great rock on Malham Cove has proven serious. After a few days of seeming to diminish and even vanish, the pain returned and became so searing and intense that walking long distances felt impossible. My hurt foot needed treating, I had been advised by an expert climber. It needed rest and bandaging or I would end up writing How to Hobble Half of the Pennine Way.

The element of discontinuity has other virtues, giving me the perspective to reflect on my journey so far and feel again the emotional pull of places. In the case of my hometown, there has been – as is often so with our first homes – a paradoxical pull to both escape and to return. During my time here, I explore the place I grew up in, how it has shaped and grown through me, the ways I've drawn from it as a source of strength then and now, and the stereotypes people have about the place.

I've often crashed up against the barrier of the North–South divide. I have throughout my life encountered huge prejudice and class snobbery towards the North. After writing about how Prince Charles told me I didn't look as if I was from Manchester, the messages I received from around the world sharing global preconceptions of the city included observations that I don't look like Liam Gallagher or Bet Lynch, wear a shell-suit, or look 'drunk and dishevelled' like most people from Manchester apparently do. Of course, some of these comments were poking fun, but behind the veneer of humour lie deep-seated prejudices about place and identity.

I first moved away from the North for university, where I almost was at risk of becoming that silent girl again as I'd open my mouth to speak and have my broad accent, its flat vowel sounds, mocked, and be told I sound like someone from *Coronation Street* or *Hollyoaks*. Why are there such stereotypes? Growing up, I rarely heard a northern accent on television aside from a couple of soaps, or on the radio or in wider culture, and when a northern person did appear, they were caricatured, figures of fun or unintellectual – as if the locus of intelligence is to be found within the Home Counties.

In terms of class, the US has the American dream of being able to move beyond the strictures of one's birth, but Britain is more rigid in the notion of class fluidity: those who move beyond their class or region can too often be regarded with suspicion and as imposters – there's a sense that people need to 'know their place' and not move from it.

The media and cultural industries have for so long been London-centric; only relatively recently have there been rumblings of change. Is it any wonder that – if attempting to make it in such industries – you might develop imposter syndrome? Even if you had steely self-confidence, it would be impressive to keep your cool when mocked, belittled or patronised. Those from non-traditional backgrounds can be regarded with hostility and we have to prove even more our right to exist and belong in such worlds. Imposter syndrome is imposed from without, in multiple macro and microaggressions of prejudice. Such feelings can be internalised as unsettlement in the self. To be made to feel as if you are an outsider incites a feeling that you do not belong in your own life. How can you feel settled when you're treated like this? I had internalised such hostility so much I did not believe I belonged – and had to gain that self-belief.

Writing about anything beyond the M25 is still not respected enough in the industry, not seen as 'universal' but Northerners are just as human and intelligent as Southerners and care as much about nature; what's more, we are capable of reading too. When I mentioned to someone (a Londoner) my plan of writing this book, they said 'No-one cares about the North and don't use the word Pennines as it won't sell.' It only fuelled my determination to write this; what's more, I love the word 'Pennines', it holds within it 'pen' and 'pine' – and I was pining to turn my pen to the Pennines.

Shifts and relocations of regional power need to be deep and permanent. In 2020 Boris Johnson proposed moving the House of Lords to York while the Palace of Westminster, which is literally a crumbling edifice, is renovated, but the proposal has been axed. There have also been reports that the government is considering establishing a new 'hub' in the North but nothing has yet been confirmed.[78] The North's political landscape changed in the 2019 general election as voters lapped up empty promises of a northern renaissance, with former Labour working-class heartlands that have been hit hard by austerity going to the Tories, from Redcar by the North Sea (the man who racially abused me resides in Marske-by-the-Sea part of Redcar and Cleveland, North Yorkshire), to Darlington (where he was arrested) to the Blyth Valley in Northumberland, and Bishop Auckland. Such areas also had majority Brexit votes. Manchester, though, had a strong percentage voting Remain.

Go back to where you're from.

My journey through the North ends up taking me right back to the beginning of where I am from, to my first home, around the corner from The Smiths' former frontman Morrissey's childhood home and on the same road as the hospital where Ian Curtis of Joy Division was born. I grew up at a literal crossroads, an intersection, and have always been aware of the intersections of experience. The diversity of both landscape and people in the North is often overlooked, including by the so-called 'Northern Powerhouse' slogan; it is not a homogenous region – there is a gulf between its inner cities, such as the one I grew up in, and the salubrious suburbs and surrounding countryside. As always, it's important to remember the nuances and intersectionality of experience – how regionality intersects with class and race and gender when it comes to our identities, life chances, how others judge us, our experience of being in the world and moving through place.

I hadn't intended this stop-off. I am at the mercy of my sore foot rather than guided by my gut. Yet this stay in the place I'm from proves to deepen my understanding of how it shaped the person I am. It has shown me how deeply we need to reclaim the lost or overlooked history of places, and how human history and natural history comingle, which affects our sense of belonging.

First, I will walk you through the forgotten feminist history of the area in which I grew up.

Where were the first steps you took and what place did you most spend your early life walking through? I walked down the street of my childhood home thousands of times without knowing that the feminist campaigners Sylvia and Christabel Pankhurst were born and raised there. A hundred years after the first women in the UK were allowed to vote, a statue of Emmeline Pankhurst was unveiled in Manchester's St Peter's Square thanks to the campaigning of the WoManchester Statue Project which set out to celebrate and restore the significant role that women have played in the city, a city in which sixteen out of seventeen city-centre statues are of men. It is important to also shine a light on more neglected places of feminist history. While growing up, I was not taught that Emmeline was born in Moss Side on what is now the Alexandra Park estate bordering Whalley Range – a much-maligned area of the city, known more for its crime rates than its campaigners. Nor that her daughters, Sylvia and Christabel, were born in Old Trafford, known more for its football than its feminist history. The houses in which they were born, including the one that stood near my childhood home, have since been demolished and no plaques mark their birthplaces. They deserve blue plaques rather than their existence in these places erased. Moves to redress such geographical ignorance include the Pankhurst in the Park project on the Moss Side/Whalley Range border, which aims to 'empower the local community' by celebrating its connections to the Suffrage movement. As a young girl forging my place in the world, such knowledge would have felt inspirational. It does now, as an adult. I now walk through the local Alexandra Park and imagine The Great Demonstration that took place there in 1908, when thousands marched in a political rally campaigning for women's rights. I imagine the Pankhurst sisters walking down my home street, planning how to make the world a better place.

Celebrating the unsung history of places helps tackle all kinds of prejudice and ignorance and when our knowledge about a place expands, so does our imaginative landscape. I can now feel proud to be from such a postcode, for its feminist history and not only its football. I reclaim these Pankhurst sisters as part of my local history, my sisters in place, from my neck of the woods. Whether here or elsewhere, such restored memories can play a part, however small, in making the world a more equal place.

Gaining deeper understanding of the feminist history of where I am from has inspired me in my journey along the backbone of Britain. But as well as walking in the footsteps of the feminists before me, I know I must go further than the limits of 'white feminism', for we need a more intersectional feminism which acknowledges how the multiple marginalisations of race, gender and class affect how we move through the world. I take this knowledge with me in every step I make on my journey through the North – in both its urban and natural landscapes – and every step I will make beyond.

Places make us, but people also make places. Manchester's immigrant history helped to build the backbone of the city and country, and yet that too has been variously written out of history or distorted and needs to be reclaimed and restored. For far too long people of colour have been viewed by some as pestilent, burdens on the country, leeching its resources, and yet so many immigrants came here to help bring into being a better Britain. Immigrants were members of the army. Immigrants worked in service roles such as in hospitals, as my mother did, arriving in England to train as a nurse. (As to the welcome she got, when working as a midwife in hospitals, including the one in which Ian Curtis was born, some would refuse to have her deliver their baby, saying: 'We don't want a black nurse touching our baby.') The notion of a 'white working class' is toxic, overlooking the many black and brown people of working-class backgrounds who have often been wiped out of the narrative propagated by media and culture.

I am on the train back to Manchester when I receive a tweet from a stranger to help spread the word about the funeral of a hundred-year-old man. There is a link to a *Manchester Evening News* article: 'An RAF veteran with no family has died aged 100 – you are invited to salute him at his funeral.' It tells how Oswald 'Ossie' Dixon was the oldest resident at Broughton House care home for veterans in Salford. Oswald had joined the RAF in Kingston, Jamaica, in November 1944 and then moved to Britain to serve before the conflict ended. He had become a leading aircraftman, remaining in the service and teaching new recruits until his retirement. Oswald was registered blind, but Broughton House told how he would not go to sleep without a torch in his hand. Like many others, including Gary Lineker, I retweet the article and it soon goes viral. The response shows the power of online community, how the state of isolation can be breached through positive use of virtual realms. People reply from near and far, expressing their condolences and that they will attend.

I am moved by his story and decide to attend his funeral. Ossie has no family to attend. I have always believed in a broader concept of 'family' than mere flesh and blood. I believe that water can run as deep as blood. Having throughout my life found support from those who are of no flesh and blood 'family' relation whatsoever, I believe that friendship and community can be and must be as powerful as conventional family. While Thatcher posited a view of the family as the dominant societal structure, this felt alienating to me. What if – like Ossie – you have no actual or conventional family? What if you are estranged from or disowned by your family? What if you do not find a sense of belonging in your birth family but must seek that belonging in other groups or else find an entirely new sense of belonging?

The day of the funeral lashes with torrents of rain and intermittent patches of sunshine breaking through huge clouds of such immensity they feel like living things. I find the bus stop outside Manchester Art Gallery and remember bus journeys of the past, trundling through the city on Magic Buses, and think how public transport is such a democratiser, and environmentally friendly. The bus passes concrete buildings and an industrial estate, and finally I see the green of the crematorium gardens ahead.

I join mourners. On a grey day the flowers in the cemetery bloom bright against the gravestones. I arrive to hear words of tribute praising Ossie's gentle, unassuming personality and wicked humour and how he was able to live out the last of his life with dignity and respect. Tribute is paid to people who served during the war, to those who died and those who suffered life-changing wounds. The honorary consul to the Jamaican High Commission gives a tribute: 'Oswald was a member of the Windrush generation who, as you are aware, contributed significantly to a modern, prosperous and multicultural United Kingdom. Many servicemen came from all over the Commonwealth. Oswald, thank you for your service and rest in peace.' Another tribute drifts into hearing range: 'It is with great sadness I stand here today. Not least as I didn't know him. Like many of you here today, I heard the plea on social media...' The strains of 'Amazing Grace' resound and everyone joins in singing and I feel my voice rise.

After the service, we filter outside into the pouring rain and biting cold. Through a gathering of people dressed in RAF uniform I see white doves suddenly soar out and I gasp at the flurry of beating wings. I have to blink to believe what I have seen, such beauty here on a bleak day. I think of Ossie and all the flights he made in the skies around the world.

The rain begins to pour more heavily and I look out over the cemetery gardens and see the raindrops gathered in flower petals. The rain beats down more ferociously by the minute. It feels as if the whole world is weeping.

I get chatting to people on the way out who also saw the appeal on social media and were moved to attend. We talk about the importance of caring about even those we don't know personally. I talk to an Asian man who served in the bomb disposal unit of the British army and is dressed in a military suit with badges. We talk about how many people don't realise that black and brown people served the country on land, sea and in the air, and dedicated their lives to Britain.

On the bus back, I get chatting to an elderly lady who tells me her daughter was the primary carer for Ossie. After he died, she dressed his body, rubbed coconut cream into his skin, and put on his best pyjamas. He was laid out with his torch and medals and cremated with them. We talk about what an important job such carers do, in bringing dignity to the last years and days of life and in death itself. We talk about the importance of community. We talk about how beautiful the doves were, and I see them again in my mind, their wings spreading and soaring.

By the time we reach Manchester city centre, I am soaked and shivering, and my body brings back muscle memory, perhaps skin memory, of all the other times I have walked through this city freezing cold after foolishly forgetting to bring an umbrella. Yet I am warmed by the beautiful send-off Ossie got, by hope for the possibilities of community and the coming together of people of all races and social backgrounds as one family, for the kindness of strangers.

I look into the skies of my home city, and see birds swirling there in a symmetrical pattern amid great gatherings of clouds; they look set to be beginning their long migration to escape the bitter cold of winter. I have long been enchanted by the migratory patterns of birds, their instinct to know when to leave and where to go and how to find the way, flying towards better conditions for their survival. Their migration moves me, perhaps because I too come from people who have migrated thousands of miles in the hope of better conditions for survival. I imagine those doves soaring away into the skies somewhere in Manchester, symbols of peace. They are soaring through my heart too, wings spread wide.

It is the first time I remember seeing real-life doves, not ones on greeting cards. Nature in the city added to the beauty of the ceremony today, those bright flowers blooming and those glorious doves released into the skies. I remember how I drew strength from what nature I did find in the city during childhood, for it was not possible to venture to the countryside as frequently as we would have liked. I am curious about the birds that inhabit my hometown and I search 'doves birds in Manchester' online and alongside search engine hits for Noel Gallagher's High Flying Birds, I learn about Greater Manchester's most common garden birds. A 2020 RSPB Big Garden Birdwatch survey reveals that they are: 1. house sparrow; 2. starling; 3. blue tit; 4. woodpigeon; 5. blackbird; 6. magpie; 7. goldfinch 8. long-tailed tit; 9. great tit; 10. robin. Since the RSPB began its survey in 1979 the house sparrow has declined by 53 per cent and the starling by 80 per cent, though there have been increased sightings of goldfinches.[79]

The turtle dove is the UK's fastest declining bird species, now on the brink of extinction, according to The Wildlife Trusts (Lancashire, Manchester, North Merseyside).[80] These birds with mottled chestnut and black wings have long inspired non-winged humans, fluttering throughout literature, music and art – from Shakespeare to Elvis Presley – as an emblem of renewal and love. I search 'turtle dove extinction' and the word 'vulnerable' shows up in large black letters against the white screen, and beneath it the words 'population decreasing'. In 2019 it was reported that the European Commission had launched legal action that could protect turtle doves from extinction, stating that they were 'now under threat, illustrating how pressures from agriculture and hunting contribute to biodiversity loss'.[81] Thousands of turtle doves are being shot by hunters (with the French government reportedly allowing up to 18,000 European turtle doves to be shot in 2019).[82] We are facing a crisis of extinction, failing to value, care for and respect the natural world, the creatures inhabiting it and their homes.

Operation Turtle Dove is a partnership of the RSPB, Conservation Grade, Pensthorpe Conservation Trust and Natural England and is dedicated to 'saving a bird on the brink'. Turtle doves are ecologically unique, being Europe's only long-distance migratory dove. They spend a third of the year on their breeding grounds in Europe and the winter on their non-breeding grounds in sub-Saharan West Africa.[83] The main factors associated with the decline of turtle doves include loss of suitable habitat such as the destruction of wildflower meadows and dense hedgerows. Operation Turtle Dove is working hard to understand these threats so that conservation solutions can be developed and delivered, helping these beautiful creatures to have a home in which they can safely belong.

Manchester is the gateway to so much glorious country-side, to spectacular natural landscapes such as the Pennines, the Peak District and the Lake District. The city itself is not absent of nature; indeed, there is wildlife in the very heart of the city, and it is crucial to ensure that it is cared for, nourished and allowed to flourish. Nature not only in the countryside but also the city is vital to us, and we are vital in ensuring we protect nature properly. Green spaces in the city should be abundant and safe. My earliest memories of parks were not of safe spaces to walk in. The inner-city area where I grew up was beset by gang violence, those youngsters themselves searching for a sense of belonging. One of the layers of trauma I peel back is the violence on the streets as well as inside the home.

During my time in my home city I come close to notions of 'the wild' and 'wilderness' that were the first I knew growing up in an urban landscape. I see how the wild first grew within me, as a small child learning to spot sudden startling growths of nature in the city. The first daffodil to bloom in our small garden. The unexpected sight of a dandelion growing between the gaps in a grey pavement. And the ladybirds that crawled along the concrete and fluttered onto my hand, tickling my heart line. I liked looking at ladybirds, their intricacies; it helped, in this great blur of a crowded city, to focus.

The first time I saw one opening its wings I thought it was dying, the way its body seemed to be splitting open, but then it flew, flapped about in the air, dived back down and became again a small oval solid thing. It was so unmoving that the first time I saw one I didn't know it was a living creature and thought it might have been some kind of colourful pebble – until it flew. I started to paint ladybirds so they could be with me even when they weren't, moving my paintbrush over the page and retrieving them with each brushstroke, until they were flying again, inside my head.

Now I begin to remember how a garden first grew, how something began to flourish out of nothing, amid the screech of sirens and honking of horns. When the garden grew there, it became a lifesaver. The earth was covered in coldness, which stretched itself over our lives like a dull, thumping headache. My mother had slumped into a pit of depression and I seemed to absorb her mood, mirroring the melancholy overcast sky. Then one day my mother was not in her usual place in bed. She was outside. She had begun cultivating the garden. Where once there was a concrete strip fringing the house and leading to the blaring crossroads, now there was rich black soil. I peered closely at colours I had seen every day but not really looked at, inspecting the brown bark of the trees with swirling patterns like those on a palm. The colours of the body – which I had been teased about by the boy in the street, by the girl in school – there in the garden I could see they too were a natural part of the world.

The next task was the planting of the bulbs. Mum wore thin garden gloves, burrowing out a home for those bulbs, deep enough for each one to be safe, for life to grow. She spent long hours in the new garden, passing her sadness away into the soil. I came to understand that the bulbs – small, oval-shaped, colourless – would one day sprout a shock of life, would one day flower. Their sowing had planted new emotions in my heart – a small but potent sense of anticipation. In the barren earth there was now a small seed of something new: hope.

It was lucky that we planted the bulbs when we did, for if we had left it a few days longer the earth would have been too hard for humble human fingers to interfere with. That soft soil would have grown solid and rocky, impenetrable.

It was lucky that we planted the bulbs when we did for just a few days later it became too cold to stay outside for very long at all – seconds even and the breath came out in curling white smoke, the body shivered and the teeth chattered.

It was lucky that we planted the bulbs when we did for that winter was one of the longest on record. The frost clung fiercely, tightening its grip, clutching our skulls so that the journey to school was painful in the cold, wind lashing against the skin, pulling tears out of the eyes.

Plant new worlds, quickly, quickly, before the light fades.

All through the cold days, those small bulbs gave me something to imagine. Something to hold on to. Then one morning, an astonishment of golden-yellow in the black, a daffodil burst open. I gazed long and deep at the daffodil so that I could carry it inside my mind once I had left to go to school – and throughout the grey day, the daffodil bloomed within. I loved the daffodil.

The deep depression that had burrowed its way into our bones and hearts was lifted and lightened, for now.

It wasn't only the purposefully planted bulbs that were enchanting, but the accidental growths. For, even among the rubble and concrete, even among the litter and debris, the tip of discarded dreams, can something grow. Life grows in places you least expect it; the dandelion springs in an astonishment of colour between the gaps in the grey pavement. Its delicate body was battered by the weather, for it was born in an unfortunate location and it was pounded by fierce rain and whipped by ferocious winds, so it would sway and bow and bend yet still it did not die. It blazed briefly, that flower, so that all who passed along the path, the concrete roadside, the supposed wasteland, on the otherwise forlorn day, could glance down and – should they chance to see it – perhaps their hearts too would bloom and fill with a sudden moment of joy.

I knew it wouldn't last, the glory of the garden in full bloom. So when the leaves started to fall and the flower petals curled and wilted, and the sweet scents evaporated to leave the smog, and the birds stopped singing and migrated to Africa, I didn't entirely despair. I knew this was the rhythm of the earth. I knew it would happen again, the opening-up of the world.

Now that forgotten first garden is growing within. For a long time it had been buried beneath darker memories, but now it is growing within me, its roots and its branches, its soft, fierce soil, its determination to grow where growth was least expected. Now I feel anew its ferocity of life-force, a thing of beauty yearning to grow, despite everything.

Having been to two funerals in the space of a few months – of a twenty-eight-year-old friend and a hundred-year-old stranger, it is impossible not to think about how all of our lives will one day be extinct. What do we want to leave behind to the earth? How should we best treat the world and the people within it during the relatively brief time we belong here? We will all one day lose our lives, but what of us will live on?

I would like to leave behind this story of hope. I would like to leave behind a record of what the life I knew was like during my time on earth, its pain and fear and hate and love and joy and hope, for those who come after to perhaps learn from, to know something of the times through which I was living. I would like this book to be available to all backgrounds. I'd like it to be stocked in libraries as well as bookshops, where I first gained my passion for reading.

Libraries are one of the backbones of communities, but heartbreakingly threatened with extinction as the UK closes ever more.

In 1852, Charles Dickens opened the UK's first free public lending library, in the heart of Manchester.[84] It evolved to become the Manchester Central Library in St Peter's Square, opposite that Emmeline Pankhurst statue. The library was built upon the philosophy of providing wisdom for all, regardless of background, 'knowing no sect, no party, no distinction; nothing but the public want and the general good' as Charles Dickens said in his stirring speech at the library's opening ceremony. 'In this institution, special provision has been made for the working classes, by means of a free lending library... this meeting cherishes the earnest hope that the books thus made available will prove a source of pleasure and improvement in the cottages, the garrets, and the cellars of the poorest of our people.'[85]

During my childhood, local libraries were a lifeline to books and the sense of a safe space. Those who support library closures argue that the internet provides information and e-books – but a significant percentage of the population still doesn't have internet access, and for many the library is also a place of community, a crucial connection to the world. Providing 'a source of pleasure and improvement' to all, regardless of background, is not an outdated principle but a democratic ideal that needs to be protected.

At the library's opening ceremony, writer and politician Sir Edward Bulwer-Lytton said of the library: 'What minds may be destined to grow up and flourish under the shade of this tree of knowledge which you have now planted, none of us can conjecture; but you of the present generation have nobly done your duty and can calmly leave the result to time.' That metaphor of the library as a 'tree of knowledge' is an apt one, uniting books and nature imagery, uniting too books and breathing; after all, without trees turning the sun's light into oxygen, none of us would exist. Without books, those strange worlds made of trees, I am not sure I would still exist now, for there were times when books were a lifesaver.

'Until I feared I would lose it, I never loved to read. One does not love breathing,' wrote Harper Lee – one of the quotes engraved into the green-domed Reading Room walls in Melbourne, where I undertook a writing residency. I was lucky as a child to have a free local library where I could live and breathe books; this may not be so for the next generation. The threat of losing our libraries, and the appetite for reading fostered by them, should make us stop and contemplate what it is about them that we so love, should make us declare that love before their oxygen supply is cut off. We don't want to be haunted by libraries as a thing of the past.

Books have long provided me with a sense of both belonging and unbelonging for, while I could disappear into the pages for hours, I would at times encounter a stereotype or prejudice about an aspect of my identity – the undercurrents of racism in *The Water-Babies*, for example, or in adulthood the misogyny in *A Pennine Journey*. There are some who have been marginalised so much that they have been made to feel as if their stories don't belong in books. I write this book to create a home for my story, to give it somewhere to belong, to hopefully help others who feel alienated to find a sense of belonging, to help them keep breathing. It's when writing that I feel like I most belong.

I wrote up part of this book in Manchester Central Library – the same place I spent time in teenagehood, high up on the top floor, burrowed in a corner near books of poetry – not long before all libraries in the country closed due to coronavirus. This library truly does feel like a refuge, a place to belong, and I feel stress seep away beneath its tall domed ceiling. I love writing in fountain pen, and swear by blue-black Parker cartridges, us descendants of immigrants creating rivers of ink not rivers of blood. In the heart of the city, I am writing the rivers.

Between sessions of writing, I walk through the city. I walk and walk and each footstep lasts a mere second yet contains a lifetime within it. Each footstep stirs memories of my younger self, working in the library and walking through the city, dreaming of one day being a writer and making worlds come alive out of words and wounds. Each footstep echoes not only with my own life but all the lives that have been before here. I pass the Pankhurst statue and think of the Peterloo Massacre that happened here a hundred years ago, during which more than 600 people were wounded and several died fighting for freedom.

My sense of belonging in the world has always felt so contingent, so easily snatched from me, that I came to feel that if I could build a sense of belonging in writing it could not be taken from me. I could make a home for myself out of words. I feel how language is a landscape of sorts, and I burrow out a place for myself in the curves and arcs and peaks and valleys of words and sentences and chapters. I find that words can burrow their way into the body too, find new places, open up sealed spaces and heal, move through us.

To anyone who feels like they don't belong, I say: build a sense of belonging in your own mind, body, and in nature, a sense of belonging that no one can take from you. Learn to inhabit yourself.

13

Areas of Outstanding Natural Beauty

I love my home city, a backbone of sorts, but am eager to continue on up through the North Pennines and complete my journey. I long to breathe clean air. Walking through the city, breathing the smog of pollution, my ears filled with blaring traffic, I feel panic and claustrophobia. Air pollution, besieging all major cities, is endemic and studies reveal just how toxic it is: a Public Health England report stated that 'Air pollution is the biggest environmental threat to health in the UK, with between 28,000 and 36,000 deaths a year attributed to long-term exposure.'[86] More people of colour live in polluted cities, a comorbidity with coronavirus. Class and race and regionality literally affect the air we breathe. There is vast inequality within the North and elsewhere in the UK in access to the natural world. I wish for cities to be redesigned as greener, cleaner spaces. I wish for closeness to nature – the abundance of trees on streets, the plentifulness of parks – to be improved for all including in urban areas so that we don't just have to exist in the countryside to breathe clean air. I wish for greater access to the countryside and Areas of Outstanding Natural Beauty too, and a sense that all backgrounds belong there.

The gulf between socially deprived areas and the countryside was highlighted in a report from the

Campaign to Protect Rural England (CPRE, 2019)[87] revealing that almost half of the country's most socially deprived areas are more than 25 kilometres by road from ten national parks and forty-six Areas of Outstanding Natural Beauty (AONB). The CPRE launched detailed maps that show 36 per cent of England's population live too far from the current network of national parks and AONBs for these areas to be classified as easily accessible, and it has called for better, more sustainable public transport. Emma Marrington, senior rural policy campaigner at CPRE, said: 'When the most beautiful parts of England's countryside were given national park status, or designated as AONBs, they were done so as a public good – so that everyone could enjoy the benefits that access to them can bring. But the mapping demonstrates that a huge amount of people are currently missing out.'

One day I'm delighted when the North Pennines, an Area of Outstanding Natural Beauty slips through the letterbox, compressed into two-dimensions. I had ordered a second-hand OS map, not being able to afford an original one, and a frisson of excitement courses through me as I unfold it, wondering who held this map before I did and the journeys they made with it – like second-hand books, such maps are haunted. I'm staggered by the sheer scale of the map when I open it out. Its vertical length reaches up to my breastbone and it is wide enough to wrap around me entirely. I spread it out and it absorbs me for hours as I pore over its markings. The Pennine Way runs through it in a green line with green diamond-shaped markings, rivers inked as if by a blue cartridge.

I feel my breath catch as I see the explanations for 'magnetic north' and 'true north' – distinctions I confess I hadn't been fully knowledgeable about. 'True north' or geographic north is the direction towards the fixed point of the North Pole. 'Magnetic north' is the direction towards the north magnetic pole, which is a wandering point on the surface of the earth's Northern Hemisphere where the planet's magnetic field points vertically down.[88] That autumn of my journey, compasses at Greenwich pointed true north for the first time in about 360 years.[89]

I can't wait to let myself be pulled further and deeper by the magnetism of the North, and to step inside that map. It is not very practical and opening it up on a rainy day would not be ideal, but I will take it with me, nevertheless. I also try to memorise as much of it as possible, poring over it until its lines and contours run through me.

Before beginning the final stages of my journey, I research the emotions I felt during the earlier stages, the ways and extent to which nature and walking can be ameliorative to symptoms of PTSD and trauma, and evolving notions of a so-called 'nature cure'.

I speak with Professor Dacher Keltner, who co-authored the paper 'Emotions in the Wilds of Nature' showing declines in PTSD symptoms among poor teenagers and veterans when they went white-water rafting. I ask why nature is so healing to symptoms of PTSD. 'There are multiple things that happen when you have suffered a hate crime as you did, and I'm really sorry about that, or a child who's been bullied or you've been sexually assaulted or you're coming out of war, or you've been in poverty,' he tells me. 'With nature – the sounds, the scents, the colour, they directly calm down your stress response. Our bodies are like antennae that pick up these natural cues. The second thing is the effect on your mind: you feel you're not so vigilant, you can open up your attention. The third thing is awe: when you get out in the wonders of nature you feel awe and you feel there's a lot more to life than the trauma, there's more to this story. Those three pathways of how we sense nature, how it calms our minds, and that powerful awe really are good ways to heal. Certain chemicals that calm your body are emitted by plants, and hearing running water calms your body. Parts of our body evolve to experience awe-inspiring nature.'

I'm fascinated to learn more about those physiological reactions: one of my symptoms of PTSD was anxiety, essentially a very intense fear. I tell him that I read the study 'Emotions in the Wilds of Nature' while specifically researching the after-effects of my experience of hate crime yet it also chimed deeply in other ways too. We discuss how traumatic experiences can trigger the trauma of earlier experiences, so causing greater susceptibility to PTSD. For some, such early experiences can actually increase resilience. I wonder if nature can heal the deep-rooted fear that we've kept in our bodies and mind since childhood.

'I believe it will through these pathways, or what are called mechanisms, and that is the radical thesis,' he says.

'Which is why I think it's so important to write what you're writing and show how nature can be healing. I think we're moving in the direction of using nature as a source of healthcare. Some countries are ahead of us, such as South Korea and Japan – they have the concept of "forest bathing" ["shinrin yoku"].'

His study describes analysing people's facial expressions, and I tell him that if you looked at my face I would be tense and anxious, but then when I'm in nature my breathing changes, which is going to affect my body and mind.

'That's exactly how to think of it,' he replies. 'Take the trauma stress profile: breathing really shallow breaths, facial pressure, cortisol. What the studies show is that being in nature calms all that – you breathe more deeply, your heart rate slows, your cortisol levels drop, your immune system functions better. So the body is sensing the environment, and when it's beautiful around you it calms down. The radical part of these possibilities is that you take a child who's been bullied and maybe if we get them out walking in the woods they'll handle the trauma better, and I think that would be a good thesis to get people thinking about and it has a lot of physiological support.'

I recall that dictionary definition of the word scar, 'a lasting effect of grief, fear or other emotion...' I tell Professor Keltner that it was welcome that his study focused on emotion and that, when experiencing PTSD, I might not be thinking about the traumatic incidents themselves but the emotion is still there of fear and anxiety and seems to have become embedded in mind and body. We can feel trapped by past experiences, whereas walking in nature can bring us back to the present moment.

'Well put, and I think that awe is relevant there because one of the things about fear and trauma is that you're locked in this very vigilant, hyper-aware, narrow view of the world, and locked up in the mindset of trauma – awe is a powerful antidote to that.'

What happens to us when we experience the awe of nature has been pontificated on for hundreds of years, evolving throughout the centuries. 'This begins with Edmund Burke, Immanuel Kant, Wordsworth,' he says. 'The sublime, which triggers awe, is vast and mysterious, and so your present knowledge can't immediately categorise and make sense of it. So you begin with vastness and mystery and then the next theme comes in, which is that when you've been traumatised you often feel like your self has been injured.'

'The "core self" as well,' I say. 'Hate crime is an attack on protected characteristics, which is the core of a person. In bullying too you feel like the core of yourself has been damaged, injured or wounded.'

'Yes. What awe does is that momentarily all of the processes involved in that core self being hurt are quieted and your mind opens up to other possibilities. The next thing – which is critical for awe, which is why we get the goosebumps and chills – is that you feel connected to something larger, supported by something larger. If you're out in nature and you ask people to draw their network and community, awe will make us draw bigger networks. If you've been wounded by one person or a set of bullies, you start to think they're just one part of the story, there's so much more. Finally, there's wonder, where your mind is opened and you're curious – awe is literally a wonderful emotion. There's a lot of awe: in walks in the woods, in great music. Your story will inspire others, and they will feel awe. So there's awe around that is not just sublime poetry or religion.'

The problem with establishing a network after trauma, from my experience, is that your trust can close down, I say. Fear and PTSD can stop you trusting people enough to form a relationship and therefore to have that network with others. 'Yes, and identity-based trauma and PTSD can make you isolated. I was talking to a veteran yesterday and he said a lot of veterans return with trauma and become very isolated, and if you're a person of colour and are a victim of hate crime, you can feel alone and often are, so that compounds the problem.'

Walking in nature seemed to make me more open and lessen that fear of trusting others, I say, and I also felt like it changed the neural pathways of my brain and made me more open to new experiences and to both remember and let go of the past. I tell him about my walk through the vast Pennine range and my craving for wilderness.

'I think we have a biological need for natural awe,' he replies. 'It's like a hunger or thirst or the desire for good sleep or sex, and when that becomes activated your systems have to have more of it. My daughter rock climbs here and loves it. There's a hunger in people for awe.'

I am keen to get more expert perspectives on my experiences of walking in nature and their effect on trauma. I am also understanding more about the extent to which I agree with notions of a 'nature cure' – for me it is more 'nature care', since my symptoms of anxiety and depression can recur, which is why it is so important to be able to integrate regular contact with nature into the fabric of life.

Lynne Frederick of the No Panic charity tells me: 'Walking is excellent because people with anxiety use a lot of energy, so are often quite tired, but going for a walk helps the body to burn off the adrenalin and stress hormones. It can help calm the body down. When walking you release endorphins that make you feel better. With anxiety your brain can get tired and your body is preparing for flight or fight. It's going back to basics of how the body works and how the body and thoughts are connected because there is not enough awareness around that.'

I speak with Alan Kellas, a nature-based psychiatrist who is Green Care lead at the Royal College of Psychiatrists (RCP). Green Care is an emerging approach supported by the RCP, an umbrella for different projects that explore and promote nature connections in mental healthcare. He also points out wildlife organisations such as The Wildlife Trusts, Forestry England, the Woodland Organisations, the Canals and Rivers Trust, city farms and community allotments, and the NHS forest scheme, which do work that is also essential for people's health.

'I feel that there's a bridge to be built,' he tells me. 'There are ways in which mental health provision could be delivered outside of buildings, and in the natural world.'

I ask what actually happens to us when we're out in nature.

'We've evolved over thousands of years as biological as well as social creatures,' he replies. 'Our attention begins to change, becomes more focused and less peripheral. We notice differently. It engages all of our senses – visual, auditory, aesthetic. It often brings us back into the present, stops ruminations and helps us achieve what mindfulness practice does, which is coming into the moment. We start to breathe in a more relaxed way, which may mediate the change in our emotional regulation.'

Kellas points out that theories of how we develop as people, how our emotion and identity develop, are often based on our relationships with parents and family backgrounds, but he does not think there is enough attention on how a child relates to the natural world. Every cultural tradition has a story of relationship to the land and to place, which will be an influence. He adds: 'I think that what happens when in nature is that we access core biological memories that have evolved over centuries and generations. In that sense it helps reconnect us to a core self.'

Trauma happens at a very visceral level 'that goes much beyond words,' he says about experiences such as my own. Psychotherapies are moving towards more of a sense of integration of mind and body. Experiences can get 'burned into our physiology', so are not only at a cognitive level but also at a core physiological level.

'What is so shocking is that more people who observe such incidents as the one you went through don't side with the victim and show support – that can be for various reasons including going into a frozen state. With trauma there is the act that was perpetrated and then others' responses to it. The therapeutic challenge is to address not only the act, which was so abusive, but the neglect and lack of response of people who otherwise should be responsible and responsive.'

I tell him about my walking journey through the Pennines, and he asks if water featured at all.

'Absolutely,' I tell him. 'I've been following the course of rivers. I was in a state of anxiety but, as soon as I heard the water, it was like the stress drained away.'

'Being near water can make a difference physiologically. Think of the phrases we have such as "water under the bridge", "flow states", and so on. There's growing research on blue care as well as green care.' He continues, 'From a state of being frozen or trapped – the simple act of going for a walk to begin with, it's taking a degree of control or agency. Simple walking and movement itself can be transformative. We think about things differently when we move rather than sitting. Then what you describe powerfully is the idea of a journey as both internal and external. That's implicit in pilgrimages of all sorts. Landscape has been sacred in many cultures and the idea of walking through that landscape. Making a walking journey can be a creative as well as a spiritual act.'

He says that at times of existential conflict, we're trying to connect with core features of ourselves, which can prompt a quest-like journey, leaving the familiar, crossing a threshold and becoming immersed in the natural environment, and then returning and telling your story.

'What I love about the idea of such journeys,' he says, 'is that people might start out needing to do something for themselves but what they find is a gift both for themselves and for others – it's a social as well as individual process. You're bringing a gift back to other people.'

I tell him that some people advised me after my attack not to travel alone again but that's partly why I made this journey, to say: I'm not going to let this affect me in such a negative way or make me inert. Quite the opposite: I'm going to let it expand my world.

'A trauma can set off triggering reactions and then what happens is avoidance. It's the holy grail of therapeutic work, how you find the little flame inside a person when they move from freezing, stuckness and avoidance to thinking, "I could do that again." We begin to choose how we react to a situation.'

He mentions the psychiatrist and Holocaust survivor Viktor Frankl, who wrote about preserving the freedom to choose one's attitude in any set of given circumstances, to choose one's own way.

At the heart of sustainability questions and the climate and environmental crisis is our own relationship with the natural world, says Kellas. We need better understanding of how people and place connect: 'There are evolutionary, biological and cultural ways of looking at the history of human and place connections and there can be core traumas around our dispossession from the land.'

He goes on to make a powerful point: 'Where people have basic relationship problems, I think it should be the next step to ask: well, what about your relationship with water, or trees, or a dog or a bird? Our psyches aren't entirely defined by the human world alone and mostly, in unbearable mental states, where people can also turn to is the natural world.'

14

Forces

The sound of the river makes the heart soar, the River Tees rushing so forcefully, containing a music all of its own. I have been walking for a long while through Middleton-on-Teesdale in the North Pennines, aiming to find the track that leads to Langdon Beck, one of the remotest areas in the country, when I hear the river. Earlier, I had been curled up foetal-like, feeling a force of anxiety return and weigh me down – far worse than the weight of a backpack. In times of such anxiety it seems I can never move again, so it feels miraculous to be now putting one foot in front of the other, walking along the backbone of Britain.

The clouds have cleared to reveal blue skies and the most lucid light reflecting off trees part-green, part-golden. It is my aim to walk all the way to Langdon Beck, where I have planned to stay a few nights, before continuing onwards and upwards to Hadrian's Wall.

When I stop off for lunch at Rumours cafe in town, I ask the person serving about the journey to Langdon Beck, and other customers overhear and warn me what a long way away it is. My map is showing it is just two hours and eleven minutes' walk away, which does not seem too arduous, but the faces of the customers staring back tell a different story.

'It's very, very isolated there,' frowns one lady fore-
bodingly. 'And there's no phone signal further up, so
you won't be able to call anyone or use the internet.'
She pauses from eating to impart this warning,
reiterating just how remote the place is where I am
heading.

Despite the warnings, I'm feeling calm about the
journey ahead which looks straightforward, down a
single track along the River Tees, so it will – seemingly –
be difficult to get lost. The weather forecast is also
showing an interlude in rain for the next two days,
and I am determined to make the most of it. This
window of light is surrounded either side in the forecast
by heavy cloud and rain. It seems a window of hope, as
well as light, saying: get out and walk, and keep walking,
keep going.

'I wouldn't like to be walking on my own', says an
elderly man sitting at a table in the cafe with a lady,
eating lunch.

'You see more young ladies coming this way these
days, walking alone,' says the man at the counter. 'I always
worry for them.'

Despite their apprehensions, I am cheered by the
glimmers of light outside and by actually being here.
I finish off my salad and jacket potato, pull on an extra
layer of leggings in the cafe's Ladies, then stock up on
supplies from the shop next door including noodles,
scones and chocolate; sweetness will surely help soothe
any sense of isolation I might feel being alone tonight in
such a remote place.

I walk through the small town, stopping off at the
village bookshop and then onwards, relieved when

my map shows I am on the right route, heading deeper into the Area of Outstanding Natural Beauty in Upper Teesdale.

I walk along the River Tees lined with yews, beeches, silver birches, ferns, feeling its pulsing and pounding. Soon enough my backpack starts to strain my shoulders. I slept terribly last night, and it is mainly the lucidity of the light that is powering me on. I keep on, but when the pain worsens I consider flagging down one of the passing cars or vans and hitchhiking the rest of the way. I brush this thought aside, deciding to press on despite the pain.

I am feeling each footstep and the sheer fatigue to be all but unbearable, when a van pulls up and a young man with sandy-coloured hair and beard calls after me through its open window. I'm startled by the voice but turn towards it.

'I'm going to High Force,' he says. 'Feel free to have a ride there if that's where you're going.' He holds out his identification card showing his name and that he was born in 1993 and says: 'This is who I am, so you know I'm not some kind of weirdo. You can take a picture of it too if you want.'

I do take a photo of it for reassurance. Weighing up my sense of stranger danger with the pain in my shoulders, I decide to hop in and take the ride to the waterfall. Inside the van, there is a clutter of open energy drinks, food wrappers, a pair of children's shoes. He says he has two toddlers but has split up with their mother. He starts talking about his troubled home life and history of homelessness, and how he has often slept in his van. He is renting a place at the moment in

Doncaster, and has just come to visit the waterfall to 'get away from it all'. We reach the High Force Hotel, gateway to the waterfall and pull up in the car park and the man starts rolling a spliff and says he will need to smoke it before continuing. A part of me feels apprehensive, yet a part of me is intrigued, as I try to discern what colour his eyes are, shifting from hazel to green to brown.

I tell him I am going to leave my bag in the hotel before walking to the waterfall, and hop out of the van. The hotel kindly keeps my bag in a storage room, and sells me two tickets to the waterfall before I step out into even brighter sunshine. I consider venturing off on my own, but then in the distance I spot the young man walking in my direction, and we set off towards the sign pointing the way.

A sign 'High Force Walk and Woods' tells us how, one night in January 1992, Upper Teesdale was hit by one of the most severe gales in living memory and part of High Force Wood, through which the path passes, was 'totally devastated by the wind' and has had to be cleared. The trees that made up this part of the wood were a mixture of softwoods over a hundred years old and many over thirty metres high. The cleared area on the northern, high side of the path was replanted with a mixture of exotic and commercial conifers. The sign also tells how the footpath down to the bridge was so severely damaged by the falling trees and lifting roots that it had to be virtually rebuilt.

We head down the track and are soon walking through High Force Woods, amid trees of such stunning beauty, ablaze with all the colours of the season, some still green, others turning golden and amber in their death. I walk upon a path filled with leaves I want to linger to look at, but we press on.

Then I hear an enormous thundering, as if the earth is splitting open, and yet cannot see where the sound is coming from. We follow the sound, spirits raised and with childlike excitement, almost forgetting we are total strangers.

There it is in the distance, crashing down, gleaming white and rushing into the river, with bright sunlight behind making it sparkle like liquid diamonds: the waterfall. The word 'force' comes from 'foss', the Old Norse word for waterfalls, and derives from Viking settlers around 1,100 years ago, along with other local landscape words such as 'beck', 'dale', and 'fell'. *Force.* This local word for 'waterfall' is a word full of force itself, resonant with symbolism, drawing me to explore further.

As we draw closer, I can see that the water crashing from High Force and plunging over the precipice has strains of a metallic coppery colour due to the peat of the Pennines. The Force itself is formed by the River Tees dropping twenty-one metres into the deep gorge below.

We follow the path down towards the force. We walk and walk until the path ends and I step out onto rocks right beside the waterfall, so close to its power and energy. I look out over the waterfall as it cascades down from amid dark grey-black rock face, the first time I have laid eyes on the Great Whin Sill. A sign reading 'Force of Nature' produced by the North Pennines AONB Partnership tells me more about what this astonishing natural landscape is made of, and how it formed.[90]

The Great Whin Sill over which the Force plunges formed 295 million years ago from molten rock that solidified underground between older layers of rock, and is a key feature of the backbone of Britain. Whin Sill is quartz dolerite igneous rock, dense, hard and black and more resistant to erosion and weathering than limestone and other sedimentary rocks.[91] It can also be seen elsewhere in this region of the North including Low Force, Holwick Scars, Cronkley Scar, Falcon Clints and Cauldron Snout as well as in Hadrian's Wall. Below the Whin Sill at High Force are rocks that formed 330 million years ago when the North Pennines were still at the equator. There is a layer of sandstone that was once sand in a river delta, and of limestone formed from limy ooze in a tropical sea.

What is the North made of? And how did the North make me? These are questions I've been probing throughout my journey. I learn what the North is made of literally here, how molten rock was pushed up from the earth's surface, cooled and crystallised to form the Great Whin Sill. The hard black rock's resistance to erosion is a quality that created the astonishing geomorphological landscapes such as High Force and Low Force. It also helps to support Alpine/Arctic flora including bird's-eye primrose, spring gentian, mountain avens and the Teesdale violet.[92]

Meanwhile, the gorge I spend a long time gazing at was sculpted by water, a process that began at least 15,000 years ago with ice-age meltwaters, and continues with the action of the river today. The waterfall is progressively moving upstream as the water wears away the rock. Trees grow right to the edge of the river, and just by the Great Whin Sill yellow-gold-amber-green leaves are a glory of colour against the black rock.

Beneath the Force, I clamber over giant, dark rocks upon which patches of emerald-green moss grow. It truly does feel like walking through and on a backbone, with such ancient rock formations. Yet there are also substances of such softness all around, not least the waterfall cascading into a deep gorge. That combination of rock and running water, that hardness and softness, is powerful. I think of the quality of magma,[93] a semi-liquid, molten rock with a temperature over 1,000 degrees Celsius that, in rising up from deep within the earth due to stretching of the earth's crust, caused the Whin Sill to come into being.

My companion has walked all the way to the furthest rocks, right by the water and as close as possible to the waterfall, and he calls out encouraging me to do the same. He seems so at home here, navigating the wild.

'Come on over, it's perfectly safe…'

I'm apprehensive at first but I put one foot carefully in front of the other, feeling the footholds beneath, until I am close enough for him to reach out a hand and my heart quickens at the contact. I clamber over one of the particularly large rocks until we are standing on the same one and we watch the water for a while.

It is true that walking with so much 'deep time' beneath my feet and all around, and surrounded by those awesome forces of nature, takes me out of my own anxiety, albeit temporarily. Anxiety can be such a strong force, sucking everything into its dark vortex. But the force of life crashing over the Great Whin Sill is more powerful today, and it absorbs my entire attention.

The great stones I walk over have such a luminescence to them they seem alive. I am walking over rocks when a rainbow appears, arching over the Force. It seems a miracle, and I drink in the sight of its strong colours, from red through to violet, marvelling at its existence and yet how unpalpable it is, how I can see it yet if I reach out my hand not touch it. I look at my companion's eyes as they subtly change colour depending on the light and I see the rainbow reflected in them.

What is the North made of? And how is it making me? Be hard like rock, but tender too. Oh, to have backbone as strong as the Whin Sill of the North, to be resistant and unbreakable. To be able to gleam bright after storms. Yet to be soft too, tender enough to feel life in all its glory. I think of the landscape all around me, the solidity and softness, the Whin Sill and the moss and the water. I think of the landscape of the human body, the bone and the lifeblood and the water, the oxygen flowing through the veins, that hardness and softness both essential for existence.

I want to stay in this place for as long as possible, savouring the light and colour and sounds. It is little wonder that J.M.W. Turner chose High Force as a scene to immortalise in an artwork one morning in 1816, before he made his way to Cauldron Snout, which I also plan to visit. We linger for a while longer, drinking in the light.

My companion tells me how much he loves the place, and how he visited the place once as a child with his father. As we walk back through High Force Woods,

I ask him if he knows much about nature, and he says not much but then reels off the names of the trees and plants and bushes. I see a great leaf fallen to the ground, startlingly green amid brown leaves, and he identifies it as a fern. We pass a tree with a thin bark, bowed over the river as if yearning for it. He tells me the branches of beech trees drop without warning and grow again, self-regenerating. He hands me an oak leaf, dark green at its heart, green still in its main body, yellowing so far only in the outer edges.

'This is a spruce tree, which is a good insulator if you need to sleep outside,' he says, pointing up at a tree so huge I crane my neck to see.

'Have you slept under a spruce before?' I ask.

'Many a time,' he says.

'Where?' I ask

'Many places, when I was homeless. And I was drinking half a bottle of whisky every night.'

'So whereabouts?'

'All the villages around here.'

We pass dead ferns that have turned golden, very beautiful in their dying and death. I look at the delicacy and beauty of leaves. There are some bird feeders in a beech tree, and I spot a bird feeding before fluttering away. I hear birds singing but cannot quite identify the sweet sound. I look at silver birches; with the eye-engravings in their bark they seem to be looking at us too.

We pass another tree that has blown over – 'probably another beech,' he muses – and walk on past the most enormous tree –'perhaps an oak'. I stand under it for a few moments, marvelling and gazing through its branches at the burnished leaves and startlingly blue sky. We continue to walk back to where we set off from, savouring each moment of the light, past bright-red berries in trees, on along the River Tees, and look back to see the Force shrinking away into the distance, disappearing around a bend, and then it is out of sight.

I recall the poet Robert Frost's phrase 'talks-walking' – that potent combination of walking and talking, of place and people (Frost coined the term for his walks with Edward Thomas) – and how, although I set off on this journey alone, I have had so many talks-walk experiences with strangers along the way who have shared some of the most painful parts of their lives, as well as being living maps and encyclopaedias to the places through which we've walked.

My companion tells me about a point in the River Tees where it joins the River Greta and creates an optical illusion that the water is flowing uphill. I gaze out at the glint of the river and remember the folklore figure of Peg Powler, a green-haired, green-skinned water spirit and witch inhabiting the River Tees who lured people into the river to drown and would drag children into the water if they got too close to the edge. The foam floating on the river is called by some 'Peg Powler's suds'.

We walk on through the woods until we reach the entrance and an arrow 'To the Falls'. I notice a sign reading: 'High Force Charges. (Adults 16+ £1.50. Children .50p)'. Beneath the charges is written: 'Warning and Conditions of Admittance. Persons visiting High Force do so at their own risk and will indemnify Lord Barnard, the Upper Teesdale Estate and its employees against any claim of whatsoever nature arising in connection with their visit.' An astonishing amount of land in this area is owned by

the Raby Estate, headed by Barnard. I think of how deeply
the class system is still a reality, aristocrats owning vast
amounts of land and my companion homeless and
sleeping curled up beneath a spruce tree. I remember the
Manchester Ramblers and the footsteps they took all
those years ago to open up access to countryside owned
by the rich – and their legacy, why I have been able to
walk through this Area of Outstanding Natural Beauty
today at all, albeit paying £1.50 for the privilege.

We sit for a while together inside the hotel and I
drink a cup of tea. I check social media and my heart
lurches as I see tributes to the writer and journalist
Deborah Orr flooding Twitter. Tears well. I say that
someone I know has died, what a shock it is. Although
I only met Deborah twice, she was one of those people
who quickly get past 'small talk' and we had chatted
deeply about topics including class and the literary and
media world, and the barriers of class that can stop
someone from getting a foothold in the industry. We did
have some actual 'small talk' too, laughing about how
short we both were, what a relief it was to stop wearing
heels to affect a greater height, how liberating it was to
be ourselves. We were also both scheduled contributors
to a forthcoming nature-writing anthology, *Women on
Nature*, and had become friends on Twitter and Instagram.
I knew that Deborah was in hospital with cancer,
following her updates about it, but the shock nevertheless
is intense. She had recently liked my post on Instagram
of some purple and white flowers: 'When in severe pain
even continuing to exist for another minute can seem
impossible to do; sometimes only remembered moments
of joy, respite and beauty take one moment to the next.'

I was alluding to emotional and psychological pain, though Deborah of course was also in extreme physical pain. How odd the digital age is, how we form connections online, through a name flashing up in affirmation and acknowledgement, how weird to learn about someone's death online in this way, to see them go from present to past tense: 'Deborah was…' How oddly disembodying is the age we are living in. I feel another hole torn in the world, the shock of a death, the way a small part of us never believes that people we know will die, that they will go on living for ever and ever – and the ways they do, their words living on always, the memory of the smile of recognition she gave me and the warm hug before we parted ways.

My companion offers to give me a lift up the long road to Langdon Beck and I accept with gratitude. My knees have buckled beneath me on news of Deborah's death and the world feels vertiginous. We drive in silence up the long and deserted road, deeper into isolation with no humans in sight at all, driving into miles of moorland.

'I'd seen you walking through town earlier from the Co-op, and I waved at you but you didn't wave back so I drove after you…'

A chill passes over me. He followed me. I think back to when I was walking through town and vaguely remember seeing a young man from the corner of my vision loitering and looking my way. I remain silent. Then the van stops on a spookily remote stretch of land, and I glimpse a large building in the distance, which is apparently the hostel where I'll be staying – it being too cold for camping – but looks like no hostel I have seen before. A sliver of fear steals through me. A small part of me wonders if he will try and come in, if all those people in the cafe warning me not to walk alone, if Bob and Kathleen the elderly couple I met in Settle beseeching me not to travel alone, if they were all right and I will in fact be raped and murdered out here in the wilderness. But he does not pursue anything other than giving me a lift and bidding farewell.

I come to learn more about the fascinating geology of the North Pennines during this stage of my journey, about what the earth is actually made of and what made the earth, about the ground beneath our feet.

I visit 'the Geology Room' which is part of the Langdon Beck Hotel, apparently the most remote hotel in the country. In this area there is only the hostel and hotel, surrounded by miles of moorland. There, I learn how rich the area is in minerals. Veins of lead ore (the mineral galena) and other minerals formed around 290 million years ago when mineral–rich waters flowed through fractures underground, warmed by heat from the buried Weardale Granite. While the fluids cooled, mineral veins were formed by dissolved minerals crystallising in the fractures. Such mineral deposits were the bedrock of the North Pennines economy for centuries, with mining booming in the eighteenth and nineteenth centuries when the area's lead mines were of global importance. The landscape of Upper Teesdale bears the scars of its mining past with shafts, opencast workings and spoil heaps. Other minerals that were mined in the area include iron ores, zinc ore (sphalerite), fluorite, and barium minerals. It is little wonder that, as well as being an Area of Outstanding Natural Beauty, the North Pennines is also a UNESCO Global Geopark and part of the European Geoparks Network.

If this section of my journey is themed around 'Feet', I have also been yearning for flight, to be a creature who can be more than earthbound. Those dreams come closest to being fulfilled when looking out for the birds of the North Pennines as I go for a walk alone through the moorlands. I set out to walk along the backbone of Britain alone, and yet my journey has become peopled with those I have met along the way, young and old, with strangers who have become walking companions. Walking with another is a way of experiencing the world with extra senses: Rori hearing the roar of Hull Pot so we could follow it there, my companion today spotting the spruce trees and sharing his story of sleeping homeless beneath them. Yet it is also blissful now to walk completely alone, immersed fully in the landscape. It is bitingly cold now the sun has sunk, taking its wintry warmth, and the cold whips tears from my eyes, but I am wrapped up well and eager to explore, to lose myself in the landscape.

Although many are beginning to make their great migratory journey for the winter, as we draw ever closer to the end of British Summer Time, there are some birds that hang around, inhabiting the area even in the harshest of winters. I delight in trying to identify the birds, in listening to their songs and trying to pick out their defining features. They are frequently far too fast for me, though, soaring away when I lay eyes on them.

As I walk alone over miles of open moorland around Cronkley Scar, I look out for birds that inhabit the North Pennines high moors, including merlins, a small falcon with quick wingbeats that hunts larks and pipits, enjoys perching on rocks and has a call that sounds like '*wik, wik, wik*'. I look out for dunlins and their tiny, fast, twisting flight and shrill '*tsee*' call. I look out and listen out for golden plovers. I watch for red grouse who fly low and fast in quick bursts and glide always near heather, and stay tuned for their call that apparently sounds like 'go back, go back'. I learned such identifying features on a helpful poster on the wall outside Langdon Beck's Geology Room, such places filled with the kind of distinct knowledge that locals have.

Then I hear a flurry of wingbeats, see a flash of fierce eyes and am sure it was a short-eared owl, flapping away suddenly from a fence-post before vanishing into the growing dusk.

As I walk on, I look out for grassland birds, including black grouse and lapwings, which have a tumbling flight on their black and white wings and a distinctive crest and a '*pee-wit*' call and are rarely to be found perched on posts or walls but always in the air or on the ground. I yearn to see a curlew and hear its wild, bubbling call, to see its long, down-curved bill and see it soaring on its arched wings. As I walk, I slip through a time-gap and am a child again, longing to be a bird so much that I became one in my dreams, feeling the sensation of flying, soaring way above the chimney-tops, high above my hometown, far beyond bruises and bad words, soaring all the way to the glorious Lakes. I looked down on my bedroom from on high and saw myself in there, saw the street where I lived and saw the great beyond. Looking down upon my life in this way, I felt all the turbulent emotions drain away. I felt a great peace wash through me. I flew in my dreams, somersaulted through the sky in great arches, stretched out so that all the stiffness drained out of my limbs and I flew all the way to the Lakes whenever I wanted and watched the moonlight glinting on the black expanses of water. I knew that, whenever I felt trapped in the house, I would be able to escape; in my dreams I soared and soared and soared.

The sound of the Forces rushes through my dreams and I dream too of the hot magma at the core of the earth, bringing the Whin Sill into being. While surrounded by 'forces', it's a symbolic place to consider the forces that have propelled me throughout my journey, forces of hate and hope, fear and courage. At moments when my journey has felt toughest, when I have felt like giving up and turning back, when the road has felt too rocky for another step, it has been hope that has driven me on, a determination not to let despair win out, to try and have some magma or 'fire in the belly'.

There are other forces that can shape a life, including those of systemic inequality, social and racial injustice, and I consider the extent to which we can fight back. I think of my earlier companion slipping into a rut of homelessness and sleeping under a spruce tree, and of those times when I too have had no home. While I have found a sense of home in the wild, we all need actual homes too and not to be rendered literally homeless.

The next morning I wake into mist hanging over the Cronkley Scar, which looms near the hostel. I walk through the mist to the strange formation jutting out of the earth, it too made of the Great Whin Sill. It was due to faults in limestone layers, and magma oozing through those faults and hardening, that such landscape formations came into being. It was movement of the earth's tectonic plates during the Carboniferous period that caused the igneous intrusions of magma across much of northern England.

I head to the pub, which is part of the hotel, for lunch and am tucking into fish and chips when I get chatting to two elderly men who offer advice about where I should walk next. One of them, Frank, is ninety. He asks me about my travels and I tell him the short version. When he asks further, I tell him the whole story including about being racially abused on a TransPennine train, and he congratulates me for making this journey, and condemns what happened to me. He tells me about the landscape and the flower of the area, the gentian.

I walk to Low Force, in much gloomier weather. Low Force itself is impressive and I watch the river cascade over a ledge of rock into a plunge pool then continue on its way to the North Sea. I gaze at that tough dolerite Whin Sill that no water can erode, the reason these waterfalls exist at all due to the strength of that rock.

I contemplate the difference between being alone and being lonely. When alone walking through these vast natural landscapes, I have not been feeling lonely. But when I see a family together near Low Force a sense of loneliness does creep in. Perhaps it is the gloom of the weather, so different from yesterday. I am also feeling the loss of loved ones, dear friends, thinking how much they would have loved it here.

I walk on through juniper woods and feel that seep of loneliness slip away as I admire the woods, and the peculiarly arched trees, shaped by winds. Juniper trees are a species that are 'protected'. They provide habitat for lichen, fungi and insects and are a source of food. Yet this important tree – one of the first trees to inhabit Britain at the end of the Ice Age – is at risk due to a fungus that has been killing them off.[94]

Here, high in the North Pennines, is one of the few places in Britain where you can see the most ancient plants, such as lichens, mosses and fungi in autumn and winter, gentians and wood anemone in spring, and globeflowers and heather in summer, which have so far managed to survive since the Ice Age.[95] Thinking about such deep time all around draws me out of my loneliness, as I feel how fleeting a human life is, how miraculous that mine has for these moments crossed paths with such astonishing lifeforms, which provide a kind of companionship. I feel how the natural world can be in friendship with us and we with the natural world. I recall Viktor Frankl's description of a dying woman in a concentration camp who through the window could see just one branch of a chestnut tree with two blossoms upon it; she described the tree as 'the only friend' she had in her loneliness.

The highest and largest National Nature Reserve in the country, comprised of 8,800 hectares of upland country, is here in the North Pennines: Moor House-Upper Teesdale National Nature Reserve, straddling both Cumbria and County Durham. It was designated a UNESCO biosphere reserve in 1976 and there is nowhere else in Britain that has such a diversity of rare habitats in one location.[96] A large part of the River Tees – from its source near Great Dun Fell (the second highest mountain in the Pennines, after Cross Fell) to High Force waterfall – flows through the boundaries of this nature reserve. The Trout Beck flows entirely through it and is an ECN Freshwater Site. The Pennine Way also passes through both halves of the reserve.

I wake early to try and walk to and through Moor House-Upper Teesdale National Nature Reserve, Cow Green Reservoir and Cauldron Snout. I step outside and walk towards light reflecting off a fell, turning it silvery and emerald-coloured. After the gloom of yesterday, it is another bright day, and the fell looks like a different creature entirely with light reflecting off it. Whereas yesterday it seemed imposing, frightening, a beast sleeping in the land and something to keep away from, today it looks enticing, full of secrets, something to enter into. I walk towards the fell, whose name I later discover is Cronkley Fell, and am awed each step I take closer. I follow a path and see signs pointing towards the Pennine Way. As I reach the top of the path I see a cluster of cows coloured white, black, dark brown, beige, and one cow reflecting the sun looks like it is made out of gold. Most of them are oblivious to me and continue grazing, though some look towards me with their large, oval eyes.

I walk on and see another sign pointing towards the Pennine Way and Cauldron Snout and follow it, but then all tracks seem to disappear. I follow my map, and it leads me to a small stone wall with stone steps. Clambering over the wall, I reach another hay meadow, this one thick with mud and cow pat. I continue walking and glance down at my map, which shows I have strayed off the right path. I turn around and look for the right direction, but I am truly lost. Whichever way I walk, my map shows I am going off grid. I spend more time seeking the right path but then, with a sigh of resignation, walk towards the one lonely tree in the meadow. The Pennine Way seems to have vanished entirely.

There is a great shudder and the sound of whirring, loud and strong, and at first I think it is some kind of engine, until an enormous bird beats its wings and soars away from the tree so quickly I don't have time to inspect it or try to identify it. It is the largest bird I have ever seen, a flurry of brown wings, and making a sound of such great force the like of which I have never heard from a bird.

I look again for the path, but it is as if it has disappeared into a strange no-man's land, some kind of vortex, and I shiver with a sudden sense of eeriness, a true shiver even though I now feel anything but cold with the light which has risen and warmed both myself and the landscape.

I decide to abandon the pre-set path and instead walk through the meadow, letting my feet guide me, forging 'desire lines'. I turn around to catch a glorious sight of the River Tees glinting as a slick of silver under the sun, a brilliant sheen glowing against the green. Hearing the rushing of water too is so soothing, and I follow the

sight and the sound of the river. I walk along it upon
the greenest grass I have seen, the skin of the earth.
Skin. Backbone. Lifeblood. Heartbeat. Feet. Of what am
I made? I am made of skin, bone, water, blood, minerals,
trace elements. I am made of some of the same stuff as
the earth. As I walk I let my journey so far flow through
my mind, and my body seems to merge with the body of
the landscape.

I let my feet watch the earth (inspired by Nan
Shepherd, who wrote: "My eyes were in my feet").
I walk along a path whose puddles reflect the sky with
huge white fluffy clouds threatening no more rain for a
while. On reaching a stone wall and seeing a shed with
an ominous red warning triangle in the distance, I decide
to about-turn and find another route along the river.

I am so in love with the river and decide to take a path
that runs alongside it. I have not been feeling well – still
the churning anxiety – and walking by the river and
hearing it takes me out of anxious thoughts. I let go of the
Cow Green Reservoir in my mind, leaving it out there as
a place not for me today but for another time, and it slips
away from my desires and becomes like Malham Tarn, a
place out there but too far beyond the bounds of my
capacities or wishes. Such places are like boundary markers
of what I am physically capable or wish for, and walking is
a way of finding such markers, sometimes reaching and
even going beyond them, sometimes accepting the limits,
and on some occasions encountering unexpected but
most welcome natural wonders.

I find a silver gate that would be easy to miss, then
push it open and step onto a very narrow path, and clink
the gate shut behind me. It is not so much a footpath,

more a way to walk by the river, over pebbles and grass, which takes all my care. Here is a place where every footstep must be taken with care, and I recall Malham Cove and those great limestone boulders at the top, how every step required all my concentration so that walking became a kind of meditation.

As I walk, the way beneath my feet opens out and it becomes easier in some places, flatter, and then narrows in again and becomes more filled with rocks to clamber over. Then I step out into meadowland by the river and the river suddenly seems swollen and larger, with great black boulders silhouetted on its surface. I look down on the map and see how the river is joined by another tributary. Beyond the gorgeous gleam of the river fells rise in the distance.

I now sense how alone I am in this immense landscape and am so glad I did not follow the original path but instead followed my gut. I am so grateful for another day of light. Someone had warned me that it was not a sensible season to be going to the North Pennines due to the cold, but I end up taking off my coat and stripping off a layer, peeling off my purple woolly polo neck in the autumn sunshine. I take a sip from my water bottle and am revived by the cold liquid flowing through me, as by the sight of the water running beside me, and consider how important water is to the land, and to our human body.

I hear and feel a flurry of beating wings, so close as if coming from within me, and then a bird soars as if from me, I see its body and its wings and then it is gone. So much for identifying birds; they are way too fast for my eyes to linger upon.

I continue walking along the river with not another soul in sight. I walk and walk and walk and it seems as if my heart is beating in my feet.

Then I see a bridge and walk over, towards one of the great emerald fells, over the silver sheen of river beneath, and on the other side I see a sign: 'Welcome to Moor House-Upper Teesdale National Nature Reserve'. I exhale. My heart soars and I feel more delight than I have in a while. I made it. It turns out I have already walked through part of the nature reserve, as the juniper woods stretching between High Force and Low Force form part of it, but it is a joy to see a marker for it, having been so lost earlier but now reaching where I had wanted to go through an unexpectedly beautiful route. The sign tells me that the nature reserve rises to 876 metres and covers some 88 square kilometres of special upland habitats. It is Britain's leading site for research into the effects of a changing climate on the natural environment. The nature reserve is rich in unique Arctic-alpine plants that have survived here since the last Ice Age and are conserved by moorland management and traditional farming. The sign also urges visitors to help look after the site by following the Countryside Code.

My heart always sings to see a detailed map embedded in the landscape showing where I am. The map on the board in front of me shows the words YOU ARE HERE with an arrow pointing to a yellow line that winds its way through a great expanse of green. Yellow marks the Pennine Way, the large red dashes are the bridleway, the small red dots are public footpaths, the thick red line is the Nature Trail, while a red box with diagonal lines inside means MOD Danger Area. I inspect where I am: right

on the Pennine Way and beside the River Tees, and in
the country's largest, highest nature reserve in the heart
of the North Pennines, on the backbone of Britain.
To my west a jagged black curve with toothpick-like
protrudings marks Cronkley Scar, further south-west is
Cronkley Fell. To the west, past Widdybank Fell, is Cow
Green Reservoir and Cauldron Snout, and Great
Cocklake. To my south, beyond the green area, are many
amber lines and the words LUNE FOREST, and to the
east, LUNE MOOR. To my east is High Force and
beyond are jagged black markings showing Holwick
Scars. I see several caves and crags and mines marked,
some named, some unnamed. To the north of me is
Langdon Beck, and then beyond the green edge a large
area of swirling amber lines and the words LANGDON
COMMON. To the edge of the map is a black arrow
pointing up and the single word: NORTH.

I drink in the map in fascination, trying to learn by
heart all those lines and curves and colours delineating
the landscape, before leaving it to walk back into the
landscape for real, letting my feet again be my guide.

I continue walking through hay meadows, limestone
grasslands, blanket bog with high fells all around, truly
like giant emeralds in this bright light. I hear a clear,
high-pitched sound of a bird and treasure the sound
without yearning to name it. I hear the rushing of the
river, the sweetest sound. I hear nothing else, no beeping
of my phone, no chatter of people, no engines growling
or car-horns shrieking or alarms blaring.

I head up the only path I can see and at the top of the
hill there is the first trace of human habitation I have
seen in a while – and a delicious one too: a little stall

with a sign saying 'Tuck Shop' with cans of Tango, Coca-Cola, 7up and a box of Mars Bars. There is a jar of money too, pound coins glinting. How trusting people are here, to leave money and food out like this, how unthinkable seeing this in a city. I walk through the open gate of a farm, calling 'helloooo', hoping to find a human who can point the way since I am lost again, but my voice echoes and there is no response. I walk back down the hill, then the memory of Tango calls me back, and I return to the tuck shop, leave a pound and take a drink.

I walk back down the hill towards the river and become lost again, and cannot find the route towards High Force. I walk along the river until I reach a thin wedge of wood stretched across the water. It is the only way to cross the river here and, after some hesitation, I do so and continue walking over large boulders and rocks, past a tree with bright berries. I grow more apprehensive as it becomes harder to walk, the land so much boggier beside the rushing river. I stumble and almost slip into the river, and Peg Powler the river-witch flashes into my mind.

I am suddenly startled out of my skin by a loud cawing, and a giant bird beats its wings, and the blood rushes to my head as the bird caws again while also making a sound like its own heart thrumming, before it disappears from view. Ahead I see a gate that looks locked so I about-turn and rapidly walk back the way I came, filled with fear. This is wildness. Despite such signs of human habitation as the cute tuck shop, there is also such wildness here, creatures of the like I have never seen and cannot name, and creatures I can sense are wild and belong to the wilderness. Not the kind of creatures to be found prowling our cities – although there is a kind of wildness to be found in cities too – but those creatures belonging to and beloved of these remote fells, these great open skies. I walk back, unsettled by such an eerie and unfamiliar sound from that great bird, the hugest winged living thing I have ever seen. I am so filled with fear by the force of its sound and beating wings, imagining it flying after me and attacking me, so filled with fear I slip and lose my footing often and take the wrong path, right into a prickly bush filled with red berries. I look to my right and see that perilously narrow ledge across the river I had walked across and head back towards it. I breathe deeply, trying to slow my heartbeat. I reach the ledge and see just how thin it is, large enough only for one foot. Beneath it churns the river, rushing with such great force; how deep it is I am not sure. I put my left foot on the ledge and it creaks and sinks then I bring my right foot over and jump onto the grass ahead. I have done it, I am over the river and with miles of open moorland stretching ahead, the green skin of the earth beneath me, and I walk and walk until my heartbeat has again stabilised.

Beside the river rushing silver, I gaze at black rocks protruding, the glory of the earth's green skin, the blue skies and white clouds, golden maize, a sudden startle of red berries. I follow the path back and Cronkley Fell looms closer, a part of the Whin Sill. I get lost again, until the blue heartbeat of my map shows I am back on the right path. I hear a sweet, high-pitched singing though cannot see the bird. I feel again the huge force of that great bird earlier, the thrumming of its wings, and what sounded like the beating of its heart, and I wonder what it was communicating in the sound it made. *I belong here*, it seemed to say, right here, in its element, amid the elements. How threatened so many bird species are, by those who do not believe they belong here or who don't care that they do and would shoot them dead or pollute the environment or destroy their habitats, their homes, so they cannot survive.

I recall reading how the moorlands of Upper Teesdale are a vital refuge and breeding ground for the black grouse, one of England's rarest birds, which once existed in abundance but is now restricted to a few places in the North. The North Pennines is the home of over 80 per cent of the population of England's black grouse birds due to the mix of habitats needed for the birds to flourish. A Natural England sign told me the unforgettable nugget that black grouse are famous for the males' flamboyant courtship displays known as lekking, in which male grouse dance around and call to female birds who attend the leks to select a mate. These leks occur throughout the year at gathering sites.

I walk the long path back to the hostel to retrieve my beast of a bag; it has been a delight to do some walking without its weight upon my weary shoulders. I lug it out from the storage cupboard and sit for a while. The lady working there comes to say goodbye. I see a glitter from the corner of my eye and it is a large crystal. She tells me it is purple fluorite, which is good for emotional balance. She tells me how her partner died of cancer three years ago, and how purple fluorite is precious to her since he gave her a piece of it, how it reminds her of him. I express my sympathies for his death and we chat for a while, about how suddenly illness can come on, how

fleeting life is. Then she tells me about how she also saw
the mineral when she was climbing Cross Fell, how she
hadn't realised it was the highest mountain in the North
Pennines, but it was one of her greatest senses of
achievement to be climbing it, and how she saw purple
fluorite glittering on its surface.

Glittering minerals and crystals surround me in the
Geology Room of Langdon Beck Hotel, where I am
staying one night before moving further north. It is a
haven of blissful respite to step into my light-filled room
there, warm and dry and so quiet, with a window
overlooking the moor. I had been awoken early at the
hostel – which became more hostile than hostel – by a
loud knocking. I shouted through the door that I was
still in bed, and a man's voice thundered through the
door, demanding I leave the hostel as it closes at 10 a.m.
I insisted I didn't have to leave since I had paid for the
night and had checked that guests could stay during the
day. It turns out he was a volunteer who was not aware
of the regulations that allowed people to stay during the
day. It is a relief to be spending a night in a place I won't
get shouted out of my dreams.

That evening I attend an event called the Science of
the Sun and Moon as it is Stargazing Week in the North
Pennines and, although too cloudy that night for actual
stargazing, I nevertheless dream of future nights watching
the stars. After the event, I sit by a roaring fire in the pub,
researching the journey ahead, and the landlady offers
me a lift to Middleton-on-Tees dale the next morning.

I ask if anyone happened to be going to Alston the next day, a place in the Pennines I have only dreamed of going as it seems so remote and wild, so hard to reach by the humble human feet (well, by my feet anyway, which are growing sorer by the day). Theo who is working at the bar does not look hopeful as he points out that it is over 30 kilometres away. Later that evening, he mentions that someone called Emma will be heading to Alston the next morning and might be able to give me a lift.

The next morning is so misty that I cannot even see an inch ahead. I nevertheless walk for a while, enjoying the sense of being submerged, the bodily vanishing, the eeriness of an element that can blot out the world in this way. Walking in the mist, I sense how high up I am, for surely this is a cloud itself I am walking through, so many hundreds of feet above sea level am I.

I head back to the hotel and have a hearty breakfast during which the landlady tells me she is originally from Moss Side, Manchester, and we laugh at how us Mancunians are to be found in every corner of the globe. She also tells me that her late husband, the long-time landlord of the place, had a passion for geology and the Geology Room is his legacy. An image surfaces in my mind of those glittering crystals and minerals, so strong, permanent, living on long after the person who loved them passed away; seeming to store in them some of that love. How haunted places are.

Emma and I head for Alston. Emma is nineteen, lives locally, and tells me how only four people were at her village school, how she learned maths through counting sheep on the farm she grew up on. We swerve through the fells, the mist still so dense it is impossible to see beyond it, but Emma seems to know the twists and turns of this place like the lines on her hand. She tells me about the way of life here on the remote fell, how in the winter of 2010 the fell was snowed in for a fortnight, how every winter there is such deep snow, and how the community of villages and villagers help each other out if anyone is in trouble – kindness that makes the backbone of such remote communities.

We see Alston in the distance, a cluster of rooftops amid the trees, and my excitement grows to be finally arriving in a place that is both in the North Pennines and in Cumbria, and reputedly the highest settlement in England, rising 300 metres above sea level. It is a place W.H. Auden called his 'great good place', his 'Mutterland', and had a map of it hanging over his desk – how Auden loved limestone landscapes such as this.

Emma drops me outside The Angel Inn, where I will be staying. It is closed and so I step into the nearby Cumbrian Pantry: empty. I hesitate before ordering tea and settling down to use the Wi-Fi. The cafe fills up with a father and son, both with long white hair and beards, who chatter about Hadrian's Wall, about the formidable amount of footsteps that have fallen in the area, about what it is made of, the chatter punctuated with the son's urge to his father that he is doing well to be out here. Soon an hour has passed, during which my anxiety has risen again, clutching my throat. I start to feel claustrophobic, but it has hit 11 a.m. and so the Angel should be opening. The innkeeper tells me I am the first here so can choose my room, and I am delighted at the sight of a room with artwork of autumn leaves and another of a gentian flower – all for a third of the price of the room I have just paid for, for my forthcoming stay in Newcastle. I leave my bag and head out to explore.

The day has brightened as I head towards the historic South Tynedale Railway station, England's highest narrow-gauge railway. I buy a ticket for the 1 p.m. train, which runs a roundtrip through the valley, and then set off on a walk. I find the path down to the river, and very soon the small settlement of Alston gives way to the astonishments of the natural world; signs of human habitation vanish in place of the rushing of the river, rowan trees, an abundance of amber leaves. Already that snake of anxiety clutching my neck and gripping my heart unwinds itself and soon slips away, and the river soothes and calms; the river is so much stronger. How beautiful are these leaves even as they are dying, burning golden in their final days. It is only a few days until Daylight Saving Time, and how precious this light is, how rare and special this clarity, for the forecast just yesterday had been for rain and cloud.

After walking alone for some time, I see two men in work uniforms sweeping away leaves. One looks at me, and I smile and comment on what a beautiful day it is.

'What country are you from?' he asks.

'England,' I say and he looks a little bemused.

I walk on and stand on a bridge, and there in front of me is another 'force', the Seven Sisters Waterfall, plunging into the river. Six separate columns of white water rush down into the river. It is a baby force compared to High Force and even Low Force, but a force nonetheless.

Alston does feel like a great place and a good place today, as Auden described it. The quality of light today is truly great, and the air I breathe is so good that I breathe more deeply than I have in a long time, letting the light warm my skin. I recall the scaremonger who told me I was foolish to be going to the North Pennines in this season, that I would probably perish in the Pennines so cold and bleak and inhospitable would it be.

I walk for a while longer, following the force as it flows into the river and becomes the river, and let my mind be clear of everything but the water, the trees in all their turning colours, the blueness of the sky and the lucidity of the day.

Soon there are only twenty minutes left until the train departs so I hurry back to the railway station and buy a hot tea for the journey ahead. Settled into the train already is a family with young children. I take a seat in a carriage with open windows and soon it sets off.

'You'll die of hypothermia!' a disembodied voice shouts after the train as it speeds away into the fells, and I laugh though cannot place who the voice belongs to, and soon we are far away from the station.

I do feel the wind cold on my skin but it is refreshing and enlivening to be moving through the world on a train with no window between me and the world, no glass blocking off the landscape. As I begin to feel colder, I put on my woolly purple turtleneck and am soon snug again and far from dying of hypothermia. The train engine growls, I remember that great bird and the thrumming of its heart, the bird who seemed to be saying *I belong here*.

I look out over fir trees on the fell in the distance, dark green and gold, and try to identify the other trees we pass, so close to the carriage: lime trees with bright yellow and green leaves, sycamore trees, oak trees, the startle of a rowan, or possibly rose-hip, and many marvellous maple trees. The train passes under some stone arches but mostly through miles of meadowland and moorland, remote and wild. I watch so many brilliant gold leaves against blue sky. Shadows fall into the carriages, shadows of silver birch trees, shadows of leaves, shadows of barks and branches and our bodies.

The train pulls up at a place called Slaggyford, where we wait for a while – an unfortunately named place, you might think, but it is interesting to discover the original meaning of the word 'slag', now become yet another abusive term to describe a woman. 'Slag' is the glass-like by-product left after a desired metal has been smelted, or separated, from the raw ore.

A light rain has begun to fall and the train is ready to take us back to Alston. The family with children move to sit inside the sheltered train carriage. I dither for a while about whether to sit inside or in the open-air carriage, eventually choosing the latter. It is empty but for a man who tells me he is eighty-four years old, and I ask him if he knows the name of the trees we pass, and he helps to confirm that I am identifying them correctly.

'You can see most types of trees in this area,' he says, 'Firs, beeches, sycamores, limes…'

What is so unique and special about this area is its biodiversity. We talk about how the sheer diversity of species in the natural world is vital for the survival of the planet – and so too the diversity of human beings. Considering human and biodiversity together throughout my journey is showing how people and place are inextricably connected, how we must care both for the earth and for each other.

The train pulls into the great, good place of Alston. I am standing at the platform, soaking in the scene in the distance of the tracks disappearing into miles of golden leaves, when a small child with curly brown hair runs towards me and wraps his arms around me. A hug from a stranger, a small child, on this cold day here in one of the remotest settlements in the country – what a lovely thing. His father approaches and apologises. We laugh and I ask the young boy his name, and he tells me he is Ezra. I chat for a while with the father and his two sons who are staying in a nearby caravan. I compliment Ezra on his hero Superman top, and then we part ways. I am still on the platform, taking a photo with the train guard in his traditional uniform and cap, when Ezra bounds up to me again and gives me another hug. The three of us pose for a picture with the train guard and chat some more before parting ways.

I realise I haven't been hugged by a human for a long time, how an epic walking adventure such as this creates a kind of tactility with landscape rather than human, how instead it feels I have been hugged by the wind, embraced by the light itself, by the curve of earth when lying upon it. I nevertheless savour the moment of uncomplicated affection from another human being and it lifts my heart.

I walk back down to the river and, as the hug fades away, I let the last of the day's sunlight envelop me, for it is still bright and the pattering of rain has stopped. I hear a fluttering of wings but the bird is too quick for me. I yearn to see some winged things, and run over in my mind what I have learned about the birds of the North Pennines, what species inhabit these wildernesses. I look out at the golden glints of sunlight on trees and wonder if I have just seen a golden plover, though I did not hear its liquidy '*pyou*' call so perhaps it was an illusion.

I look out and listen out for birds beloved of the rivers and streams of the North Pennines, such as grey wagtails, which are found almost exclusively at the water's edge, wagging their long tails, fluttering up to snap insects from the air, and making a high-pitched call. As I walk and the sun turns the rocks an even deeper black, I think I see camouflaged on a rock a dipper bird, and the dipper then seems to dive into the river, but I cannot be sure if it is a trick of the light. I look out for oystercatchers with their long, bright red bills and fast flight and loud '*peep-peep*' calls. I see a sandy-coloured bird bobbing along and wonder if it is a common sandpiper. I see a bird soar away, showing off a bold white patch before disappearing amid the trees, and think perhaps it is a goosander, though I did not have a chance to spot its long, thin, serrated bill.

As the river opens out into more grasslands, I look out for grassland birds such as ring ouzels with their white necklace mark upon black feathers, beloved of crags and screes and moorland edges, though perhaps they have already begun their flight towards North Africa for the winter. I look out for meadow pipits with their streaky identifying marks and their '*sett, sett, sett*' and '*pip-it*' calls, and see a bright flash and wonder if it is a yellow wagtail – I am sure I hear its fluting '*tu-lip*' call but perhaps it too is a trick of the senses and instead the sound of the river or a child in the distance. I hear the singing of a bird then, a sweet singing that sounds like a skylark, but cannot see where that sweetness is coming from.

Human beings are one of about 50,000 species of animals that have a vertebral column, which enables us to walk upright. The major group of vertebrates include fishes, amphibians, reptiles, birds and us mammals, but 97 per cent of all animal species are invertebrates. While walking through the backbone of Britain, I have been thinking too of those creatures without a backbone. Indeed, during my research I discovered a North Pennines project called Cold-blooded and Spineless, 'celebrating and recording invertebrates in the North Pennines'.[97] There are 30,000 different species of invertebrate in the UK, from crustaceans to corals. The project sheds light on the underappreciated role of those creatures with no backbone or bony skeleton who yet make a vital contribution to the functioning of our ecosystem, from soil nutrient cycling to pollination, while also being an important food source for many birds, fish and mammals. Sadly, the State of Nature report revealed large declines of invertebrates in the past fifty years.

While walking, I look out for all creatures great and small, not only those with a backbone but the spineless too – though there are those I will never see with my naked eye, tiny creatures such as almost invisible flies and microscopic mites.[98] While Nabokov believed we should be proud to be vertebrates, I also celebrate the many wonderful invertebrates that inhabit our shared home.

I walk until the light begins to fade, and then head back into Alston and the place called The Angel Inn where I will be staying. How strange and marvellous are these uplands, these natural landscapes of the North, at once distinctive for their hard backbone of limestone and Whin Sill, and for their spineless creatures.

As I walk, I watch the curves of the mountains and fells begin to darken magnificently here in the highest settlement in England. I savour these moments of walking alone, the sense of self falling away, of losing myself in the landscape. *I am the river, and the river is me –* the Maori saying comes to mind. *I am the mountain, and the mountain is me –* so it feels now, surrounded on all sides by their great archings, as I walk and watch them until there is nothing left in the mind but the mountains.

15

Walking and Witnessing

My spirits have been fluctuating, and I think of High Force and Low Force waterfalls and the great ascents and sudden descents of the mountains, and how they seem to mirror my mood.

Yet I am so grateful for these days of rare autumn light, the last few days as we inch towards the end of British Summer Time, for enabling me to take all the footsteps I have made through the great outdoors, leading to this point. What a gilded landscape the North Pennines has been, gifting itself up in so much glorious light, despite the forecast before I set off showing unrelenting rain and cloud and cold.

My hunger to walk by Hadrian's Wall is growing, a wall that runs through natural landscapes as well as cityscapes. I have been inspired to head there ever since reading that it was Wainwright's destination in *A Pennine Journey*. It is a potent symbol of empire and the fear of immigration, and seems increasingly resonant in our era of wall-building, with the leader of the most powerful country on the planet propagating the chant of 'build the wall'. The vast territory of the Roman Empire stretched throughout Europe, North Africa and the Middle East, governed by the ideology of 'empire without end', captured in the Latin phrase *imperium sine fine*. At its largest expanse, under the Roman Emperor named Trajan, the Empire encompassed an area of 5 million square kilometres with a population estimate of 55–60 million inhabitants.

Hadrian's Wall runs a route of 135 kilometres through northern England, from the banks of the River Tyne near the North Sea to the Solway Firth on the Irish Sea. Built as a defensive fortification, it marked the northern limit of the Roman Empire beyond which were lands of the northern Ancient Britons, or what Emperor Hadrian called 'barbarians'. Hadrian's motivation in building the wall, according to a restored inscription on fragments of sandstone found at Jarrow, was the supposed 'necessity of keeping intact the Empire', which he believed had been bestowed on him 'by divine instruction'. Construction began in 122 AD and was completed in six years, starting in the east and moving westwards, with soldiers from all occupying Roman legions participating in the work. There were milecastles, turrets and forts, including Vindolanda, which offered supplies and protection.

Of what is the wall actually made? To the north in its best-preserved section the wall runs along the Whin Sill, that hard, resistant rock escarpment that is so characteristic of the backbone of Britain. Local limestone was used in much of the construction, except for the section to the west of River Irthing where turf was used, later rebuilt in stone. Milecastles in this area were built from timber and earth, turrets from stone. Some substances used in certain sections were not the best and made the wall vulnerable to collapsing, such as a clay-bonded core.[99] The remains of the wall are the largest Roman archaeological feature in Britain.

Hadrian's Wall Path marks the way that people can follow the remains of the wall by foot, from coast to coast,

either east to west (beginning at Wallsend and ending in
the Solway estuary in the Lake District) or west to east
(beginning in the countryside and ending in the city).

When people say 'Go back to where you're from',
they could do with a history lesson at the Wall and its
evidence of diverse cultures inhabiting the country for
hundreds of years; people of many skin colours quite
literally helping to build aspects of this country, though
history has failed to adequately bear witness to their
existence. In the tiny village of Burgh by Sands in
Cumbria, a plaque commemorates: 'the first recorded
African community in Britain guarded a Roman fort at
this site. 3rd Century AD'. It was writing on a stone
discovered in 1934 that revealed that soldiers from
North Africa were part of the fort's garrison. The fort,
Aballava, was built during the Roman occupation of
Britain to guard two forts on the Solway that were
popular with border raiders from the North. St Michael's
Church, which now stands on the site, was built with
stones taken from Hadrian's Wall. David Olusoga's
television series *Black and British* explores such
overlooked history, from the African Romans who
guarded Hadrian's Wall to the black trumpeter of the
Tudor court. In the first episode, 'Black and British: A
Forgotten History,'[100] archaeologist Richard Benjamin,
Head of the International Slavery Museum in Liverpool,
details evidence of people from the African part of the
Roman Empire in northern Britain including
inscriptions on stone tombs.

Re-examining well-known Roman cities such as York
is also shedding new light on the ethnic make-up of
Britain's past. Estimates suggest between 10,000 and

15,000 black Georgians were living in Britain in the eighteenth century, and evidence shows some of those to have lived in northern areas including York and Cumbria. There were parts of Roman York that were more multicultural than contemporary York. The skeleton of a woman known as 'the Ivory Bangle Lady' was discovered in Sycamore Terrace in York in 1901, and was revealed to be a female of North African descent, aged between eighteen and twenty-three, who was found with objects suggesting a high status including ivory bangles, a bracelet of blue glass beads, silver and bronze pendants, yellow glass earrings, a blue glass flask and a glass mirror. A piece of bone inscribed with the words, 'Hail sister, may you live in God' was also found with her skeleton.

A now quintessentially English village in East Sussex is where the 'Beachy Head woman' was discovered – the most ancient black Briton currently known of; forensic facial reconstruction revealed her features to be those of a sub-Saharan African. Isotope analysis indicated that she grew up in south-east England around the years 200 to 250 AD. The discovery was made as part of the Eastbourne Ancestors project, during which 300 sets of human remains excavated from Anglo-Saxon cemeteries were re-examined. I remember walking through Eastbourne and along the Seven Sisters cliffs including Beachy Head with a group of refugees, asylum seekers and migrants from The Refugee Tales group. Us people of colour stuck out in an overwhelmingly white seaside place, yet Britain was a multicultural community thousands of years ago.

What is the North made of? This is a question I have been inspired to explore in terms of both the physical composition of its natural landscapes, the wildlife inhabiting it, and also the people who comprise the North and have historically done so, whose lives and labour contributed to its characteristics.

Go back to where you're from. I belong here, and there have been people of colour inhabiting Britain from long before my parents' generation, for thousands of years. That belonging is not superficial but a deep kind of belonging, as deep and strong as those ancient substances of which the earth is made. Yet such histories have not been widely taught due to the 'whitewashing' of the curriculum, wiping away such existence from between the covers of books. It is such eradication that is one of the motivations impelling me to put pen to paper, to tell this story, to form a home out of words for this story of belonging.

It is impossible to walk by the remnants of Hadrian's Wall without feeling its resonance to our own era. Chilling chants of 'Build the wall, build the wall' have resounded from Trump and his supporters after those words became a political slogan of his presidential campaign, referring to a proposed expansion of the Mexico–United States barrier. While the official campaign slogan was 'Make America Great Again', the chant of 'Build the wall' became a rallying cry. The 'Build the wall' slogan was developed by campaign advertisers as something Trump could use to link his anti-immigration policy proposals to his history as a property tycoon. Trump claimed that Mexico would pay for the wall but the President of Mexico refuted this claim.

Those 'Build the wall' chants are another example of language inciting division: after Trump won the election there were reports that the chant was being used by some children to bully their Latino classmates. A *Washington Post* article entitled 'White Texas teens chant "build that wall" at Hispanics during high school volleyball match'[101] revealed how school was far from an equal or safe playing field but one filled with racism and hostility. In another incident, video footage revealed schoolchildren chanting 'Build that wall' at Latino students in Michigan. The *Detroit News* reported that twelve-year-old Josie Ramon, who filmed the video, was left in tears.[102] One parent who posted the video on Facebook wrote: 'This happened today at Royal Oak Middle School in Royal Oak, Michigan... It is so sad. Latino children were crying. The taunts, the "Build that Wall" with such bullying power and hate from children to children. Just horrifying!'

There have been some powerful artistic responses and challenges to the wall. In summer 2019, fluorescent-pink see-saws were built across the border, a symbol of unity across divides, installed along the steel border fence on the outskirts of El Paso in Texas and Ciudad Juárez in Mexico. The see-saws were created by Ronald Rael, a professor of architecture, and Virginia San Fratello, an associate professor of design. Rael said it was about bringing togetherness at the border wall and recognition that the actions that take place on one side have a direct consequence on the other side.

The building of the wall itself comes at huge financial cost. Following his inauguration, Trump directed the US government to use existing federal funding to begin attempting wall construction. The cost to construct a wall along the remaining 2,100 kilometres of the border could be as high as $12.5 million per kilometre, with private land acquisitions and fence maintenance pushing up the total cost.

As well as the human and financial cost, building the wall has been predicted to cause significant environment damage including habitat destruction. The National Wildlife Federation called the erection of a continuous wall 'one of the biggest potential ecological disasters of our time.'[103] Congress has enabled environmental protections such as the Endangered Species Act to be waived. An article published in the journal *Bioscience*[104] signed by more than 2,900 scientists said the administration's plan would threaten some of the continent's most biologically diverse regions. The report explains how the US–Mexico borderlands traverse six ecoregions containing vegetation types that include desert scrub, temperate forests and woodlands, semi-desert and plains grasslands, subtropical scrublands, freshwater wetlands and salt marshes. These environments 'support extraordinary biological diversity'. The analysis showed that the border bisects the geographic ranges of 1,506 native terrestrial and freshwater animal and plant species, including sixty-two species listed as Critically Endangered, Endangered or Vulnerable by the International Union for Conservation of Nature (IUCN) Red List. Some of the species that may potentially be affected include pygmy owls, jaguars and Mexican grey wolves, to name but a few. Near the banks of the Rio Grande in Mission, Texas, the National Butterfly Center – where more than 200 butterfly species live – was notified that the wall will divide the hundred-acre sanctuary. The centre brought a lawsuit against the Department of Homeland Security, which was dismissed but the centre is appealing. The butterflies fluttering in abundance through the area are just some of the wildlife that has been threatened with destruction due to Trump's border wall.

Plato described in his book *Critias* how under the Roman Empire, the natural landscape was dramatically altered, including whole forests cut down to provide wood, leaving 'the mere skeleton of the land.' During our own era of border fortification, natural landscape and wildlife are also being altered for the worse, ravaged and rampaged, as during the building of the British Empire.

It is a heart-liftingly bright day when I set off on my walk, the gloom of the previous day stripped away. I want to walk alone to the Sycamore Gap Tree, which has stood for hundreds of years between two distinctive and dramatic curves in the earth caused by melting glacial waters. I want to walk beyond it too, to try and find Greenlee Lough, the largest natural lake in Northumberland, surrounded by wetlands. I am directly north of the North Pennines, just past Haltwhistle and Hexham, and I walk in nature for miles with no sign of human habitation. I walk amid giant maple trees, heathland, moors, meadows, peat bogs, and along the edge of a cliff, an outcrop of the Great Whin Sill. I walk and gaze out into the horizon and am haunted by the thought of all who once lived here. Rising in my memory are lines from Auden's 'Roman Wall Blues' poem told from the perspective of a Wall soldier surrounded by heather and hard grey stone.

'Welcome to Housesteads Roman Fort,' a sign reads.

Stay safe
The Romans built their fort at the top of a hill in a rough
landscape. Please take care on uneven ground and look out for
slippery paths and steps.
Help keep Housesteads special.
This special site and surrounding landscape is protected by law.
Please take only photographs and leave only footprints.

Protected by law. Those words again haunt my journey.

Housesteads is the most complete example of a
Roman fort in Britain, standing high on a dramatic,
scenic section of the Wall. A sign reading 'Housesteads
Vercovicium / Edge of Empire' explains that it was one
of several permanent forts built by Emperor Hadrian in
about 124 AD for his new frontier. For nearly 300 years
Hadrian's Wall was the north-west frontier of an empire
that stretched east to present-day Iraq and south to the
Sahara Desert. Now, Housesteads and Hadrian's Wall
are part of a multi-country World Heritage Site that
also includes the German Limes and Scotland's
Antonine Wall.

I walk up a steep footpath to reach the wall and fort,
through the former Roman town where soldiers' families
lived, where there once were taverns and terraces across
the hillside. I walk right up to the fort, to what were
once barrack blocks, and drink in views over the
countryside, Hadrian's Wall Country, dubbed 'The Land
of the Far Horizons'. I walk on, following Hadrian's Wall
along the natural ridge of the Whin Sill escarpment.
I see an extraordinary furry green substance clinging to

the grey stone. What is special about lichen is that they can flourish in so many different environmental conditions, from high alpine levels to sea levels, and can grow on all manner of surfaces, including rock and stone (they are often found on gravestones), and can survive extreme conditions from arctic tundra to hot, dry deserts. Lichen is a survivor, growing even when the odds seem to be against any kind of flourishing. *Be more like lichen*, I think.

I hike on one of the few sections of the Wall that it is actually possible to, on a path covered with leaves and fringed with gleamingly bright green grass and, looking to the right, I see a perilous drop from the edge, down a steep cliff. I walk along the Wall through a wood with enormous trees casting their shadows on the path and creating intense beams of light. In the distance a lake glistens blue. I walk out into open countryside stretching all around, and above, a layer of clouds the colour of pearls, and above that, clear blue sky. Underfoot is a mixture of green and golden maize-like grass.

I walk by Crag Lough, a huge expanse of steely blue water formed by glaciers in the last Ice Age, fringed by dark green fir trees, one of four Roman Wall Loughs (as many lakes around these parts are named), along with Greenlee, Broomlee and Halleypike. I see a capacious mound cresting out of the earth, Steel Rigg, made of what looks like limestone and Whin Sill, with the Wall winding up and along crags and by the lough. Beyond I see the dark shapes of conifers, Wark Forest. As I walk I realise that walking has – even when getting lost and very muddy – been helping me to find my feet, a sense of deeper belonging.

The wind has picked up, whipping against my skin, and rippling through the grass, and whirling the water of the lough in which clouds are reflected. It is an awesome sight, this giant near-vertical cliff-like drop that awakens muscle memory of Hull Pot and its sudden plummet and of the limestone cliff-face of Malham Cove, of the Whin Sill of High Force. The Emperor Hadrian incorporated this natural phenomenon of the cliff-face as a defence against so-called barbarians.[105] The Whin Sill is such an important and defining part of the North that a centre called The Sill has opened in tribute. I spend some time there, browsing exhibitions devoted to humans' relation-ship with landscape and to the story of when and why the national parks and Areas of Outstanding Natural Beauty came into being.[106] I am technically in the quirkily named village of Once Brewed and a nearby inn takes the name of Twice Brewed.

Fortified by tea, I keep walking, forgetting all about the time. Soon I'm on the edge of Wark Forest. All human habitation falls away and I see a great expanse of water gleaming between trees and I walk towards it until it feels like I am walking into the landscape, becoming a part of it, with water and trees visible from every corner of my vision. I am walking through a Site of Special Scientific Interest consisting of more than 80 per cent water, through a mosaic of habitats now rare in Britain, forming a home for much flora and fauna, for sphagnum moss, cranberry and sundew, and caterpillars in cottongrass that turn into large heath butterflies. I try to spot wildflowers including valerian, skullcap and yellow flag iris. It is so bracingly cold; it feels much colder here in a wilderness away from the lights of the city. I shiver and inhale and delight in the scent of meadowsweet and mint. What a wild and remote place.

A white bird soars overhead and another group of birds flock together and soar away, migrating. There will be birds, though, that will make this sheltered environment their home even in winter, such as whooper swans, geese and goldeneye.

I walk on but the sycamore tree is still nowhere in sight, and beyond are a few more hills to climb before reaching it. The sun begins to sink, turning the sky a drama of deep gold and orange spreading out behind dark clouds. What a joy to drink in the sight of these open skies, so dramatic in the coexistence of brightness and dark.

Walking down a valley, I suddenly set eyes on the sycamore, resplendent under light gleaming off its branches, growing between two curves of the earth. The tree seems to set eyes on me too, and as I walk deeper into the Sycamore Gap, I shiver to think of the ways in which the natural world witnesses our existence. 'The Watchful Tree' is the folk-name given to the silver birch and aspen because of the eye-markings gazing out of the trunks, either natural bark-markings or scarring left where branches have dropped.[107] This sycamore also seems to see. It seems splendid standing there in isolation, and I walk closer, seeing the leaves it has been shedding all over the grass, coppery brown with distinctive black markings. Walking and watching seems to have sharpened my perception. I have looked more closely and deeply at the world than I have looked before – looking not only into place but through time. How important that we all learn to pay close attention.

The light slips away from the tree then, and my heart sinks. When it grows gloomy it is so difficult to imagine that light will ever be back, and I curse myself for having missed the light to photograph the sycamore. Then slowly the light begins to return from behind a cloud, reaching out long gold fingers and then touching the tree so its branches blush, and the grass and the leaves on the grass all glow.

EPILOGUE

Up From a Past that's Rooted in Pain

'You only are free when you realize you belong no
place – you belong every place'

— Maya Angelou

I think more about the notion of belonging. Can anyone
truly 'belong' to a place and can a place 'belong' to you? I
hesitate at the notion of ownership implicit in aggressive
forms of belonging; people are not possessions; another
person cannot 'belong' to you, for that would be slavery. So
much of this land, though, its natural landscapes and man-
made terrains, has been aggressively owned by a tiny
proportion of the population, the wealthiest percentage,
excluding so many. I remember those Manchester Ramblers
walking at Kinder Scout and how we must continue their
spirit, continue to protest against systemic exclusion, too
many people in places regarded as if they don't belong as
much as others do. We need to move more deeply beyond
conquest and ownership to mutually respectful inhabitance.

With those in power intent on pushing minorities to
the peripheries, it is also important to know when to say
'I don't belong here!' as well as asserting your right to
exist in places where you do belong. If you're wrongly
pigeonholed, given the smaller space – the cramped seat
in the worst section of the bus, as it were, wrongly put in
Yarl's Wood detention centre for not being able to

evidence your identity, forced from systemic inequality
to live in a squalid hovel in a place starved of nature –
these are not places you should have to belong or find
your sense of belonging. Nobody should be forced to fit
themselves into a place that's ultimately fatal.

Walking through such wild, ancient landscape brings a
strong awareness of how we are all temporary guests on
this earth. We will take nothing of it with us.

How changing it feels to have seen and heard and felt
the wilderness, felt it creep within, seep beneath the skin,
the greatness of those vast expanses of wilderness and the
sense of peace in existing it brings. The feeling of living
things – the trees breathing, the water lapping – calms the
turbulence of thoughts and brings the sense of being a
part of something greater than the self, a part of the
natural world. I must do everything to hang on to that
feeling of fully inhabiting time and place; a dissolving
into the present moment instead of flailing against it, the
sheer realness and life of the here and now blasting
hypotheticals away. To say 'I belong here' is not only
about place but time, too, about being fully present in the
moment. I must try to feel this always, to keep a place for
this peace within the landscape of my mind and heart.

My journey has shown me that my anxiety cannot so
easily be 'cured' but rather managed with regular doses of
nature – for, when indoors again, that anxiety can seep
back in, become searing, and it takes further walking and
engagement with the great outdoors to quieten it once
more. I remember walking through Hope Valley and how
it soothed the edges of the searing anxiety and, although

the anxiety returned, how then climbing up Malham Cove and clambering over the limestone taught me to not feel ashamed when it did return, that there was a certain strength in vulnerability. I remember walking over the Whin Sill, the backbone of Britain, feeling a bedrock of strength within. I reflect on how anxiety itself served a purpose, how that inherent sense of feeling unsettled pushed me even further beyond my comfort zone, where I learned nature's power not only to soothe but also to deeply unsettle in a different and ultimately edifying way – just as I was unsettled by walking alone through the wilderness and hearing the blood-curdling cry of a bird I could not name or see, unsettled by the fierceness of the wind and the bone-deep cold. For to be unsettled in this way was to see the world anew and my place within it. To feel true and primal fear is to set into context the background noise of everyday anxieties.

I have walked and walked and walked, so far and for so long I could feel the bones of my feet, my heartbeat pumping oxygen around my lungs. Throughout my journey I have explored things that run skin-deep but also deeper than the skin, to the very heart, to the blood and bones and water and air of which we are all made.

Whilst my journey began in a hate crime, it has turned out to be filled with so much love. As I walked, I felt a love as vast as the mountains and for them and I loved the tiniest beings I saw too. I felt love flow deep as the rivers and for them and I loved the smallest raindrop too. As I walked, I felt love for human beings and for formations made from stone, and how in this love my soul and strength have grown.

It is a clear, calm day when I walk towards the Solway Coast, one of the country's Areas of Outstanding Natural Beauty, and either the end or the beginning of Hadrian's Wall, whichever way you want to look at it. I walk closer to the sea and then step out onto the sand. I am astonished to be in such a landscape, right here in the North of England, and in such glowing light as this. It feels miraculous. This part of the coast is so empty, I glance back and am startled by my own footprints in the sand, the only footprints I see. I walk right up to the sea's edge and suddenly a great wave comes crashing in, soaking my shoes right to the soles of my feet. The sea seems to grow wilder by the minute, though the light is still bright and fierce. I feel its wildness as it crashes against me with a great roar, and then ebbs away and seems serene again, before rushing back in, another great wave breaking the surface.

Step by step I walk further and it feels like walking into the landscape, becoming a part of it, sea and sky visible from every corner of my vision. The sound of water lapping becomes everything. So clear is the sea that the sky is reflected in its surface, so I am walking upon the clouds, as the boundaries of above and below dissolve. The body itself is a landscape and for the first time in a while I feel I am fully inhabiting myself and simultaneously inhabiting this place, becoming the sea and sky.

How wide the skies, after being cooped up for so long in lockdown. What a sense of freedom to walk in this wilderness amid the blue and gold. How the heart rises to be here. The Wall has been calling me again as lockdown lifted, so my first journey has been here.

I savour each second, not knowing when again movement might once more be restricted. I walk further and a sign welcomes me to RSPB Campfield Marsh, telling me this wetland paradise is one of the most important places for wildlife in the UK, made up of a mosaic of different habitats that provide homes for species; for wading birds, for migrant warblers who settle here in spring when the coconut-scented gorse blooms bright yellow. I hear a bird though cannot see it, its sound strong and sweet.

While Whin Sill offered a geologic defence against immigrants and so-called invaders and 'barbarians', the sea offered a topographical defence. I feel more than ever how it is crucial that borders are not fortified further. What a symbol of belonging is the sea's edge, so many suffering trying to cross its shores for a safer life.

I am met with such warmth and hospitality during my time in Bowness-on-Solway. When I enter a cafe with muddy shoes and jeans after my feet became stuck in what felt like sinking mud, thick peat bog, the owner offers to wash them for me. I leave for the next stage of my journey with clean shoes on my feet, fish and chips in my belly, and the kindness of strangers filling my heart.

I continue on until I see again the Great Whin Sill and I am exultant to walk again amid it, to feel it beneath my soles, within my soul. I walk and walk on a day that is the hottest it's been all year, but with a wind too, cooling the skin. I see the sycamore once more, standing proud and magnificent, owned by no one, owning itself. How ridiculous that anyone could think this tree could in anyway be more theirs than mine or truly belong to anyone but itself. I stand beneath the tree and feel the

wind whipping through its glorious branches, making a
song all of its own.

As I walk a dandelion blows past me on the breeze, and
then another, and with it all the wishes that have ever
been made on this earth, all those that might still be made.
I wish for a world of no more wounding of places and
people. I wish for a world in which we can all make a safe
home and feel at home in ourselves, in which all bodies
and minds are valued. I wish for a world in which all are
regarded as belonging equally and truly to this earth, all
needing to breathe fresh air, therefore needing to be near
trees, which turn the sunlight into oxygen. I wish for a
world in which we value nature and wildlife, the smallest
flower, the tiniest blade of grass, and understand that we
are part of nature, and that not only humans but every
creature and lifeform great and small belongs here. I wish
for a world recalibrated to make it a better, fairer place.
I wish for a world in which hate is transformed into
love – and we realise that we cannot truly love each other
without loving nature which keeps us alive at all, which
flows through our lungs and fills our hearts.

I visit Vindolanda fort and see the ancient writing
tablets – including the oldest handwriting from a woman
in Britain. There are stylus tablets, wood with a depression
to take wax that was written in and could be erased and
rewritten. There are ink tablets too, thin pieces of wood,
the growth of one tree ring flattened and written on in
ink. I wonder at those trees, at once able to provide
oxygen and be a home for our writing. I learn of the
many trees that had their origin at the time of this
northern frontier, both native and non-native conifer
and broadleaf species.

I walk on and see encased in glass a skeleton, the bones of a child aged around ten or eleven including some of their backbone, which has survived all this time. Analysis of the teeth shows that the child was an immigrant to northern England, having grown up in the Mediterranean.

Ink. Bone. Tree bark. Stone. I walk on and feel the urgency and primacy of writing. I remember those documents that were destroyed evidencing existence – from my own ancestors to people still alive today, traces of them gone. One day we all will be gone, but traces will be left upon the earth. What evidence of our existence will we leave behind, that we once walked here? What will we leave to the earth from the relatively brief lifespans during which we belong in this world?

I continue on to the Northumberland coast. I can smell the sea before I see it and taste the fresh, salty air, and I hear the seagulls calling. Walking a few more steps, I see the sea spread out, a deep blue today under the light, which fades every now and then, turning it into a great grey abeyance, then blue once more.

I walk along Whitley Bay, on and on along the golden sand as it stretches and curves – it is more peopled here, with paw prints and shadows and laughter echoing – on towards St Mary's Lighthouse, watching white foam frothing as I walk on towards Seaton Sluice that means 'settlement by the sea'. The light and the sight and sound of the sea seem to soak up all anxieties and leave me fully present in the moment, enjoying simply being with no barrier between myself and the landscape. I walk on and a seagull swoops so close to me I feel its wingbeat and then it soars up into the sinking sun, which sets aglow its brilliant white feathers, and I am soaring too, remembering how as a child I longed to be a bird so much I became one, how I would feel as if I was flying, how in my dreams I soared and soared and soared.

I remember the first shell I found on a beach in Blackpool and learning to hear the song of the sea forever held within its heart.

The song 'Sittin' on the Dock of the Bay' filters through my mind and I remember it was played at Sophie's funeral.

I realise how much of my journey has been about friendship and loneliness: grieving the loss of one, understanding the ways friendship lives on, discovering its true meaning, finding a friendship of sorts in wildlife and the natural world. I feel how friendship can flourish from and with the most unlikely of places.

I head back to the Newcastle and walk to Wallsend which in Roman times hosted fort Segedunum and now the excavated remains of the fort as well as a reconstructed Roman bathhouse. As I walk, the present moment and past seem to converge. My earlier journeys are in the present tense as much as the time that Romans once guarded this wall. The past and present occupy a single moment, one heartbeat. I realise how my journey has not been solely of reclamation but of restoration, restoring hidden histories of human and natural worlds and showing how they are comingled, a journey in itself also emotionally restorative.

I walk for a while along the river, watching great seagulls swoop and dive and soar.

I take the train to Hexham, for tonight I'll be visiting an observatory and stargazing in Wark. How I long to see the North Star. The route passes along the River Tyne and I look out into the landscape and watch the river flash and flicker between enormous beech trees, gilded in this sunshine, the river pulsing and glinting, a vein of this earth.

I listen to the chug of the train, images floating through my mind and sounds rising up over the engine. Places grow within us. What of this journey will settle like sediment within? I already feel it is layering itself inside me, becoming a part of my inner landscape, leaving traces. I see again in the mind's eye that glorious life growing in the grykes and fissures of the huge slabs of limestone at the top of Malham Cove, life flourishing where least expected, something beautiful coming into being from fault-lines and fractures. I see the lichen clinging on to stone, surviving even the harshest of climates. *Be more like lichen.* I hear again the plunging of water into the largest natural hole in England, and how the wounds of the earth have become such startling scars. I hear again the roar of the waterfall, High Force, over the Whin Sill, the insistence of that lifeforce washing away all anxieties. I think of that great bird I saw while walking lost in the North Pennines and how it too seemed to be saying, *I belong here.* I see again in my mind's eye the sycamore tree, turning carbon dioxide into oxygen, and I smell and taste once more the freshness of the air in my lungs. I remember how, for a time, I became the river and the mountains and the birds and the trees, and how for all time I love them.

I hold my hands together and clench them until I can feel the very bones in my body and think of what I am made, minerals and memories and mettle, trace elements.

I stretch my feet so I can feel the muscles, and remember walking over limestone and Whin Sill, feeling the backbone of this country, and learning what it means to have backbone. I feel the urgency to tell this story, to get it down into words before I die, this story of belonging.

I don't steel myself but spider-silk myself against any hardships that might lie on the road ahead.

I look upwards into a sky blue and clear but for the dark shapes of birds swooping and gliding and one day soon migrating to warmer climes, wings spread wide.

I think of the great mountains out there, how they have been empty of every human being during lockdown, patient and persistent. I will return one day to those fells and forces, when the doors of the world are again thrown open, but for now I close my eyes and feel how a landscape plants itself within us, its roots growing within the heart, its branches arching through the mind, its rivers running like blue-black ink through the veins, lifeblood.

Resources

Victim Support – offers a range of free and confidential services: victimsupport.org.uk

Anxiety helplines

No Panic – helps people suffering from panic attacks, phobias and other anxiety-related symptoms: nopanic.org.uk

Anxiety UK – helps with people suffering with anxiety disorders and symptoms of anxiety: anxietyuk.org.uk / 0344 4775774

Samaritans in the UK and Ireland: 116 123

National Suicide Prevention Lifeline in the US: 1-800-273-8255

The crisis support service Lifeline Australia: 13 11 14

Other international suicide helplines can be found at befrienders.org.

Organisations a part of CATCH (Community Alliance to Combat Hate)

The Monitoring Group – helps those who have been distressed or suffered from race hate crime: www.tmg-uk.org

Tell MAMA – public service that supports victims of anti-Muslim hate crime: tellmamauk.org / 0800 4561226. You can also submit a report: tellmamauk.org/submit-a-report-to-us/

Acknowledgements

I am grateful to all those who provided help and support throughout my journey along the backbone of Britain. My deep gratitude, too, to those who have encouraged me during my journey to becoming an author and given a home for my writing. This book was completed during an extraordinarily challenging period of history and never more have I felt how a backbone of support is necessary.

Thank you to...

The train staff for assistance on the TransPennine Express train journey during which I was racially abused, including Stephen, Steve and Lewis. The British Transport Police officers who worked on the case. The Victim Support officers who do such valuable work.

The experts I interviewed as part of my research: Alan Kellas, Green Care lead at the Royal College of Psychiatrists; Professor Dacher Keltner; Lynne Frederick of No Panic charity; Suresh Grover of The Monitoring Group. Anna Pincus and David Herd of The Refugee Tales and those of The Refugee Tales community who shared their stories with me as we walked.

Those who sponsored my Pennines walk including: Lisa O'Kelly, Emma Jane Unsworth, Hazel Reeves, Donna Ferguson, Rishi Dastidar, Ben Myers, Ian Mackintosh, Steve Padley. Those who sponsored my walk with The Refugee Tales (full list at anitasethi.com).

I experienced the kindness of strangers during my journey: some became walking companions along the way, some provided a smile which cheered my day. Thank you.

Thank you to the Society of Authors for an Authors' Emergency Fund grant which provided crucial help in the completion of this book during the pandemic months. Thank you to Commonwealth Writers and New Writing North.

Thank you to Robert Macfarlane, Katharine Norbury, Patrick Barkham, Nikesh Shukla and Lucy Jones, for reading *I Belong Here* before it winged its way into the world and providing heart-warming early endorsements and encouragement.

Many thanks to the editors I've been honoured to work with who commissioned/edited writing the research for which fed into this book.

Joseph Harker. Ursula Kenny. Jane Ferguson. Lisa O'Kelly. Sarah Donaldson (the chapter heading 'Onwards' was inspired by a tweet from Sarah). Harriet Green. Steve Chamberlain. Emma Cook. Sam Baker. Ben Hoare. Hugh Montgomery. Those who commissioned/edited my contributions to anthologies/journals: Katharine Norbury. Jenn Ashworth. Nikesh Shukla. Rachael Kerr. Melissa Harrison. Maria del Pilar Kaladeen. For various kinds of vital support, solidarity and encouragement along the way, including: Caroline Sanderson, Katherine Cowdrey and Philip Jones. Alice Jones. Paul Laity. David Nicholls. Stephanie Merritt. Liz Vater. James Miller. Paul Scully. Sarah-Jane Roberts. David Cooper and Rachel Lichtenstein. Alexandra Pringle. Jackie Morris (sender of the most beautiful cards). John Mitchinson. George Torode. Nii Ayikwei Parkes. Lemn Sissay. Sara Hunt. Cate & Nash at Much Ado Books for a bed in their bookshop. Early bookshop supporters including Sam Reads, Forum Bookshop and Five Leaves. Early I Belong Here foundation sponsors including: Truda Spruyt. Kate Davis. Sandeep Mahal. Molly Flatt. Victoria Cottrell. Lynn Enright. Aoife Larkin. Helen Gilchrist. During isolating times, I've been heartened by virtual solidarity and allyship from those including: Paula Hawkins. Bianca Jagger. Celeste Ng. Sanjeev Bhaskar. Nitin Sawhney. Linda Grant. Kate Mosse. Will Smith and Polly Atkin – and thank you to all my Twitter/instagram friends and supporters; each and every one of you who have sent supportive messages during challenging times is appreciated. Thank you to my Manchester cheerleaders Lisa, Bridie and Austin. My family in Guyana for support during the visit mentioned in this book.

I am grateful to all my friends living and dead.

To my late friend Sophie Christopher for 'A Little Card Full of Magic and Joy'. You were only alive 28 years, but your kindness lives on.

Thank you to the librarians in the local libraries in Manchester where my love of reading and writing flourished in childhood. Thank you to my mother and father.

In Summer 2020 I lost the room I was renting and lived out of a suitcase for a time – thank you to the lovely staff of the hotel in which I sought refuge for their kindness.

I went birdwatching with Margaret Atwood in the UK's oldest nature reserve as the setting for an interview, which deepened my understanding of nature. "Nature is inside you. You just breathed some of it in," she said. Loving one's neighbour means loving the air in their lungs: "You have to love their oxygen, therefore you have to love what makes their oxygen".

Above all, THANK YOU to my wonderful publishers Bloomsbury for providing a home for I Belong Here: special thanks to my brilliant editor Alice Ward for believing in this book from the beginning and being a fantastic support including helping me navigate the publishing process. The whole amazing team I've been fortunate to work with on bringing this book into being including: my publicist Jude Drake; Alice Graham in marketing; Jasmine Parker in design and illustrator Amy Grimes; proofreader Anna Macdiarmid; cartographer Julian Baker; Terry Lee for being a great northern champion; Rachel Nicholson, Rachael Williamson and Jim Martin.

Thank you to the trailblazers who forged paths before me and helped give me the courage to forge my own.

Thank you to each and every reader of *I Belong Here:* you've helped complete a journey, from my mind – over the Pennines - to your mind.

I am grateful to the following for the granting of textual permissions: The chapter title, 'Up From a Past that's Rooted in Pain', is from the poem 'Still I Rise' by Maya Angelou. Reprinted with permission from Little, Brown Book Group Ltd, the UK publisher and Penguin Random House, the US publisher. "You only are free when you realize you belong no place — you belong every place" – Maya Angelou, is reprinted with permission from WNET. 'People exploit what they have merely concluded to be of value, but they defend what they love, and to defend what we love we need a particularising language, for we love what we particularly know' – Wendell Berry. Copyright © 2000 by Wendell Berry from *Life Is A Miracle: An Essay Against Modern Superstition.* Reprinted by permission of Counterpoint Press (I first learnt this quote when I interviewed Robert Macfarlane, for the Daily Telegraph, to whom thank you for support, encouragement and advice). The full version of 'Dear Prince Charles, do you think my brown skin looks unBritish?' first appeared in the *Guardian.* Small portions of text appeared in my contributions to *The Pool, Common People,* and *Seasons.*

The writing of a book can itself be a mountain to climb and there were some musicians, poets, writers and artists who helped keep me going when the going got tough. A poem which was influential is 'In Praise of Limestone' by WH Auden. For further resources/ acknowledgements including an I Belong Here playlist of music that kept me company at various stages of the writing and walking (including many Northern favourites), see www.anitasethi.com.

For further information on the I Belong Here foundation, anitasethi.com/i-belong-here

Bibliography

Angelou, Maya. 1978. *And Still I Rise.* Virago, London.

Auden, WH. 1994. *Collected Poems.* Faber & Faber, London.

Berry, Wendell. 2000. *Life Is A Miracle: An Essay Against Modern Superstition.* Counterpoint Press, Berkeley.

Blake, William. 1978. *The Complete Poems.* Penguin Classics, London.

Chaucer, Geoffrey. 2003. *The Canterbury Tales.* Penguin Classics, London.

Davidson, Robyn. 1995. *Tracks: A Woman's Solo Trek Across 1,700 Miles of Australian Outback.* Vintage, London.

Dickinson, Emily. 1976. *The Complete Poems of Emily Dickinson.* Back Bay Books, New York.

Ensler, Eve. 2001. *The Vagina Monologues.* Villard, New York.

Gentleman, Amelia. 2019. *The Windrush Betrayal.* Guardian Faber, London.

Grant, Colin. 2019. *Homecoming: Voices of the Windrush Generation.* Cape, London.

Hughes, Ted. 1979. *Crow: from the Life and Songs of the Crow.* Faber & Faber, London.

Keltner, D; Monroy, M; Anderson L. C. 2018. Awe in nature heals: Evidence from military veterans, at-risk youth, and college students. *Emotion*, 18(8), 1195–1202.

Keltner, D; Monroy, M; Anderson L. C. 2017. Emotion in the wilds of nature: The coherence and contagion of fear during threatening group-based outdoors experiences *Emotion* 2018, 18 (3): 355-368

Kimmerer, Robin Wall. 2020. *Braiding Sweetgrass.* Penguin, London.

Machado, Antonio. 2003. 'You Make Your Own Path as You Walk' – from *Border of a Dream: Selected Poems.* Copper Canyon Press, Washington.

Macfarlane, Robert. 2012. *The Old Ways.* Penguin, London.

Muir, John. 2020. *Our National Parks.* Doublebit Press, Cherry, Illinois.

Nicholls, Grace. 2020. *Passport to Here and There.* Bloodaxe Books, Hexham.

Solnit, Rebecca. 2014. *Wanderlust: A History of Walking.* Granta, London.

Strayed, Cheryl, *Wild: From Lost to Found on the Pacific Crest Trail.* Vintage, London.

Wainwright, Alfred. 2008. *A Pennine Journey: The Story of a Long Walk in 1938.* Frances Lincoln, London.

Notes

PROLOGUE & MOUTH

1 www.peakdistrict.gov.uk/looking-after/climatechange/climate-change-and-the-peak-district

2 www.liverpoolmuseums.org.uk/ism/slavery/europe/liverpool.aspx

3 *A New Narrative for Africa: Voice and Agency* by Abiodun Alao (Introduction) (Routledge, 2019)

4 www.personal.rdg.ac.uk/~llsroach/phon2/artic-basics.htm

5 www.bbc.co.uk/news/av/science-environment-43420738/the-whales-that-talk-with-accents

6 www.sciencedaily.com/releases/2013/05/130508092830.htm

7 www.nytimes.com/2017/03/10/books/review/margaret-atwood-handmaids-tale-age-of-trump.html

SKIN

8 kinginstitute.stanford.edu/encyclopedia/selma-montgomery-march

9 *The Old Ways: A Journey on Foot* by Robert Macfarlane (Penguin, 2013)

10 *Howards End* by E.M. Forster (Penguin Classics, 2012)

11 www.britannica.com/topic/list-of-plants-in-the-family-Poaceae-2036227

12 www.the-scientist.com/news-analysis/microbes-of-the-skin-37335

13 www.nature.com/articles/d41586-018-07431-9

14 www.ncbi.nlm.nih.gov/books/NBK441980/

15 www.britannica.com/science/melanin

16 www.woodlandtrust.org.uk/trees-woods-and-wildlife/british-trees/a-z-of-british-trees/rowan/

17 www.buxtonadvertiser.co.uk/news/people/right-wing-group-unfurl-huge-white-lives-matter-banner-mam-tor-2909936

18 www.bbc.com/news/uk-43782241

19 www.amnesty.org.uk/blogs/yes-minister-it-human-rights-issue/seventy-years-after-windrush

20 www.theguardian.com/uk-news/2018/apr/17/home-office-destroyed-windrush-landing-cards-says-ex-staffer

21 *The Windrush Betrayal: Exposing the Hostile Environment* by Amelia Gentleman (Guardian Faber, 2019)

22 www.gov.uk/government/publications/windrush-lessons-learned-review

23 www.caribbean-beat.com/issue-117/holes-history

24 *Insatiable Appetite: The United States and the Ecological Degradation of the Tropical World* by Richard P. Tucker (University of California, 2000)

25 www.theguardian.com/world/2018/feb/25/colombia-farmers-fairtrade-bananas-civil-war-drug-trafficking

26 *Immigrants in American History: Arrival, Adaptation, and Integration* edited by Elliott Robert Barkan (ABC-Clio, 2013)

27 www.sciencedaily.com/releases/2013/05/130508092830.htm

28 *Cultures of Color in America: A Guide to Family, Religion, and Health* by Sybil
    M. Lassiter (Greenwood, 1998)
29 www.thenorthernecho.co.uk/news/14590525.the-banana-boats-coming-
    for-you-spike-in-racist-incidents-post-brexit/
30 www.independent.co.uk/news/uk/home-news/brexit-hate-crime-rac-
    ism-reports-eu-referendum-latest-a7106116.html
31 www.theguardian.com/uk-news/2018/jun/04/pensioner-given-sus-
    pended-sentence-over-racist-emails-to-mps).
32 news.bbc.co.uk/1/hi/uk/7822883.stm
33 K. Briggs 'OE and ME *cunte* in place-names' in *Jrnl. Eng. Place-name Soc.* 41
    (2009) 26–39.
    www.nottingham.ac.uk/research/groups/epns/documents/jour-
    nal/41-2009/keith-briggs-oe-and-me-cunte-in-place-names-journal-of-
    the-english-place-name-society-41-2009-pp.-26–39.pdf
    www.languagehat.com/new-words-in-the-oed/
34 www.metoomvmt.org/get-to-know-us/history-inception/

BACKBONE

35 *Invertebrate Zoology: A Functional Evolutionary Approach* by Edward E. Rup-
    pert, Richard S. Fox and Robert D. Barnes (Cengage Learning, 2004)
36 www.geolsoc.org.uk/GeositesMalhamCove
37 www.bgs.ac.uk/discoveringGeology/geologyOfBritain/limestoneLand-
    scapes/whatIsLimestone/home.htm
38 Karst/limestone landscapes are explored in *Underland: A Deep Time Journey*
    by Robert Macfarlane (Penguin, 2019) and *Stones of Aran: Pilgrimmage* by
    Tim Robinson (Viking, 1989)
39 On limestone in literature: www.theguardian.com/books/2005/may/14/
    featuresreviews.guardianreview34
40 www.yorkshire-dales.com/craven-fault.html
41 *A Guide to the Lakes in Cumberland, Westmorland and Lancashire* by Thomas
    West (1784)
42 www.malhamdale.com/malham-peregrine-falcons/
43 Relatively recent research shows Malham Cove to be older than once
    thought, at least 50,000 years old: https://www.theguardian.com/
    uk/2002/apr/23/books.humanities
44 www.gov.uk/discrimination-your-rights
45 assets.publishing.service.gov.uk/government/uploads/system/uploads/
    attachment_data/file/839172/hate-crime-1819-hosb2419.pdf
46 www.irr.org.uk/research/statistics/racial-violence/
47 www.theguardian.com/society/2019/jun/26/devastating-impact-of-hate-
    crimes
48 www.catch-hatecrime.org.uk
49 www.bbc.co.uk/news/magazine-33725217
50 edition.cnn.com/2017/05/31/us/portland-train-stabbing-what-hap-
    pened/index.html
51 David Lammy explores both the benign and malign effects of our need to
    belong in *Tribes: How Our Need to Belong Can Make or Break Society* (Constable,
    2020)

52 www.bbc.co.uk/news/uk-england-london-50892347
53 www.uefa.com/insideuefa/news/newsid=2628172.html
54 www.bbc.co.uk/news/50093931
55 www.gov.uk/check-your-business-protected-area
56 assets.publishing.service.gov.uk/government/uploads/system/uploads/
    attachment_data/file/833726/landscapes-review-final-report.pdf
57 www.gov.uk/government/publications/designated-landscapes-national-
    parks-and-aonbs-2018-review
58 Berros, María Valeria. 'The Constitution of the Republic of Ecuador: Pacham-
    ama Has Rights', Environment & Society Portal, *Arcadia* (2015), no.11. Rachel
    Carson Center for Environment and Society. https://doi.org/10.5282/
    rcc/7131.
59 intercontinentalcry.org/rights-nature-indigenous-philosophies-reframing-
    law/
60 nzhistory.govt.nz/the-new-zealand-settlements-act-passed
61 www.theatlantic.com/video/index/587689/river-me/
62 www.bbc.co.uk/news/world-asia-india-40537701
63 www.theguardian.com/books/2019/nov/02/trees-have-rights-too-rob-
    ert-macfarlane-on-the-new-laws-of-nature
64 *Braiding Sweetgrass: Indigenous Wisdom, Scientific Knowledge, and the Teachings
    of Plants* by Robin Wall Kimmerer (Penguin, 2020)
65 *Wendell Berry: Essays 1993–2017* by Wendell Berry (Library of America,
    2019)
66 www.greekmythology.com/Myths/Heroes/Heracles/heracles.html.
67 www.brainpickings.org/2011/10/24/unsung-heroes/
68 www.forbes.com/sites/startswithabang/2019/06/18/there-are-6-stron-
    gest-materials-on-earth-that-are-harder-than-diamonds/#217264dd
    3412
69 www.sciencemag.org/news/2018/11/spider-silk-five-times-stronger-
    steel-now-scientists-know-why
70 www.reuters.com/article/us-spidersilk-limpetteeth/strongestknown-nat-
    ural-material-spider-silk-or-limpet-teethidUSKBN0LM00520150218

LIFEBLOOD

71 www.theguardian.com/world/2014/jun/20/global-refugee-figure-passes-
    50-million-unhcr-report
72 www.independent.co.uk/news/world/world-history/state-of-nature-
    how-modern-humans-lived-as-nomads-for-99-per-cent-of-our-his-
    tory-1604967.html
73 www.usgs.gov/special-topic/water-science-school/science/water-you-
    water-and-human-body
74 variety.com/2020/digital/news/gone-with-the-wind-hbo-max-dis-
    claimer-horrors-slavery-1234648726/
75 archive.yorkshiredales.org.uk/visit-the-dales/discover-the-dales/caves-
    and-potholes/hull-pot
76 www.npr.org/templates/story/story.php?storyId=4675953
77 www.worldwildlife.org/species/directory?direction=desc&sort=extinct
    ion_status

FEET

78 independent.co.uk/news/uk/politics/house-lords-where-location-move-
    york-boris-johnson-a9678626.html
79 www.manchestereveningnews.co.uk/whats-on/top-10-birds-look-
    out-18123310
80 www.lancswt.org.uk/wildlife-explorer/birds/pigeons-and-doves/turtle-dove
81 www.theguardian.com/environment/2019/jul/25/eu-acts-to-protect-
    future-of-bird-facing-extinction-in-uk
82 www.birdguides.com/news/thousands-of-turtle-doves-to-be-shot-in-
    france-this-season
83 www.operationturtledove.org/turtle-doves/ecology-habitat-and-food/
84 news.bbc.co.uk/1/hi/england/2238494.stm
85 www.manchester.gov.uk/info/500325/central_library_building/4586/
    history_of_central_library
86 www.gov.uk/government/news/public-health-england-publishes-air-pol-
    lution-evidence-review
87 www.cpre.org.uk/news/helping-people-enjoy-the-benefits-of-englands-
    special-landscapes/
88 phys.org/news/2019-09-magnetic-north-true-align.html
89 www.theguardian.com/science/2019/aug/30/compasses-to-point-true-
    north-for-first-time-in-360-years
90 www.northpennines.org.uk
91 www.geolsoc.org.uk/GeositesHadrian
92 www.geologynorth.uk/the-whin-sill/
93 blogs.agu.org/martianchronicles/2008/08/22/hot-lava-where-does-it-
    come-fro/
94 www.discoveringbritain.org/content/discoveringbritain/trail%20book-
    lets/High%20Force%20trail%202016.pdf
95 discoveringbritain.org, from the Royal Geographical Society (with the
    Institute of British Geographers).
96 www.northpennines.org.uk/
97 www.northpennines.org.uk/what_we_do/citizen-science/cold-blooded-
    and-spineless/
98 www.nationalgeographic.com/animals/invertebrates/
99 hadrianswallcountry.co.uk/hadrians-wall-management-plan/
    description#BHW
100 www.bbc.co.uk/iplayer/episode/b082w9p9/black-and-british-a-forgot-
    ten-history-1-first-encounters
101 www.washingtonpost.com/news/early-lead/wp/2016/11/17/white-
    texas-teens-chant-build-that-wall-at-hispanics-during-high-school-vol-
    leyball-match/
102 eu.detroitnews.com/story/news/local/oakland-county/2016/11/10/
    royal-oak-students-chant-build-wall-cafeteria/93581592
103 www.nytimes.com/2019/01/24/climate/border-wall-wildlife.html
104 academic.oup.com/bioscience/article/68/10/740/5057517
105 www.visitengland.com/experience/walk-wall-steel-rigg
106 www.heartofhadrianswall.com/
107 twitter.com/RobGMacfarlane/status/1061151542047399936?s=20

Index